Lecture Notes in Computer Science 1553

Edited by G. Goos, J. Hartmanis and J. van Leeuwen

T0223301

Springer

Berlin
Heidelberg
New York
Barcelona
Hong Kong
London
Milan
Paris
Singapore
Tokyo

Sten F. Andler Jörgen Hansson (Eds.)

Active, Real-Time, and Temporal Database Systems

Second International Workshop, ARTDB-97
Como, Italy, September 8-9, 1997
Proceedings

 Springer

Series Editors

Gerhard Goos, Karlsruhe University, Germany
Juris Hartmanis, Cornell University, NY, USA
Jan van Leeuwen, Utrecht University, The Netherlands

Volume Editors

Sten F. Andler
Jörgen Hansson
Department of Computer Science
University of Skovde
Box 408, S-541 28 Skövde, Sweden
E-mail: {sten,jorgen.hansson}@ida.his.se

Cataloging-in-Publication data applied for

Die Deutsche Bibliothek - CIP-Einheitsaufnahme

Active, real time, and temporal database systems : second
international workshop ; proceedings / ARTDB '97, Como, Italy,
September 8 - 9, 1997. Sten F. Andler ; Jörgen Hansson (ed.). -
Berlin ; Heidelberg ; New York ; Barcelona ; Hong Kong ; London ;
Milan ; Paris ; Singapore ; Tokyo : Springer, 1998
  (Lecture notes in computer science ; Vol. 1553)
  ISBN 3-540-65649-9

CR Subject Classification (1998): H.2, C.3

ISSN 0302-9743
ISBN 3-540-65649-9 Springer-Verlag Berlin Heidelberg New York

© Springer-Verlag Berlin Heidelberg 1998
Printed in Germany

Typesetting: Camera-ready by author
SPIN: 10693203   06/3142 – 5 4 3 2 1 0   Printed on acid-free paper

Preface

Database systems of the next generation are likely to be inherently very complex due to the diversity of requirements placed on them. Incorporating active, real-time, and temporal virtues in one database system is an arduous effort but is also a commendable one.

This book presents the proceedings of the Second International Workshop on Active, Real-Time, and Temporal Database Systems (ARTDB-97), held in Como, Milan, in September 1997. The aim of the workshop was to bring researchers together from the active and real-time research communities, and to examine the current state of the art in active, real-time, and temporal database systems.

This book offers a collection of papers presented at the ARTDB-97 workshop. The papers, many of them representing proficient and tenable results, illuminate the feasibility of building database system supporting reactive behavior, while enforcing timeliness and predictability. The book contains nine papers carefully reviewed and accepted by the program committee, three invited papers written by prominent researchers in the field, and two summaries of the panel discussions held at the workshop. The program committee received seventeen submissions, where each submission was reviewed by at least three program committee members. The two panel sessions focused on predictability issues and on practical experience of active, real-time, and temporal database systems.

The ARTDB-97 workshop was held in cooperation with the IEEE Technical Committees on Real-Time Systems and Complexity in Computing, and the ACM Special Interest Group on Manipulation of Data.

We wish to express our appreciation to all the authors of submitted papers, to the program committee members and their additional referees, to the invited speakers, and to the organizers of the panels. Special thanks are due to Joakim Eriksson and Johan Lundström for documenting the panel sessions. We would also like to thank Lars-Erik Johansson, Vice-Chancellor, and Stig Emanuelsson, Head of Department of Computer Science, both at the University of Skövde, for their financial and moral support.

Skövde, December 1998

Sten F. Andler
Jörgen Hansson

Organization

Organizing Committee
Sten F. Andler, University of Skövde, Sweden
Jörgen Hansson, University of Skövde, Sweden

Program Committee
Brad Adelberg, Northwestern University, USA
Azer Bestavros, Boston University, USA
Sharma Chakravarthy, University of Florida, USA
Anindya Datta, University of Arizona, USA
Wolfgang Halang, Fernuniversitaet, Hagen, Germany
Young-Kuk Kim, Chungnam National University, Korea
Kam-yiu Lam, City University of Hong Kong, Hong Kong
Kwei-Jay Lin, University of California, Irvine, USA
C. Douglass Locke, Lockheed Martin Corporation, USA
Aloysius K. Mok, University of Texas at Austin, USA
Rajkumar Ragunathan, Carnegie Mellon University, USA
Krithi Ramamritham, University of Massachusetts, USA
Tore Risch, Linköping University, Sweden
Timos Sellis, National Technical University of Athens, Greece
Sang H. Son, University of Virginia, USA
John A. Stankovic, University of Virginia, USA
Alexander D. Stoyenko, New Jersey Institute of Technology, USA
Ozgur Ulusoy, Bilkent University, Turkey
Paulo Verissimo, Universidade de Lisboa, Portugal
Philip S. Yu, IBM T.J. Watson Research Center, USA
Wei Zhao, Texas A&M University, USA

Contents

Panel Sessions

Real-Time and Active Databases: A Survey*

Joakim Eriksson

Department of Computer Science
University of Skövde
Box 408, S-541 28 Skövde
joakim.eriksson@ida.his.se

Abstract. Active real-time databases have emerged as a research area in which concepts of active databases and real-time databases are combined into a real-time database with reactive behavior. However, this marriage is not free from complications. The main problem is that timeliness, i.e., predictability and efficiency, is of paramount importance in real-time databases, while reactive behavior may add to the unpredictability of the database. This survey addresses reactive behavior and timing constraints from a database perspective. Results of both real-time databases and active databases that have impact on active real-time databases are discussed, as well as projects which have done research on active real-time databases.

Keywords. Active databases, reactive mechanisms, real-time systems, real-time databases, predictability, timeliness

1 Introduction

As the amount of information in a system grows larger, it needs to be stored somewhere and stored intelligently, with regard to space requirements and time for retrieval. A database serves as a repository. Database technology has been thoroughly investigated with regards to query languages, database models, storage techniques, buffer management, concurrency control, multi-user access and update, etc. However, some applications that include a database system work in a real-time environment, and traditional databases have not been designed with real time constraints in mind, in particular predictability. At most, efficiency is considered, but that is not satisfactory. Moreover, traditional databases are not capable of taking actions on their own, in terms of consistency maintenance, view updates, etc.

Since the beginning of computers there have been systems that have operated in real-time environments; current examples of such technology areas are chemical processes, nuclear power plants and space shuttle control. The common denominator for these systems is that they all react to inputs from the environment and must produce some output within a specified time. The data associated with, and used by, such applications has grown steadily. Inserting a

---

* This work was supported by NUTEK (The Swedish National Board for Industrial and Technical Development).

database into such an environment cannot be done without concern for maintaining timing constraints, i.e. the database operations must be efficient and predictable, so the database does not prevent the system from meeting deadlines. Suggestions have been made on how to ensure the timeliness of databases, some of which will be described in the section on real-time databases.

In a traditional database system nothing happens unless a database action is explicitly requested. In simple systems this may be satisfactory, but in larger systems considerable added effort must be expended on the development of applications using the database, in order that they preserve database consistency. Furthermore, materialized views must be updated whenever they are affected by database updates. This could be done incrementally by the database manager. The term *active* databases was first used by Morgenstern (1983) to denote such databases incrementally updating views. Later, the application areas of active databases have come to include, for example, triggering facilities, constraint checking, etc. Today, we define an active database as a database being able to react to events and conditions in the database, or even the surrounding applications and environment.

Reactive behavior brings a new dimension into a time-constrained system. Due to the reactive nature of real-time systems, it is suggested be beneficial to incorporate reactive behavior into a real-time databases. The first project to address these issues was HiPAC (Chakravarthy et al. 1989, Dayal et al. 1988). However, the issue was considered future work. Today, substantial interest is being put in the matter, and several application proposals have been made.

This survey addresses reactive behavior and real-time aspects from a database point of view. The remainder of this paper is organized as follows: In Section 2, real-time databases are discussed. Section 3 outlines issues in active databases. The problems of combining reactive behavior and timing constraints in database systems and a summary of projects that up to now have involved active real-time database research are presented in Section 4. We present a summary in Section 5.

2   Real-Time Databases

When talking about real-time systems, it is often assumed that we are simply referring to *fast* systems. However, this is a misconception (Stankovic 1988). A real-time system is a system in which the execution time is *predictable* so that it can be guaranteed that a task will meet its time constraints. A task can never be guaranteed to meet its deadline, no matter the speed of the system, if its execution time cannot be predicted. In this section, basic concepts of real-time systems and issues and problems that affect predictability in a real-time database are presented.

2.1   Temporal Validity

Since real-time databases often work in a dynamic environment, where data values are changing frequently, much of the data becomes invalid after some time, and can therefore not be used in decision making or for derivating new data. This *temporal consistency requirement* can be divided into two parts (Ramamritham 1993):

Absolute validity: Data is only valid between absolute points in time. This arises from the need to keep the database consistent with the environment. For example, the position of a moving vehicle might be valid for one second. After this, the position has changed so much that the old value is of no use. The length of the interval depends on the purpose of the system, and on its mode. For example, a space shuttle needs to know its exact position. In order to maintain a steady course in cruising mode, the position value is valid for 30 seconds, and then needs to be recalculated. However, in a situation where the shuttle docks, and where it is crucial to have the exact position up-to-date, the position value is only valid for one second, or even less.

Relative validity: Different data items that are used to derive new data must be temporally consistent with each other. For example, a gas tank may have a pressure gauge and a temperature gauge to help decide which action to take. If the reading of the pressure is more than 5 seconds later, or earlier, than the reading of the temperature, the values may no longer be correlated since the temperature may have changed by the time the pressure is read.

Temporal consistency must be kept in mind when determining an appropriate frequency of readings.

2.2   Deadlines in Real-Time Systems

The most important correctness criterion in real-time systems, besides the correct logical behavior, is whether tasks finish within their specified *deadline*. The deadline is a point in time when the execution of a task must be completed. Deadlines can be categorized into *hard*, *firm* and *soft* (Ramamritham 1993). Transactions with hard deadlines, if missed, could cause damage to the system or environment (hard *essential*) or even a catastrophe (hard *critical*) (Ramamritham et al. 1989). Transactions with firm deadlines, if missed, bring no value to the system, but no harm is done to the environment. When transactions with soft deadlines are broken there is still some value in completing the task despite the deadline being missed. These different types of deadlines are best illustrated using *value functions* (Locke 1986), where a positive value is favorable and a negative value means damage or disaster. Such value functions can be used to illustrate the above mentioned categories of deadlines, as shown in Fig. 1.

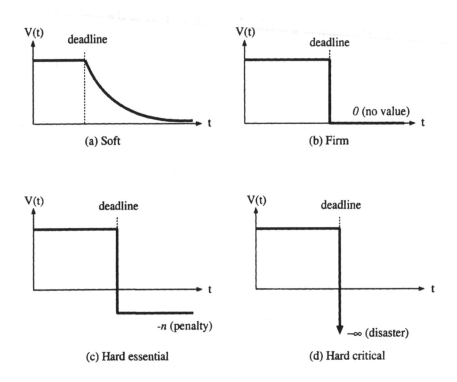

Fig. 1. Deadlines represented with value functions.

Scheduling. The most researched area within real-time systems is scheduling, in which each task is given its share of system resources (often CPU, or disk in database systems). The task of the scheduler is to schedule the tasks and their use of the resource(s), while meeting a certain correctness criterion, such as "no deadlines missed", "minimum number of deadlines missed" or, if value functions are used, "maximum value density". Schedulers can be *static* or *dynamic*. A static schedule is determined off-line and used by the system as-is. In a dynamic system, tasks are presented to the system at runtime and the scheduler determines on-line at every schedulable point how to run the different tasks.

In dynamic systems the scheduler could be presented with too many tasks to be able to give every task its share of the system resources within specified deadlines, in which case an *overload* situation occurs. This situation can be resolved, for example by dropping certain tasks or by not allowing more tasks into the system while the overload condition exists. By definition, overload does not occur in a static system, otherwise a failure has occurred. It has been claimed that dynamic systems cannot guarantee hard deadlines because of the inherent overload risk, but research is underway on dynamic scheduling with guarantees for hard deadlines in systems including both hard and soft deadlines.

Contingency Plans. Since hard transactions must meet their deadlines, they cannot be discarded in an overload situation. But when there is a risk that one or more deadlines cannot be met, alternative actions can be executed for some or all hard transactions, which do not give exact results but which will be complete before the deadline. Liu et al. (1991) list examples of such imprecise computation techniques. Note that there is overhead associated with these techniques. This overhead must be taken into account when choosing a contingency plan technique.

2.3 Sources of Unpredictability

When putting a database into a real-time environment, new demands are put on its behavior. It must not only be able to handle database operations properly, but it must do so *within a predictable amount of time* to be able to meet the timing constraints. However, there are fundamental concepts in traditional database techniques that are in conflict with predictable responses, that is, which make databases unpredictable. Ramamritham (1993) identifies four sources of unpredictability.

Dependency on Data Values. The execution sequence of a transaction can depend on the data retrieved from the database and/or data calculated using data from the database.

Data and Resource Conflicts. Locking of data is used to prevent harmful interleaving of transactions and thereby preserve consistency. When data is locked, other transactions may have to wait for an often unpredictable time until the data is unlocked. This means that a transaction could be delayed past its deadline. On the other hand, particularly if the granularity of the lock is large, there might not be a conflict, even if the transactions should access the data simultaneously.

One approach to avoid this unpredictable waiting is not to put locks on data, but to allow transactions to access the data without restrictions and wait until the transactions have run to completion to check if any access conflicts have occurred. If any such conflict is detected, the completed transaction is aborted and restarted at a later point in time, or all the other transactions that have touched the same data are aborted. This approach of deferring checks until completion is called *optimistic* concurrency control (Kung and Robinson 1981) as opposed to *pessimistic* concurrency control such as two-phase locking. There are also mixes of these approaches such as Wait-50 (Haritsa et al. 1990).

There is a variant of optimistic concurrency control, called *speculative* concurrency control (Bestavros and Braoudakis 1994), in which a transaction is not restarted from the very beginning, but only from the point in time when a possible conflict is detected. This is obtained by making a copy of the transaction at the point of potential conflict and suspending the copy. If the conflict becomes a fact, the original transaction is aborted and the copy is made runnable. If no conflict arises the original transaction is run to completion and all suspended transactions are discarded. However, the number of incomplete transactions can be very large, since one must be stored for every possible conflict detected. Variants of this algorithm limit the number of transaction copies. This lowers the administrative overhead and the storage requirements for all incomplete transactions, at the cost of having to restart a transaction to an earlier point than necessary.

Dynamic Paging and I/O. In traditional databases, data is stored on secondary storage such as a hard disk. To retrieve data, one or more pages first have to be read from disk into buffers in main memory, before the data can be used. Likewise, to make written data persistent, pages have to be transferred from memory to disk. Of course, if the page to be read already is in memory the page does not need to be re-read. However, the time to read a page from disk is several orders of magnitude slower than reading a page already in memory. Therefore, worst case scheduling will be hopelessly pessimistic. For example, if a page must be read into memory each time an object is read, which must be assumed when calculating worst case execution times, and if the pages already are in memory, the transaction will complete much faster than expected leaving the processor idle, thereby wasting a lot of valuable execution time. One possibility to avoid this waiting is to place large portions of the database or even the complete database in main memory, thereby minimizing or even eliminating disk I/O and its unpredictable behavior. In Section 2.4 main-memory databases will be discussed.

Transaction abort with rollback and restart A fourth source of unpredictability is the possibility of a transaction being aborted and restarted. This may occur several times in succession and a deadline may therefore be missed before the transaction completes. By not having an upper bound on the number of restarts, the total execution time can also increase unpredictably.

2.4 Main-Memory Databases

As described in Section 2.3 the main reason for disk-based databases not being predictable is that fetching of pages residing on disk into buffers in main memory is orders of magnitude slower than if the page was already in main memory. To solve this problem, the main part of a database, or even the complete database, can be placed directly in main memory, thereby eliminating disk I/O handling (Garcia-Molina and Salem 1992). Moreover, if transactions can be kept short they can be run to completion before letting a new one access the database, since execution time can be kept much shorter than on a disk-based system. Thereby concurrency control is no longer needed.

However, new problems then arise. Very often main memory is volatile, meaning that data is lost when the system fails or is turned off. Therefore, since some data must be kept in spite of the system being turned off, some form of persistent storage is needed. Likewise, the data needs to be restored before the database system can function after a failure. The memory can, however, be made *stable*, for example by being battery powered, and thereby remain intact despite the system being shut down.

If a main-memory database cannot be made stable, more problems arise if a system shutdown is unforeseen, e.g., a power failure. All data written after system start is lost. Therefore some form of logging must be done (Eich 1987). Logging of database activity should always be done, via stable main memory to secondary storage or directly to secondary storage. See (Levy and Silberschatz 1992) and (Kumar and Burger 1992) for main-memory database recovery algorithms.

2.5 State of the Art in Real-Time Databases

During the last years, research in real-time database technology has experienced a tremendous boost. Several journals with special issues on real-time databases have been presented (e.g. Son 1988, Özsoyoğlu and Snodgrass 1995a, Bestavros 1996, O'Neil and Ulusoy 1996), and workshops have been held (e.g. Berndtsson and Hansson 1995, Liu and Son 1996, Bestavros et al. 1996). There are also extensible surveys and bibliographies in the area of real-time and temporal databases (e.g. Ulusoy 1994, Özsoyoğlu and Snodgrass 1995b, Tsotras and Kumar 1996).

Since the behavior of traditional database systems are in conflict with the nature of real-time systems, trade-offs are needed to obtain timeliness. Often it is suggested to relax correctness criteria for the database, such as consistency of data. For example, it might be beneficial to use an old value in the database, should a new value be retrieved too late. Lin and Peng (1996) suggest it be allowed to update certain data values in the database, although transactions are already using the data. Thereby, transactions need not wait for data to be updated, and data is kept fresh.

Alternative concurrency controls have been proposed, one being the aforementioned speculative concurrency control (see Section 2.3). Another approach is to use lock-free objects (Anderson et al. 1996) which is a variant of optimistic concurrency control. Locking of objects is replaced with "retry loops" on objects, and the number of these retry loops can be guaranteed to have an upper bound.

Contingencies are being investigated for use in hard real-time environments, where a transaction cannot miss its deadline. A proposed admission control strategy (Bestavros and Nagy 1996) divides a transaction into two parts: one main part with no a priori knowledge and one predictable contingency part. The system won't admit a transaction into the system if it cannot be guaranteed that at least the contingency action can complete within the deadline. It has also been suggested (Soparkar et al. 1995) that time constraints should not be associated with completion of transactions, but with states in the database. A safe state is explicitly defined using "consistency" constraints, and if such a constraint is violated, a correcting action is started.

Main-memory databases are being exploited, mainly due to falling memory prices making it economically possible to have large databases in main-memory. Since disk based and main-memory resident databases differ in their behavior, modifications of traditional algorithms and mechanisms have been investigated. For example, a concurrency protocol is proposed by Ulusoy and Buchmann (1996) in which transactions, based on a priori knowledge of read and write sets, locks complete relations instead of individual tuples, thereby increasing CPU utilization. Furthermore, time cognitive scheduling for main-memory databases has also been looked into (Tseng et al. 1996).

While there are some commercial high-performance databases available such as Smallbase from HP Labs (Listgarten and Neimat 1996), commercial databases enforcing timing constraints are virtually non-existent. Despite this, there are numerous areas which would benefit from using database technology, including process industry, manufacturing, and multimedia and telecommunication systems. Although there are real-time database systems in use, these are most often ad hoc systems tightly connected to the application. Whether this is due to immature RTDB technology, or lack of promotion and technology transfer is an open question Applications showing how existing systems can be improved using current RTDB technology are needed (Buchmann 1995).

3 Active Databases

Within traditional databases there has always been a requirement that the data in the database be consistent with the environment. Moreover, enforcing constraints on data has also been desirable, e.g., a certain value must not grow above a given limit. It has also been beneficial to be able to activate alarms on detecting certain events in the database. Traditionally all this has been done in two ways on passive databases (Chakravarthy 1989):

1. The database is frequently polled to check if something of importance has happened.
2. All constraints and consistency checks are implemented in the applications and not in the database management system.

The former approach has the drawback of very large overhead if the polling is done too often, as the database has to process queries which often return nothing. However, if the polling is done too infrequently, some events might be missed. The latter approach is better from an efficiency point of view. However, letting the database management system perform all checks instead of every application has the following advantages:

- Each update of a constraint only needs to be done centrally in the database manager and not in each application.
- Since constraints are defined centrally they are the same for all applications. No two applications can have inconsistent constraints.
- A new application does not need to be programmed with all checks before startup, since all information already is stored in a centrally maintained database manager.

By extending a database manager with rule mechanisms, reactive behavior can be obtained.

3.1 Rules

The first approach to defining rules was to specify conditions which, when satisfied, would trigger an action (e.g. Hanson and Widom 1991, Stonebraker 1986). Although easy to understand, this method suffered from several drawbacks such as implementation difficulties and expressiveness limitations (Stonebraker et al. 1989).

In HiPAC (Chakravarthy et al. 1989, Dayal et al. 1988) is was suggested to use modified *production rules* which was used in AI systems such as OPS5 (Brownston et al. 1985). These "ECA rules" are divided into an event part, a condition part and an action part. The semantics are

> **on** \<event E\>
> **if** \<condition C\>
> **then** \<action A\>

Furthermore, it was suggested that rules should be represented as objects themselves, instead of having data and rules separated. The reasoning behind this is:

- Rules can relate to other objects and have attributes. This suggests grouping rules by context. Moreover, rules may be associated with classes, that is, only triggered by objects belonging to specific classes. This increases the efficiency of rule searching by reducing the scope of possible rules to trigger.

– Rules can be created, deleted, retrieved and updated using ordinary transaction mechanisms with read and write locks.

There is a distinction drawn between when a rule is *fired* and when it is *executed* (Branding et al. 1993). A rule is fired when its corresponding event is triggered. This initiates the execution of a rule, which involves establishing a correct execution order and establish control structures, such as independent transactions and subtransactions. In time-constrained systems, the time between triggering and execution should of course be as short and predictable as possible.

When an event is triggered it must be determined which rules, if any, are triggered by the event. For efficiency reasons a linear search through the rulebase is unacceptable. A better approach is to associate rules with classes. For example, in Sentinel (Anwar et al. 1993) a rule can *subscribe* to a reactive object. Thereby events generated in that object will trigger only subscribing rules. A further refinement is to let rules subscribe to specific *events* (Berndtsson 1994), thereby further limiting the search space. Rule triggering can thus be kept to a minimum, which is essential in a time constrained environment.

Events. In order to trigger rules in an event based system, the system needs to handle events and send them to the rule manager for further evaluation. Therefore the system needs to be instrumented with hardware or software sensors to detect events. Event monitoring is much too large an area to be covered in full in this paper. The following section provides a brief overview of vital aspects of event monitoring in an active database system, with bias towards time-constrained systems. The reader is referred to, for example, Mellin (1995) for a more comprehensive study of event detection.

Events can be divided into *primitive* events and *composite* events. Primitive events are simple events detected in the system or in the environment, and composite events are, as the name suggests, events composed of other events using logical expressions such as conjunction and disjunction. An event can carry parameters, for example a timestamp denoting the time of the event. Several active database event languages have been suggested, for example in Snoop, the event monitor used in Sentinel (Chakravarthy and Mishra 1994), Ode (Gehani et al. 1992a) and SAMOS (Gatziu and Dittrich 1993).

Another vital issue in composite event detection is how events are *consumed*, as they are used by the composite event detector. One event instance *initiates* a composite event and another event instance *terminates* the composite event and thereby raises it as a new event. For example, consider the sequence $E1$ followed by $E2$, as described in Fig. 2. If two instances of event $E1$, here denoted $e1a$ and $e1b$, are raised in that order, and then two instances of event $E2$, called $e2a$ and $e2b$, are raised, the question is how to combine those events. Chakravarthy et al. (1993) describe four different *contexts*. The simplest one, *recent*, throws away earlier event instances of a given event and uses the most recent. In the example above one composite event should have been raised consisting of $e1b$ together with $e2a$. The recent context is the context most likely to be used in a real-time environment where sensors are read periodically. In the chronicle context, event instances are combined as they arrive. In the example, $e1a$ would be matched with $e2a$, and $e1b$ with $e2b$. If constraints are put on the time between the initiating and the terminating event instances, this context could be useful also in a real-time environment. The remaining two methods described, continuous and cumulative context, are less interesting for practical use, especially in real-time databases.

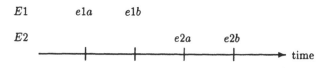

Fig. 2. Event occurrences

Different systems use composite event detection techniques based on different models. For example, SAMOS uses Petri Nets, Ode uses Finite State Automata and Snoop has event graphs. See (Deutsch 1994) for a comparison of different composite event detection systems.

As mentioned in (Branding et al. 1993) there is a trend towards modeling composite events using more complex condition parts. Primitive events are used to trigger rules and the condition part of such a rule queries the event history to determine whether its action is to be executed. The gain from this is simpler event monitoring, but there is no clear semantics of rule triggering. Moreover, there is an overhead incurred since rules are triggered more often and thus rule retrieval and condition evaluation is more frequent. This is still an open area of research.

Conditions. A condition in an ECA rule is used to check whether all prerequisites are satisfied for an action to execute. The event indicates *the need* to check, whereas the condition determines *what* to check. In its simplest form a condition is just a simple logical operation, for example on an event parameter, as in "updated value of x is larger than a threshold n". Another condition mechanism, usually used in relational systems, issues a query to the database, and if the query returns a non-empty answer the condition is satisfied. The returned tuples could also later be used in the action part. It may also be possible to execute an arbitrary function which returns true or false. Method execution in object-oriented systems is suited to this type of condition testing.

Condition evaluation can be done at the time of the event, at the end of the transaction, or in a separate transaction. This will be detailed in Section 3.2.

There have been suggestions to include a condition on the event and not only on a rule, thereby reducing the number of events that are signaled. The resulting events are called logical events. One approach is denoted E_CCA rules (Berndtsson and Lings 1995). The main motivation is that the rule manager is invoked as little as possible with unnecessary events, thereby potentially increasing efficiency. However, this puts more emphasis on the event detection. Ode (Gehani et al. 1992b) uses only logical events and no conditions on rules. In SAMOS it is possible to specify that events in a composite event must be raised by operations on the "same" object (Gatziu and Dittrich 1993).

Actions. If a condition of a rule is satisfied then its action will be executed. Actions could be database operations including deletion, update, or even refusal of the original operation. Other types of actions are external actions such as automatic ordering of stock items, signaling an alarm to a supervisor or launching missiles.

The rule also specifies a coupling mode between the event detection and action execution (see Section 3.2).

3.2 Execution Semantics

Coupling Modes. In early systems like POSTGRES (Stonebraker et al. 1990) and Ariel (Hanson 1989) every condition evaluation and action execution was done immediately upon event detection. However, in some situations that is too limited. Dayal et al. (1988) identify three different points in time where condition evaluation and action execution can take place, relative to the triggering event, with the constraint that condition evaluation must be performed before action execution:

Immediate: Upon event arrival the transaction is suspended, and condition evaluation and action execution is performed immediately. Execution of the triggering transaction is continued when the condition evaluation (and the action, if condition is true) is completed. This is useful, for example, in checking authorization.

Deferred: Condition evaluation and action execution are done at the end of the triggering transaction, after the transaction has finished execution and just before it commits. Integrity checks are well suited for this mode.

Detached (or decoupled): Condition evaluation and action execution are performed in one or separate transaction. This is useful in situations when an audit trail is required, since even if the original transaction is aborted the logging is executed.

The detached mode can be further separated into *causally independent* in which the triggered transaction is executed regardless of whether the triggering transaction commits or aborts, and *causally dependent* in which the triggering transaction must commit before the triggered transaction can commit or else the triggered transaction is aborted.

Branding et al. (1993) state that a system which interacts with the real world, as real-time systems always do, is likely to have side effects that are irreversible if the transaction should abort. Therefore two additional coupling modes are presented. In a *sequential causally dependent* coupling mode the triggered transaction cannot start its execution until the triggering transaction has committed. In an *exclusive causally dependent* coupling mode the triggered transaction is run in parallel, but it cannot commit until the triggering transaction *aborts*, otherwise the triggered transaction is aborted.

Dynamic Rules. In a dynamic environment it is important that the rule-base is allowed to be dynamic, i.e. that rules can be changed, inserted into or deleted from the rule-base. This means that rules cannot be statically compiled into the database system. However, since rules are sharable they must be put under the same concurrency mechanism as the rest of the database. Therefore when a rule is triggered, a read-lock should be applied to the rule, and when a deletion or update is requested a write lock should be applied.

Since dynamic rules could incur some unpredictability if used, it should be better to use a static rule-base in a time-constrained environment. If this is not possible, for example different rules is used in different situations, some form of *mode change* (e.g. Sha et al. 1989) could be used. That is, on a mode change the rule-base is switched, along with schedules, processes, etc.

Cascade Triggering. When actions are executing, or even when conditions are evaluated, events might be raised that could trigger other rules. This *cascade triggering* can continue and could in the worst case result in a circular triggering where rules trigger each other infinitely. Unless the rule-base can be analyzed, and potential unacceptable cascade triggerings be detected and avoided, the only way to avoid such uncontrolled triggering is to put a limit on the *depth* of triggering. In the extreme case, no cascade triggering is allowed at all. However, the semantics of an interrupted triggering is not clear and could leave the database inconsistent if the triggering transaction is not aborted. Therefore, if the limit is reached it should be viewed as a signal that the rule-base is incorrectly designed.

Conflict Resolution. When an event is triggered it could be associated with more than one rule in the rule-base. To determine in which order to execute those rules some form of conflict resolution must be performed. One solution, used in AI systems such as OPS5 (Brownston et al. 1985), uses what is called the *recognize-act cycle*. On an event, all rules that are triggered are collected, conditions are evaluated on those rules, conflict resolution is undertaken on the rules eligible to run, and finally the action is executed on the chosen rule. Then the cycle is repeated (collect all triggered rules, etc) until no more rules are triggered or 'halt' is executed.

However, there are issues that need to be addressed. For example, should all triggered rules be run concurrently, or in a certain order? If only one rule is to be executed, which one? If rules are discarded, does that bring damage to the system? There are no absolute answers to these questions, but different applications require different rule semantics. This is certainly the case in a time constrained environment.

3.3 State of the Art in Active Databases

Reactive mechanisms have been developed in databases for more than ten years and a multitude of prototypes have been developed. Refer to Jaeger and Freytag (1995) for an extensive bibliography. Today active database technology is mainstream and these ideas have been incorporated into commercial systems like Oracle, and also into standard query languages such as SQL3.

However, as with real-time database systems (see Section 2.5), active database technology has difficulties in reaching out into real world applications, despite the fact that there have been several application proposals, such as computer integrated manufacturing (Berndtsson 1994) and stock market/trading applications (Adelberg et al. 1997). There are obstacles that need to be addressed to be able to produce real world applications.

- System developers are not familiar with the active database paradigm. Design methodologies and tools should be developed that support the use of reactive mechanisms, and encourage developers to do the transition from non-active to active database systems (Díaz 1998).
- Although database vendors have incorporated reactive mechanisms into their products, they do not seem to be technically supported at a level desired for its wide usage. Moreover, performance of these mechanisms are often not satisfactory enough to be used in critical applications.

Researchers have argued that active databases are beneficial for use in real world applications. But in order to prove it, emphasis needs to be put on producing working prototypes, not research vehicles or "yet another research paper" (Buchmann 1995).

4 Real-Time Active Databases

There has been recent interest in the development of active real-time databases, that is, active database systems with time constraints that must be enforced. However, the problem to be addressed is not simply one of introducing reactive mechanisms into a real-time database. As mentioned earlier, predictability is of paramount importance in a real-time database and reactive mechanisms *add to unpredictability*. The following sections will discuss some of the issues relating to unpredictability and also give examples of restrictions of the reactive mechanisms in order to obtain timeliness.

4.1 Rules and Predictability

Coupling Modes. When a rule is triggered the execution time of the transaction in which the action is executed will increase. This means that the slack, i.e. the time between the estimated end of transaction and the deadline, will decrease. In extreme cases the slack will become negative and the deadline will be missed. Therefore, to be absolutely certain that the execution time is not changed[2], every rule action should be run in *detached* mode, i.e. in a transaction of its own. Note that this does not increase the execution time of the transaction but it does increase the load on the system, if the transactions are run concurrently.

An alternative is to actively take the extended execution time into account when triggering actions and re-scheduling transactions when needed. If a legal schedule cannot be obtained, the action could be rejected, the transaction could be aborted, or a contingency plan could be executed (see Section 2.2). However, caution is needed and before letting actions execute in immediate or deferred mode there should be careful analysis of the rule-base so that situations like those described above cannot occur.

Cascade Triggering. In active databases enforcing time constraints, cascade triggering of rules can be problematic. The fact that just a few unpredicted rule triggerings can make a transaction miss its deadlines makes the situation more delicate than in other active databases, which only notice some period of degraded service (see Section 3.2). The ultimate solution, albeit the most restrictive, is not to allow rules to trigger other rules at all. However, a well-defined rule-base, complemented with rule analysis tools, is a necessity to achieve predictability under cascade triggering.

Composite Events. The available composite event detection mechanisms mentioned in Section 3.1 were not primarily designed for efficiency, but for expressibility. For example, Geppert et al. (1994) show that for very large rule-bases the composite event detection used in SAMOS becomes a bottleneck with detection of events taking up to several seconds.[3] Of course, in a real-time system this is totally unacceptable. This is especially true when using immediate or deferred coupling mode. Therefore, Buchmann et al. (1994a) suggest that composite events only should be allowed to trigger rules that are executed in detached mode, thereby avoiding unpredictable increase of the execution time of the triggering transaction. It is also suggested that event composition should not be done in one monolithic event composer, but in several small event composers executing in parallel. This will make garbage-collection of semi-composed events simpler, and cater for distributed event detection and composition.

4.2   Real-Time Rule Management

Contingency Plans. As described in Section 2.2, a situation in which not all tasks can meet their deadlines is called an overload situation. In a system with hard timing constraints, deadlines must not be missed. In order to meet deadlines, alternative actions may be executed. A contingency plan, in the form of

---

[2] Note that event detection and transaction creation always will take some time.

[3] The composite event detection in SAMOS has been improved since the test was conducted (Geppert et al. 1995). Further research is to be undertaken to investigate other systems applying other composite event detection algorithms.

an alternate action (see Section 2.2) could be invoked when there is chance of the original transaction not meeting its deadline, and there is enough time to complete the alternate action. The problem is to determine the point in time at which the switch should take place. Branding et al. (1993) introduce a special periodic temporal event, called a *milestone*. A running transaction is monitored against an "ideal" execution consisting of such milestones. If the running transaction misses a milestone an alternate action can be triggered.

Time Cognizant Rules and their Definition Language. To be able to specify time constraints in an active database we need a notation for describing those time constraints. There have been proposals for how to include time within the ECA rule paradigm.

Ramamritham (1993) suggests a simple notation in which the maximum allowed time to complete a task is given. It is stressed that the deadline should be *actively* taken into consideration, i.e. it should not be seen as just a time-out, but the task should be completed by that time. In the following example the landing procedure of an airplane is to be interrupted within five seconds if the initiating landing steps are not completed within 10 seconds from the start of the procedure.

> **ON** 10 **SECONDS AFTER** initiating landing preparations
> **IF** steps not completed
> **DO WITHIN** 5 **SECONDS** abort landing

A contingency action can be given in a rule (Chakravarthy and Mishra 1994). The semantics are that if action1 cannot be executed within the specified time, action2 should be executed.

> **ON** event
> **IF** condition
> **DO** action1
>   **WITHIN** time
>   **OTHERWISE** action2

The notation described by Buchmann et al. (1992) includes a value function (see Section 2.2) which is used in the scheduling. There is an understanding that rules are triggered by more or less complex events and that the timing constraints should be able to refer to parts of such a complex event. The rule definition algebra is also extended by the operators AFTER, BEFORE and UNTIL. An example is given below in which a temporal validity constraint on two measurements is introduced. This example states that the measurements must each have been taken within a certain time interval (temporally consistent) before they are propagated to other sites.

> **ON** measure1 **AND** measure2
> **IF** ok(sensor1) **AND** ok(sensor2)
> **DO** analysis ; propagate result;

TIME CONSTRAINT (AFTER trig_event,
  BEFORE min (ts(measure1)+6s, ts(measure2)+10s),
  value(t)=a*(ts(trig_event)+min(ts(measure1)+6s,
  ts(measure2)+10s)-t)/t

Although there have been proposals on parts of time-cognizant rules, no real proposal have been presented, and no implementation has been made.

4.3 State of the Art in Active Real-Time Databases

Increasing interest has been noticed in the area of active real-time databases. Workshops have been organized (e.g. Berndtsson and Hansson 1995, Ramamritham and Soparkar 1996) and several papers on the area have been published. Ramamritham et al. (1996) and Datta (1996) list several issues which have an impact on an active real-time database system. A number of papers describes different approaches to maintaining temporal consistency using reactive mechanisms (Chomicki and Toman 1995, Xiong et al. 1996). Transaction models are also investigated. Sivasankaran et al. (1996) investigate the assignment of priorities to certain transactions (those which trigger immediate and deferred actions) with respect to missed deadlines.

Application areas have also been identified in which active real-time databases could be beneficial. Telephone network services (Sivasankaran et al. 1993), cooperative distributed navigation systems (Purimetla et al. 1993), and stock market/trading applications (Adelberg et al. 1997) are a few examples of active real-time applications.

A number of projects have been presented that incorporates reactive behavior in a time-constrained environment. The first project addressing these issues was HiPAC (Chakravarthy et al. 1989, Dayal et al. 1988), where a straw-man architecture of a combined active and time-constrained data manager was presented. However, the combination of active and time-constrained database features was considered future work.

Three current research projects of active real-time databases are REACH, DeeDS and STRIP. REACH (Branding et al. 1993, Buchmann et al. 1992, 1994a) is a database system which incorporates active features with timing constraints working in a heterogeneous environment. Their contributions to the development of the technology include the additional detached coupling modes (see Section 3.2) and a suggestion on how to include timing information in the rule definition language (see Section 4.2). The DeeDS prototype (Andler et al. 1994, 1996) integrates reactive mechanisms, distribution, dynamic scheduling of hard and soft deadlines and integrated monitoring. The approach is to take existing components and implement only those features necessary to obtain the required functionality. STRIP (Adelberg et al. 1996, 1997) is a main-memory database with support for soft timing constraints and the ability to share data with other components in an open system. The rule system is used for incremental maintenance of derived data and has the ability to group several updates into one action through the use of *unique transactions*, thereby increasing efficiency of recomputation of data

4.4 Future Research Areas

As previously discussed, it is almost impossible to combine all concepts of active databases and all concepts of real-time databases and expect the resulting database system to perform as required. There are a number of concepts that cannot be combined without a mismatch; these have been identified and described in this paper.

In (Buchmann et al. 1994a) the following properties are stressed for active real-time databases.

- Efficient primitive event detection. Independent of event type, the event detector should be able to detect events in a timely manner. Moreover, unnecessary event generation, e.g. raising events which cannot trigger any rule, should be avoided.
- Efficient event composition. If used, composite event detection should be executed in a timely manner so that unnecessary waiting is avoided.
- Efficient rule firing. On an event the rule manager should perform timely rule selection, condition evaluation and rule conflict resolution.

To these, the following should be added:

- A rule specification language which includes timing constraints. Since time is a central issue in real-time systems, one must be able to specify it in an easy and uniform fashion.
- Scheduling of triggered actions. Since timing constraints should be actively taken into account (Section 4.2) some form of time-cognizant transaction scheduling should be utilized, in which the scheduling criteria, for example, could be maximum value density or minimal number of missed deadlines.

The compromises made in combining the concepts cannot involve crucial real-time properties, since this would jeopardize the timely behavior of the system. Therefore, restrictions on the reactive mechanisms is necessary. Such restrictions could include limited coupling modes, bounded cascade triggering and restricted composite event detection.

Today there are few research implementations being made. There are isolated industrial real-time database applications claiming to exhibit reactive behavior, but most often these mechanisms are in the non time-critical or interactive subparts of the system.

5 Summary

Today, as the amount of data grows, a database system is essential when it comes to storing and retrieving data. In such areas as telecommunication, manufacturing and multimedia there are however several issues that need to be addressed when introducing a database. Since applications running in these environments often are time-critical, the database system needs to behave in a timely manner.

Predictability is imperative in order to guarantee deadlines of time-critical tasks, and performance is also of great importance.

Active databases have been investigated as a means for relieving applications from tedious consistency checking and alerting code through mechanisms that can handle such incidental tasks centrally in the database in a uniform fashion.

Substantial research has been made on both real-time databases and active databases, and today each of these areas are seeking to incorporate mechanisms from the other. The main problem is that adding reactive behavior also means adding to unpredictability. Therefore, research is being undertaken on how to incorporate reactive behavior into a real-time database system without jeopardizing the timely behavior of the system.

Although research and results of real-time and active databases have been presented, industry is reluctant to absorb the results emerging from this research. Therefore, one of the critical issues is to find real-world applications that can show the benefit of using active and real-time database technology.

Acknowledgments

The author would especially like to thank Prof. Sten F. Andler for invaluable advice and encouragements in writing this survey. The author would also like to thank Prof. Sharma Chakravarthy, Dr. Brian Lings, and Prof. David L. Parnas for their valuable comments and suggestions. Also thanks to Jörgen Hansson for references.

References

Abbott, R. Garcia-Molina, H.: Scheduling Real-Time Transactions. ACM SIGMOD Record **17** (1988) 82–98

Adelberg, B., Kao, B., Garcia-Molina, H.: Overview of the STanford Real-time Information Processor (STRIP). ACM SIGMOD Record **25** (1996) 37–38

Adelberg, B., Garcia-Molina, H., Widom, J: The STRIP Rule System for Efficiently Maintaining Derived Data. SIGMOD Conference, Tucson, Arizona (1997)

Anderson, J. H., Ramamurthy, S., Moir, M., and Jeffay, K.: Lock-Free Transactions for Real-Time Systems. In Real-Time Database Systems: Issues and Applications. Kluwer Academic Publishers, Boston (1996)

Andler, S., Hansson, J., Eriksson, J., Mellin, J.: Project Plan—Distributed Reconfigurable Real-Time Database System. Technical Report HS-IDA-TR-94-006, Department of Computer Science, University of Skövde (1994)

Andler, S. F., Hanson, J., Eriksson, J., Mellin, J., Berndtsson, M., Eftring, B.: DeeDS Towards a Distributed Active and Real-Time Database System. ACM SIGMOD Record **25** (1996) 38–40

Anwar, E., Maugis, L., Chakravarthy, S.: Design and Implementation of Active Capability for an Object-Oriented Database. Technical Report UF-CIS-TR-93-001, CIS Department, University of Florida (1993)

Berndtsson, M.: Reactive Object-Oriented Databases and CIM. Proceedings of the 5th International Conference on Database and Expert System Applications (1994) 769–778.

Berndtsson, M., Hansson, J., editors: Active and Real-Time Database Systems (ARTDB-95). Proceedings of the First International Workshop on Active and Real-Time Database Systems, Skövde, Sweden. Springer-Verlag (London) Ltd. (1995)

Berndtsson, M. Lings, B.: Logical Events and ECA Rules. Technical Report HS-IDA-TR-95-004, Department of Computer Science, University of Skövde. (1995)

Bestavros, A. Braoudakis, S.: Timeliness Via Speculation for Real-Time Databases. Proceedings of the 14th IEEE Real-Time System Symposium, San Juan, Puerto Rico. (1994)

Bestavros, A., Nagy, S.: Admission Control and Overload Management for Real-Time Databases. In Real-Time Database Systems: Issues and Applications. Kluwer Academic Publishers, Boston (1996)

Bestavros, A., Lin, K.-W., Son, S. H., editors: Real-Time Database Systems: Issues and Applications. Kluwer Academic Publishers, Boston (1996)

Bestavros, A.: Advances in real-time database systems research. ACM SIGMOD Record 25 (1996) 3-7

Branding, H., Buchmann, A., Kudrass, T., and Zimmermann, J.: Rules in an Open System: The REACH Rule System. In Paton, N. W. and Williams, M. H., editors, Rules in Database Systems, Edinburgh 1993. Springer-Verlag. (1993) 111-126

Brownston, L., Farrell, R., Kant, E., and Martin, N.: Programming Expert Systems in OPS5: An Introduction to Rule-Based Programming. Addison Wesley. (1985)

Buchmann, A. P.: Wrap-up Statement. In Berndtsson and Hansson, editors, Active and Real-Time Database Systems (ARTDB-95) Skövde, Sweden. Springer-Verlag. (1995) 264-266

Buchmann, A. P., Branding, H., Kudrass, T., Zimmermann, J.: REACH: A REal-time ACtive and Heterogeneous Mediator System. Data Engineering 15 (1992) 44-47

Buchmann, A. P., Zimmermann, J., Blakeley, J. A., Wells, D. L.: Building an Integrated Active OODBMS: Requirements, Architecture and Design Decisions. Technical report, Department of Computer Science, Tech. University Darmstadt (1994)

Chakravarthy, S.: Rule Management and Evaluation: An Active DBMS Prospective. ACM SIGMOD Record 18 (1989) 20-28

Chakravarthy, S., Blaustein, B., Buchmann, A., Carey, M. J., Dayal, U., Goldhirsch, D., Hsu, M., Jauhari, R., Ladin, R., Livny, M., McCarthy, D., McKee, R., Rosenthal, A.: HiPAC: A Research Project in Active Time-Constrained Database Management. Final Technical Report. Technical Report XAIT-89-02, Xerox Advanced Information Technology (1989)

Chakravarthy, S., Krishnaprasad, V., Anwar, E., Kim, S.-K.: Anatomy of a Composite Event Detector. Technical report, CIS Department, University of Florida (1993)

Chakravarthy, S., Mishra, D.:Snoop: An Expressive Event Specification Language for Active Databases. Data and Knowledge Engineering 14 (1994) 1-26

Chomicki, J. Toman, D.: Implementing Temporal Integrity Constraints Using an Active DBMS. IEEE Transactions on Knowledge and Data Engineering 7 (1995) 566-581

Datta, A.: Databases for Active Rapidly Changing Data Systems (ARCS): Augmenting Real-Time Databases with Temporal and Active Characteristics. International Workshop on Real-Time Databases (1996)

Dayal, U., Blaustein, B., Buchmann, A., Chakravarthy, S., Hsu, M., Ladin, R., McCarthy, D. Rosenthal, A., Sarin, S., Carey, M. J., Livny, M., Jauhari, R.: The HiPAC Project: Combining Active Databases and Timing Constraints. ACM SIGMOD Record 17 (1988) 51-70

Dayal, U., Buchmann, A., McCarthy, D.: Rules Are Objects Too: A Knowledge Model for Active, Object-Oriented Database Systems. Proceedings of the 2nd International Workshop on Object-Oriented Database Systems, Bad Muenster am Stein, Ebernburg, West Germany (1988)

Deutsch, A.: Method and Composite Event Detection in the "REACH" Active Database System. Master's thesis, Technical University Darmstadt (1994)

Díaz, O.: Tool Support. In Paton, N. W., editor, Active Rules for Databases. Springer-Verlag. (1998) To appear.

Eich, M. H.: A Classification and Comparison of Main Memory Database Recovery Techniques. Proceedings of International Conference on Data Engineering (1987) 332–339

Garzia-Molina, H. Salem, K.: Main Memory Database Systems: An Overview. IEEE Transactions on Knowledge and Data Engineering 4 (1992) 509–516

Gatziu, S. Dittrich, K. R.: Events in an Active Object-Oriented Database System. Technical Report Nr. 93.11, Institut für Informatik, Universität Zürich (1993)

Gehani, N. H., Jagadish, H. V., and Shmueli, O.: Composite Event Specification in Active Databases: Model and Implementation. Proceedings of the 18th VLDB Conference Vancouver, British Columbia, Canada (1992a)

Gehani, N. H., Jagadish, H. V., and Shmueli, O.: Event Specification in an Active Object-Oriented Database. Proceedings of the ACM SIGMOD International Conference on Management of Data, San Diego (1992b) 81–90

Geppert, A., Gatziu, S., Dittrich, K. R.: Performance Evaluation of an Active Database Management System: 007 Meets the BEAST. Technical Report Nr. 94.18, Institut für Informatik, Universität Zürich (1994)

Geppert, A., Gatziu, S., Dittrich, K. R.: A Designer's Benchmark for Active Database Management Systems: 007 Meets the BEAST. In Sellis, T., editor, Rules in Database Systems, Second International Workshop, Glyfada, Athens, Greece. Springer-Verlag (1995) 309–323

Hanson, E. N.: An Initial Report on the Design of Ariel: A DBMS with an Integrated Production Rule System. ACM SIGMOD Record 18 (1989) 12–19

Hanson, E. N. Widom, J.: Rule Processing in Active Database Systems. Technical Report WSU-CS-91-07, Department of Computer Science and Engineering, Wright State University (1991)

Haritsa, J. R., Carey, M. J., Livny, M.: On Being Optimistic About Real-Time Constraints. Proceedings of the 1990 ACM PODS Symposium (1990)

Jaeger, U. Freytag, J. C.: An Annotated Bibliography on Active Databases. ACM SIGMOD Record 24 (1995) 58–69

Kumar, V. Burger, A.: Performance Measurement of Main Memory Database Recovery Algorithms Based on Update-In-Place and Shadow Approaches. IEEE Transactions on Knowledge and Data Engineering 4 (1992) 567–571

Kung, H. T. Robinson, R. T.: On Optimistic Methods for Concurrency Control. ACM Transactions on Database Systems 6 (1981)

Kuo, T.-W. Mok, A. K.: Real-Time Database—Similarity Semantics and Resource Scheduling. ACM SIGMOD Records 25 (1996) 18–22

Levy, E. Silberschatz, A.: Incremental Recovery in Main Memory Database Systems. IEEE Transactions on Knowledge and Data Engineering 4 (1992) 529–540

Lin, K.-J. Peng, C.-S.: Enhancing External Consistency in Real-Time Transactions. ACM SIGMOD Record 25 (1996) 26–28

Listgarten, S., Neimat, M.-A.: Cost Model Development for a Main Memory Database System. In Real-Time Database Systems: Issues and Applications, Kluwer Academic Publishers, Boston (1996)

Liu, J. W.S., Lin, K.-J., Shih, W.-K., Yu, A. C-s., Chung, J.-Y., Zhao, W. Algorithms For Scheduling Imprecise Computations. IEEE Computer (1991) 58–68

Liu, J. W. S. Son, S. H., editors: The First International Workshop on Real-Time Databases: Issues and Applications, Newport Beach, California (1996)

Locke, C. D.: Best-Effort Decision Making for Real-Time Scheduling. Technical Report CMU-CS-86-134, Department of Computer Science, Carnegie-Mellon University, USA (1986)

Mellin, J.: Event Monitoring and Detection in Distributed Real-Time Systems: A Survey. Technical Report HS-IDA-TR-96-006, Department of Computer Science, University of Skövde (1995)

Morgenstern, M.: Active Databases as a Paradigm for Enhanced Computing Environments. (1983)

O'Neil, P. Ulusoy, O.: Guest Editorials: Real-Time Database Systems. Information Systems 21 (1996) 1–2

Özsoyoğlu, G. Snodgrass, R. T.: Guest Editors' Introduction to Special Section on Temporal and Real-Time Databases. IEEE Transactions on Knowledge and Data Engineering 7 (1995a) 511–512

Özsoyoğlu, G. Snodgrass, R. T: Temporal and Real-Time Databases: A Survey. IEEE Transactions on Knowledge and Data Engineering 7 (1995b) 513–532

Purimetla, B., Sivasankaran, R. M., and Stankovic, J. A.: A Study of Distributed Real-Time Active Database Applications. IEEE Workshop on Parallel and Distributed Real-Time Systems (1993)

Ramamritham, K.: Real-Time Databases. Journal of Distributed and Parallel Databases. Kluwer Academic Publishers, Boston (1993) 199–226

Ramamritham, K., Sivasankaran, R., Stankovic, J. A., Towsley, D. T., Xiong, M.: Integrating Temporal, Real-Time and Active Databases. ACM SIGMOD Record 25 (1996) 8–12

Ramamritham, K. Soparkar, N.: Report on DART '96: Databases: Active and Real-Time (Concepts Meet Practice) (1996)

Ramamritham, K., Stankovic, J. A., and Zhao, W.: Distributed Scheduling of Tasks with Deadlines and Resource Requirements. IEEE Transactions on Computers 38 (1989) 1110–1123

Sha, L., Rajkumar, R., Lehoczky, J. P., Ramamritham, K.: Mode Change Protocols for Priority-Driven, Preemptive Scheduling. Real-Time Systems Journal (1989) 243–265

Sivasankaran, R. M., Purimetla, B., Stankovic, J., Ramamritham, K.: Network Services Databases—A Distributed Active Real-Time Database (DARTDB) Application. IEEE Workshop on Real-Time Applications (1993)

Sivasankaran, R. M., Stankovic, J. A., Towsley, D., Purimetla, B., Ramamritham, K.: Priority Assignment in Real-Time Active Databases. VLDB Journal 5 (1996) 19–34

Son, S. H.: Guest Editor's Introduction: Real-Time Database Systems: Issues and Approaches. ACM SIGMOD Record 17 (1988) 2–3

Soparkar, N., Korth, H. F., Silberschatz, A.: Databases with Deadline and Contingency Constraints. IEEE Transactions on Knowledge and Data Engineering 7 (1995) 552–565

Stankovic, J. A.: Misconceptions About Real-Time Computing. IEEE Computer (1988) 10–19

Stonebraker, M.: Triggers and Inference in Database Systems. In Brodie and Mylopoulos, editors, On Knowledge Base Management Systems, Springer-Verlag (1986) 297–314

Stonebraker, M., Hearst, M., Potamianos, S.: A Commentary on the POSTGRES Rules System. ACM SIGMOD Record **18** (1989) 5–11

Stonebraker, M., Rowe, L., Hirohama, M.: The Implementation of POSTGRES. IEEE Transactions on Knowledge and Data Engineering **2** (1990) 125–142

Tseng, S.-M., Chin, Y. H., Yang, W.-P.: Scheduling Value-Based Transactions in Real-Time Main-Memory Databases. International Workshop on Real-Time Databases (1996)

Tsotras, V. J. Kumar, A.: Temporal Database Bibliography Update. ACM SIGMOD Record **25** (1996) 41–51

Ulusoy, Ö.: Research Issues in Real-Time Database Systems. Technical Report BU-CEIS-94-32, Bilkent University, Department of Computer Engineering and information Science, Ankara, Turkey (1994)

Ulusoy, Ö. Buchmann, A.: Exploiting Main Memory DBMS Features to Improve Real-Time Concurrency Control Protocols. ACM SIGMOD Record **25** (1996) 23–25

Xiong, M., Stankovic, J. A., Ramamritham, K., Towsley, D., Sivasankaran, R.: Maintaining Temporal Consistency: Issues and Algorithms. International Workshop on Real-Time Databases (1996)

Invited Talks

Design of a Real-Time SQL Engine in the Distributed Environment *

Deji Chen and Aloysius K. Mok

Department of Computer Sciences
University of Texas at Austin
Austin, TX 78712

Abstract. Real-time database research has reached a point when a practical approach need to be found to combine academic research fruits with real world problems. It is generally believed that the transaction scheduling principles of the traditional database management is too stringent to meet real-time constraints. In this paper, we look at the real world problem and argue that the future will see the proliferation of federated database consisting of distributed heterogeneous subdatabases. We propose the similarity predicate to unify real-time constraints on applications of the federated database system. We then design a real-time SQL engine that sits between the distributed database and the applications that separates the database design from individual user application. The real-time part of the engine benefits from SQL standard and can be scaled from empty to very sophisticated.

1 Introduction

People have been working on database for a long time. A database is simultaneously used by multiple clients, and each client transaction must satisfy ACID (Atomicity, Consistency, Isolation, Durability) property [13]. The commercial database has been evolving from relational to object-oriented. The standard query language SQL is also going through a major revision to SQL96. We see a mature market for database technology.

The real-time research has also been very active. As computer technology advances rapidly, we are facing the problem of managing large data with real-time requirements. The database world frequently has real-time applications; and the real-time world often faces applications with a large amount of data that simply could not be *ad hoc* managed. There has been much work from both worlds. Based on real-time expertise, there are papers on adding database to real-time applications [4, 8, 10, 11]. They analyze what the database design should be to satisfy real-time requirements. Many insights have been obtained from real-time database experimentations [3, 11]. Based on database expertize, there are also papers on adding real-time feature to database systems. Wolfe et.

---
* This work is supported by a grant from the Office of Naval Research under grant number N00014-94-1-0582.

al. also help standard committees to enhance current (inter)national standards with real-time ability.

It is generally agreed that ACID principle is usually too stringent for real-time transaction scheduling. Even to enforce ACID in the distributed environment is a big challenge to conventional database scientist. Various relaxations have been proposed [2, 6, 9] where imprecise results are tolerated for timeliness. Despite the hardness in distributed environment, there is still research on its real-time problems [3, 8].

Most of the research comes from a real-time expert point of view. Unfortunately, the on going conventional database research, especially the industry world, largely ignores the real-time issue. What we end up is still a school database systems without or little real-time support. To make the matter worse, we are expecting the adoption of COTS (Commercial Off The Shelf) database systems by some leading real-time critical institutions [1, 12]. We may have to work with any type of database systems.

In this paper, we argue that the future real-time database will be a federation of distributed heterogeneous subdatabases that are self-contained. The individual database's support for real-time may be strong or weak. It may most likely be COTS database system. We thus proposes a real-time SQL engine that begins small but can monotonically grow into a large practical system.

The paper is organized as follows. The next section explains the challenges we try to deal with. Section 3 proposed the similarity predicate –a unified real-time constraints for the applications of a distributed database. Section 4 introduces the real-time SQL engine. Section 5 concludes the paper.

2   The Distributed World

In this section we argue that the real-time database as well as the conventional database is going distributed.

We observe that: The data number and size hence the database is getting bigger and bigger; the distribution of data has become a fact rather than an alternative; the network bandwidth has become a major factor compared to computer computation power.

With the explosions of computation power and computer permeation, every information, either already exists or man-made, is entering the computer. Text information is giving way to video and sound. Database is evolving into data warehouse. Despite previous failure on very large size database, several projects are aiming for tera databases. The database design is already very difficult without timing considerations.

Unless you are designing an isolated small project, the real-time database will be a set of subdatabases connected with network. Let us consider an avionic system. An aeroplane's mission is to fly through a hostile area and gather information. There is controlling data for flying the plane, raw satellite pictures of the area, area detail information gathered by the plane, weapon information, etc. Most of the information is consumed locally. Different data set can be more efficiently and faster managed if it is contained in a separate subdatabase. It is unrealistic to have all data managed by a central database somewhere on the ground. Besides, it is also difficult to design a uniformed database schema for various data types. In this avionic system, the aeroplane control subsystem is itself manages a distributed database. There is special subdatabases for engine performance, flight manoeuvre, target recognition, panel display, etc.

The Internet is another obvious distributed example. A web site can be considered as a database that serves browsers. It has evolved from plain text to image and (or) virtual reality. The reality is a federated system of heterogeneous subsystems. It is impossible to imagine a centralized database encompassing all the information on the Internet.

Given the fact that data is generated from distributed sources and is getting bigger and bigger, one might still suggest a centralized database system. Our answer is in the long run it is doomed. There are three ways to build a database system over the distributed environment: the centralized with only one database, the extremely distributed where each node is a subdatabase, and the schema in between where a subset of nodes forms a subdatabase. The last type can always be looked as an extremely distributed system where the subset is considered one big node and the subset itself is one centralized database. So for analytic purpose we only consider the former two types.

Let us say there is a real-time system of N nodes interconnected through some network. Node $n_i, 1 \leq i \leq N$ generates s_i data per time unit. There are $\Sigma_{i=1}^{N} s_i$ new data per time unit for the entire network. Lets say node $n_i, 1 \leq i \leq N$ accesses u_i data per time unit from the database, and a ratio r_i of u_i is from other nodes. For the centralized database, the total network traffic V_c will be the total of sending data(s_i) from each node to the database plus accessing data(u_i) from the database, i.e. $V_c = \Sigma_{i=1}^{N}(s_i + u_i)$ per time unit. For the distributed database, the network traffic V_d will only be for data accessing from other nodes, i.e, $V_d = \Sigma_{i=1}^{N}(r_i * u_i)$ bytes per second.

First we observe that the network requirement is proportional to the amount of data involved. In 1965 Gordon Moore predicted that the transistor density on the microprocessor would double every 18 to 24 months. Hence the computing power would rise exponentially over relatively brief periods of time. Consequently the amount of data involved in a database would rise exponentially. The history has verified Moore's Law and it is predicted the trend will not slow down in the near future. The network bandwidth, on the other hand, increases much slower. Judging by the data size dependent formula of either V_c or V_d, the bandwidth will never catch up. As a matter of fact, the Internet already suffers this problem. While both the number of web sites and data in each site are fast growing, the net itself is jammed more and more frequently. Recently we have seen several shut down of AOL (America On Line), the major Internet service provider. Let us assume the bandwidth increases linearly, the difference from computer power still accelerates exponential. The Internet jamming will get even worse.

What we have is a distributed network where each node has huge amount of data, while the network bandwidth is limited. The centralized database design is doomed to fail. However, there is a big difference between V_c and V_d. For the centralized database, every bit of information has to be transferred to the database, while for the distributed database data is only transferred if some remote node requires it. To further illustrate, Let us assume $r_1 = r_2 = \ldots = r_N = r$ and $\frac{u_1}{s_1} = \frac{u_2}{s_2} = \ldots = \frac{u_N}{s_n} = e$. Figure 1 draws the function $\frac{V_d}{V_c} = \frac{re}{e+1}$. From figure 1 we know the network traffic in the distributed databases is always less than that of the distributed database. While centralized database can never get over the hurdles of the Moore's law, there is a chance for distributed database. The network load reduces when e decreases, which means remote data requests decreases, or when r decreases, which means less data is requested. Figure 1 tells us there is still hope for distributed database if r and e are small. When $r = 0$, there is no network requirement. Observe in above avionic example, most of the data is consumed locally. In the next section we will introduce similarity predicate to try to trade data precision for decreasing r.

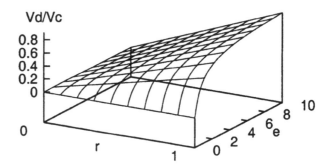

Fig. 1. The Network Traffic of Centralized and Distributed Databases

So the trend is that more and more distributed database systems will emerge. We do not, however, claim that current real-time database research misses the point. In the distributed database system, the subsystem is relatively self-contained and still need to support real-time specifications. With current ongoing research, We foresee the design of subdatabases getting more sophisticated and can be re-applied to different federated databases. The whole system will reduce cost by making use of such COTS subsystems.

3   The Similarity Predicate

In this section we extend the similarity concept to lessen database constraints and try to reduce the network load. The similarity predicate can further unify all real-time constraints so as to facilitate database management.

The advantage of centralized database is its easy management. It is suitable for small size network and for network where database is less frequently accessed. But it is not practical for large heterogeneous environment such as the Internet and military combat systems. The distributed database has less data traffic but hard to manage to make the whole confederated database consistent. When there is change in one node, it is hard for other node to be acknowledged, let alone to enforce ACID on heterogeneous databases.

It is usually unrealistic to have exact precise information of every data in a large system. And most of the time it is also not necessary. The more precise the requirement, the more time consumed to get the answer, hence the more chance of missing deadlines. Real-time application usually requires timely performance that contradicts database requirement. Research have been done to lessen stringent database requirements [2, 6]. Kuo and Mok [9] proposed the similarity concept where two values of the same data are deemed exchangable if they are within a certain similarity bound which reduces the database constraints for real-time transactions. In this paper we further extend the concept.

Similarity is a binary relation on the domain of a data object. Every similarity relation is reflexive and symmetric, but not necessarily transitive. In a schedule, we say that two event instances are similar if they are of the same type (read/write) and access similar values of the same data object. The concept of similarity can be used to extend the usual correctness criteria for transaction scheduling. By making use of the depth of data dependency in transaction schedules, the notion of strong similarity wad introduced and showed how it can be used to establish equivalence among schedules that permits a restricted form of event swapping. The results justify the weaker notion of correctness that has been employed on an *ad hoc* basis in many real-time applications where the state information is "volatile" and the value of data depends on its timeliness.

The work has been concentrated on *regular* similarity relation that is preserved by all transactions. The similarity has been measured in the time domain where two writings of the same data is considered similar if they are close enough. The similarity phenomenon is not limited. It can also be measured in other domains such as space and content; some times different client has different similarity requirement or the same client has different similarity requirement at different times. For example, the location of an aeroplane is retrieved for different purposes. The control tower accepts any value within several kilometers; but a speed derivation application need the value to be within several meters.

It is more appropriate to associate the similarity relation with individual transaction. Given any data, it is eventually used by some client. From the client's point, the data may not necessary be exactly precise. The client may only use it for reference, or gather general information, or just do not care about it at all during some periods. For example, in a combat area, participants should periodically gather position information of others. One participant A wants to make sure in the next few minutes nobody enters a bombing area. If A knows that B is far away and judged by A's information about B such as speed B will never get into the bombing area, A does not even need to poll B's position at all. In that case, any value is a similar value for B's position.

The similarity can be of various form and different client has different similarity requirement. We try to capture the this with a similarity predicate. The exact form of the predicate can be anything.

Definition 1 *The similarity requirement of a transaction T is defined as a predicate P. After T is finished, the answer X is regarded as correct if $P(X) = 1$; the answer is rejected if $P(X) = 0$. Two different answers X_1 and X_2 are considered similar if $P(X_1) = P(X_2)$.*

A transaction with 1 as P takes any result. It does not need to be scheduled at all. The example would be A's transaction to locate B in above combat system. A transaction with 0 as P can never be fulfilled and should be rejected. If P is evaluated to 0 or 1 in the beginning, system resource will be saved by not scheduling the transaction. Likewise if part of P can be evaluated, we can reduce the system resource usage. Suppose a transaction T involves two variable x, y. The similarity predicate is $P(x, y)$. The scheduler must schedule T to satisfy P. Figure 2 gives the evaluation graph of P where capital x(or y) means its value is known. Normally x and y need to be both evaluated for T. If from P we know the client doesn't care about x(It can be stated as $x = AnyThing$), i.e. $P(x, y) = P(X, y)$, $P(x, Y) = P(X, Y)$, the execution plan of T can be redesigned to ignore x, thus simplifies T and possibly reduces network traffic. In another case, if the client do cares about x but the scheduler knows its local cashed value X' of x already satisfies P, i.e. $P(X', y) = P(X, y)$, $P(X', Y) = P(X, Y)$. The scheduler may just schedule T for y and return cached x. We have seen lot's of such caching techniques in web browsers.

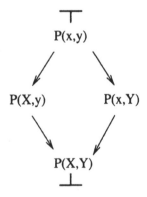

Fig. 2. Evaluation of Similarity Predicate

Example 1 *The similarity bound can be expressed as SimilarityBound =*
SomeValue. A transaction with this predicate can be scheduled with the relaxed
similar-serialization criteria.

The relaxation of ACID requirement for real-time system creates two types
of information to the conventional database system, the real-time constraints
and the similarity predicate. The predicate concept leads to a unified way to
express transaction requirement.

Definition 2 *The real-time similarity predicate P for a transaction T is the*
conjunction of a predicated clause for rel-time constraint and the similarity pred-
icate. After T is finished, the answer X is regarded as correct if $P(X) = 1$; the
answer is rejected if $P(X) = 0$. Two different answers X_1 and X_2 are considered
similar if $P(X_1) = P(X_2)$.

In a sense real-time constraint also a similarity requirement in that any answer satisfies the constraint is similar to the exact answer, and any answer fal-
sifies the constraint is not similar to the answer. A transaction with deadline
d can be expressed in predicate $FinishingTime \leq d$. If deadline can not be
met, the transaction is aborted because the answer will make the real-time similarity predicate false. We will call real-time similarity predicate the similarity
predicate, or just predicate.

The real-time similarity predicate concept introduces the powerful predicate
calculus into real-time database research. Different transaction execution plans
can be generated and compared to each other according to the predicate. if
$P = P_1 \wedge P'$ and p_i is already true, the transaction can be reduced to a new
one with predicate P'. In the distributed case, if the scheduler knows the local
lower resolution image of a remote picture already satisfies P, the scheduler do
not need to fetch the data again even the transaction uses it. Again, we are not
interested in exactly how SP is evaluated and the transaction is carried out.
There can be different ways to implement.

The exact formula of P as well as exactly how P is evaluated and the transaction is carried out is left to the specific database systems and applications.

4 The Real-time SQL Engine

In this section we briefly describes our reason for SQL, then the design and
implementation. We then concludes with the merits of a Real-time SQL engine.

4.1 Why Query Language

Cattell [5] gives two most important features of a query language:

– The language provides an English-like syntax that simplifies database access,
  so that end users and programmers have minimal new language to assimilate.

– The language provides data independence, because high-level statements may be compiled automatically into low-level operations according to the structure of the data and indexes available. The user specifies what data are desired, but the DBMS can determine how to get them

The first feature gives us a practical approach, and the second feature gives a place to optimize transaction scheduling. Not this advantage is not limited to relational database. The object-oriented database is also trying to provide query support.

The drawback of a query language is the impedance mismatch with application languages and interpretation time for interactive applications. These problems is ignorable in the distributed real-time database where network bandwidth is the bottleneck. The time spent on query analysis can be compensated by choosing an optimal execution strategy. If the query is for an image from a satellite database, we could save big if we know the user does not care too much about the quality so that the local cached copy suffices, or if we know there is a copy in a nearer host. By providing a query language engine between the federated database and the user gives us a place to optimize database access.

The SQL is already an international standard query language. The current effort is enhancing it with object-oriented feature. There is also work on real-time SQL standardization [7, 12].

The real-time SQL engine essentially opens a door to various real-time database applications. It separates the database from client applications. The applications can be procedural in which SQL queries are embedded in the application. Or it can be interactive such as Internet browser.

4.2 The Design

We assume that the data object can be of different media types and different sizes; local data access is faster than network transmission; different node has different data set and thus different database and different real-time support; and finally the SQL engine has knowledge of the metadata and network load condition. The system picture is illustrated in figure 3. The system consists of networked nodes. Each node has a specific real-time subdatabase best suited to its own requirement. The real-time SQL engine is a layer above the local database and network layer to the remote databases. It is the only interface the applications can access the federated database. Different node may implement different kinds of real-time SQL engine. The SQL syntax is the standard plus a real-time similarity predicate. Likewise the SQL engine is the standard SQL execution plan generator enhanced with plus real-time analyzer and executor. The engine will analyze and execute conventional query exactly as a normal SQL engine. The real-time application queries database with real-time similarity predicates. In this case the SQL engine will analyze the predicated while generating execution plan. The query will be reject if none of the possible execution plan can generate satisfying result. An imprecise execution plan may be generated with less network traffic as long as the similarity predicate can be satisfied.

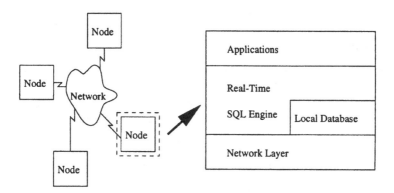

Fig. 3. The Real-time SQL Engine

The syntax for the similarity predicate can have any level of complexity. It can be empty set which equals normal SQL engine. It can include deadline requirement. It can also include syntax for expressing data similarity range. Interesting enough, we can also express periodic transaction by a single transaction with similarity predicate like $PERIOD = p$. The SQL engine will then execute it every p time units and each execution may be different as long as other oart of the similarity predicate evaluates to true. The video data has unique characteristic. In VOD(Video On Demand) the video need to be repeatedly fetch from the database, a frame at a time. This type of retrieval can also be expressed in the real-time SQL language. A video query without similarity predicate asks for the whole video at one time; a video query with $VIDEOPLAY = TRUE$ will be interpreted as continuously retrieving. The SQL engine will then fetch video frame once a time for the application. The following is the additional SQL keywords for similarity predicate.

- Real-time constraints
    - DEADLINE: DEADLINE=3 means the query must be finished within 3 time units.
    - PERIOD: PERIOD=10 means the query must be executed every 10 time units
    - PRIORITY: PRIORITY=3 means the priority of the query is 3
    - HARDNESS: HARDNESS=soft means its a sift real-time query
- Similarity constraints
    - RECENCY: RECENCY=10 means any value within last 10 time units is ok.
    - RESOLUTION: RESOLUTION=1 means data resolution must be the finest.
    - SUBSTITUTION: SUBSTITUTION=y means the value could be substituted if time is not enough.
    - PRECISION: PRECISION=1000 means data value can be round up to 1000.

– Other
  • VIDEOPLAY: VIDOPLAY=TRUE means the server will continuously send video frames.

Like normal SQL engine, the real-time engine works in two steps, query analysis and plan execution. The difference is in the first execution plan generation stage. In addition to conventional consideration, the similarity predicated is also analyzed and the information is used in execution plan generation.

The power of the real-time engine is not limited to what we discussed above. It will grow when new requirements come up and new keywords may be added. Basically this engine can monotonically grow from a non real-time engine to a sophisticated real-time engine. This is exactly why we could start our implementation without the complexity of a full-fledged real-tiem system.

4.3   The Implementation

We started by building a normal SQL engine which supports a bare bone set of SQL syntax. It manages a small relational database. The data types supported are integer and string. The limited subset of select, insert, delete, and update in addition to transaction statements are supported. It supports the join of three tables and does some query optimization. The project was done on Sun Solaris workstation using "bison" and "flex" and fully functional.

Without changing the basic SQL syntax we then add similarity predicate syntax to the "WHERE" clause of the select statement. The new keywords are "DEADLINE", "RECENCY", and "ANYTHING". For example, $"DEADLINE" = 100$ asks the query be finished in 100 microseconds; $"RECENCY" = 100$ accepts any value within 100 microseconds; $x = "ANYTHING"$ tells the engine the client do not care what x is.

Currently, however, our experimental engine is only a simulation. It responds to the similarity predicate by logging its analysis result. We do not intend to make the engine fully support all SQL syntax. Once we get hold of the source code of a conventional SQL engine, we will make it real-time aware with the testing results of our experimentation.

4.4   The Remarks

By placing a real-time SQL engine layer between the federated database and the applications gices us extra advantage in addition to the motives to the design. We summerize them in the following.

– Separation of labor. The engine is separated from the individual subdatabases that could be of any type from relational database to object oriented database, from conventional database to highly real-time supported. The SQL engine garners their information to best serve client applications. Generally most of the research result in real-time database can be incorporated into the big picture here.

- Monotonic nature. The real-time SQL engine can grow from very simply like a normal SQL engine to real-time sophisticated. This gives us a very pragmatic approach to address the realt-time problems raised in today's distributed heterogeneous systems. Through this engine, the evolution from conventional database to real-time aware database can be done smoothly.
- Easy to implement. We make use of the standardized SQL syntax and describe all real-time constraints in similarity predicate which can be easily included into standard SQL. The whole design does not put extra constraint on federated databases. This provides a way to make use of COTS databases, which again will reduce the overall cost of the system.
- Solve the key problem. We argue the bottleneck is going to be the network performance. The SQL engine sit at the right place to efficient use the network.
- Real-time service. Timeliness rather than quickness is mostly concerned here. The engine asks for extra time to analyze similarity predicate, but it can provides guaranteed real-time service. this extra time is justified by today's high computing power and relatively slow network speed.
- Powerful similarity predicate. The real-time similarity predicate can express almost every real-time constraints, including periodic requirement. The powerful predicate calculus raises an interesting topic on unifying various real-time considerations into one. Putting the predicate inside the query instead of an associated requirement to the query also offers the engine more chance to optimize.
- We provided one way of the real-time engine in this paper. The engine can actually be implemented differently, It is a combination of database, meta-database, scheduler. It can be relational or object-oriented. Ideally, it can be an intelligent agent.

5 Future Research

In this paper we analyzed the challenges faced in the database practices. We conclude as the data number and data size keeps growing, the distributed heterogeneous database is inevitable. This trend contradicts our wish in real-time research that prefers centralized controlling of all data. We first proposed the concept of real-time similarity predicate, then designed a real-time SQL engine. The distributed nature was sewed together with real-time constraints by the SQL engine.

The real-time SQL engine provides a practical and progressive way to address the real-time requirement in the distributed environment.

We plan to investigate more on the nature of the similarity predicate. We also plan to make the SQL engine into a real system and in the mean time provide more real-time service to it. For example, our engine only accepts similarity predicate with query. It can be extended to support update as well.

References

1. *Functionally Integrated Resource Manger (FIRM) Program*, 1993.
2. James H. Anderson, Srikanth Ramamurthy, and Kevin Jeffay. Real-time computing with lock-free shared objects. In *IEEE Real-Time Systems Symposium*, pages 28–37, December 1995.
3. S. F. Andler, J. Hansson, J. Eriksson, J. Mellin, M. Berndtsson, and B. Eftring. Deeds towards a distributed and active real-time database systems. *SIGMOD RECORD*, 25(1):38–40, 1996.
4. Azer Bestavros and Sue Nagy. Value-cognizant admission control for rtdb systems. In *IEEE Real-Time Systems Symposium*, pages 230–239, December 1996.
5. R. G. G. Cattell. *Object Data Management*. Addison-Wesley Publishing Company, 1994.
6. Jen-Yao Chung, J. W. S. Liu, and Kwei-Jay Lin. Scheduling periodic jobs that allow imprecise results. *IEEE Transactions on Computer*, 39(9), 1990.
7. Paul J. Fortier, Victor Fay Wolfe, and J.J. Prichard. Flexible real-time sql transactions. In *IEEE Real-Time Systems Symposium*, pages 276–280, December 1994.
8. Ramesh Gupta, Jayant Haritsa, Krithi Ramamritham, and S. Seshadri. Commit processing in distributed real-time database systems. In *IEEE Real-Time Systems Symposium*, pages 220–229, December 1996.
9. Tei-Wei Kuo and Aloysius K. Mok. Real-time database - similarity semantics and resource scheduling. *SIGMOND RECORD*, 25(1):18–22, 1996.
10. Mathew R. Lehr, Young-Kuk Kim, and Sang H. Son. Managing contention and timing constraints in a real-time database system. In *IEEE Real-Time Systems Symposium*, pages 332–341, December 1995.
11. Sang H. Son. *Advances in Real-time Systems*. Prentice Hall, 1995.
12. Space and Naval Warfare Systems Command. *Next Generation Computer Resources*, 1994.
13. Michael Stonebraker. *Readings in database Systems*. Morgan Kaufmann Publishers, 1994.

A Cellular Database System
for the 21st Century

Martin L. Kersten

CWI, Kruislaan 413 1098 SJ Amsterdam, The Netherlands, mk@cwi.nl

Abstract. The pervasive penetration of database technology in all areas of IT may suggest that we have reached the end of the database research era. This paper demonstrates that many routes and areas are still unexplored, partly because the database community sticks to a dogmatic view on the necessary functionality of a DBMS. A concrete architecture is described to exploit the distributed opportunities currently widely available.

1 Introduction

The main thrust of database research comes from attempts to deploy the technology in non-trivial application areas. The enhancements proposed to the core functionality are primarily triggered by the specific needs encountered. For example, support of multi-media applications has led to enriched data models to cope with temporal issues; support for geographical information systems has lead to improved spatial reasoning facilities, etc..

However, whether it is based on an object-relational, active, or real-time database approach progress is hindered by off-the-shelf (emerging) database technology. Simply, because development of an experimental DBMS requires too much resources. At best it results in a 'data-blade'-kind of solution, shallow layers on top of a commercial system, or a panacea offered by persistent C++.

The issue addressed in this short paper is triggered by the need to identify opportunities for innovative fundamental and strategic research in the database area. Such a discussion is considered essential to advance the state-of-the-art in a social/economic context where the risk to explore new alleys are several hindered by lack of resources or the need to bring a PhD track to a successful completion in a relatively short period.

The premises of this paper is that database technology has contributed significantly to IT over several decades, BUT it is also time to challenge the key assumptions underlying database technology. A few key assumptions considered to be dogmatic and a bottleneck for progress are:

- A database is larger then the main memory of the computer on which the DBMS runs and a great deal of effort is devoted to efficient management of crossing the chasms in the memory hierarchy.
- A DBMS should adhere to a standard data model, whether it be relational, an object-relational, object-oriented and leaving functional and deductive models as a playground for researchers.

- A DBMS provides a persistent information store through which it provides a communication channel between users separated in time and space, i.e. an electronic archive.
- A DBMS provides quick response to any query, optimizing resource usage wherever possible without concern on the effect of concurrent users.
- A DBMS should support concurrent access by multiple users and reconcile the different perspectives on the database contents.
- A DBMS provides a transaction models based on the ACID principles, or a semantically enriched version.

This list is by no means complete, but merely indicates the delineation of research activities in the database community. A prototype DBMS ignoring these point is not taken seriously in the research realm.

Furthermore, confusion on terminology and perceived mis-use of unique selling points have led to formalized descriptions of the "necessary" DBMS functionality. Illustrative examples are the standardization efforts of SQL, the object-oriented manifesto [2] and the active database manifesto [7]. They provide a milestone for product developments and a yardstick for research prototypes. But, at the same time they limit innovation in the database core as well.

The remainder of this paper is a desktop study to charter the contours of a next generation DBMS. One that is not designed to accommodate yet another important application domain, but an attempt to explore novel computational schemes and opportunities to renovate the internals of a general purpose DBMS.

It is written at a time that deployment of the Monet system [3, 4] is in full swing and it capitalizes experience gained in producing several other full-fledged systems [8, 1]. It aligns with trends of commercial DBMS providers, who have already recognized the limited growth in their core products and embrace complementary solutions, e.g. Sybase with IQ, Computer Associates with Jasmine, Oracle with Express, and Tandem with its Data Mining System. It is safe to predict that within the next decade they provide a DBMS product configured as an assemblage of specialized servers. Perhaps there is room for the architecture described below.

2   Design principles

Confronted with the task to design a new DBMS (from scratch) one has to tackle a large number of design issues without a priori knowledge on their combined effect. This requires a delineation of functionality based on a perception of the hardware/software trends. Moreover, it requires a balanced risk in following known routes or to charter a new area of research.

The basic functionality required for our system is to provide a persistent data store and query processor to retrieve data upon request. This functionality is to be realized in a distributed setting. Within this general framework the following design axioms are considered:

- Global database integrity is a convergence property.
- Indexing is incremental, dynamic and discontinuous.
- Query answering never ends.
- Transaction management is a contractual issue.
- Respect the physical limitations of the platform.

2.1 Global database integrity is a convergence property

The first design choice challenges the key assumption in contemporary DBMSs that its content obeys the integrity rules laid out in the database schema. The technical means to support it are the transaction manager and integrity controller, the datamodel semantics (e.g. logic and temporal database models), but also the features of the underlying database structures (e.g. B-tree keys). A great deal of research has been devoted to scale this rule to a distributed setting.

By setting our flag on integrity as a convergence property, we stress the fact that a user at any time sees only part of the database. It means that only his local perspective need to be consistent and not necessarily reflects the ideal global state of affairs. This property may be used in the DBMS realization as well.

For example, consider an employee database where new entries are added every day. Then the rule that a salary field should be filled is only relevant when the pay-checks have to be sent out. Moreover, it is not uncommon (in Holland) that contract finalizations cross the first payment day. Then a pro-visionary salary is being paid. This scheme works because all involved know that the system converges to a situation that the salary is paid automatically.

From a research perspective this viewpoint requires additional research in partial consistent logical models and convergence primitives in temporal models.

2.2 Indexing is an incremental, dynamic and discontinuous

This design choice challenges the practice to assume that search accelerators keep track of the changes in the underlying database files and the role of the DBA in selecting the items to index.

We conjuncture that basic search accelerators are to be selected by the DBMS itself and maintained as long as affordable. Feasibility of this approach has already been demonstrated in our Monet system.

However, a more fundamental issue related to indexing is that we have reached the end of simple syntactic-based schemes. For example, to index a multi-media database we can derive syntactic properties from the objects stored (e.g. color distributions, key frames, shapes...) to help filtering candidates, but the real gain comes from annotations, classifications by end-users and specialized computational intensive algorithms (e.g. facial recognition) to recognize meaningful objects.

For example, consider a database with a million images retrieved from the Web. Creation of a semantic meaningful index to speed-up querying requires a concept-hierarchy and capturing its relationship with every image stored.

Progress in image recognition indicates that this process is bound to remain a time consuming manual process for decades to come. This implies that either we have to involve many people to maintain the index, or change the way we use indexes.

Our design choice sets out a course where indices constructed manually or by computational expensive feature detectors are to be supported from the outset. A direct consequence of choice is that an index is always partial, it provides quick access to only a portion of the indexed set. In turn this affects all components of a traditional DBMS architecture.

2.3   Query answering never ends

A primary focus of DBMS interaction is to handle queries as efficiently as possible. Most query processors treat each query as an unique request that can be solved by the (relational algebra) engine in finite time. Moreover, the query is implicitly considered the inverse of update, it uses the same database schema to identify objects of interest.

In this area we can identify several plausible alternative routes to explore. First, we should recognize that within any given database the queries handled are driven by semantic considerations and, therefore, tend to be semantically focussed in time. This implies that we should consider keeping track of queries posed in the past and their execution plans. By analogy it is time to build an opening-book of a chess program (i.e. query optimizer).

Second, we assume that posing a query is equivalent to extending a DBMS with a stream generator. This stream generator emits objects of interest and, in principle, never stops. The stream may be redirected to applications dynamically and it can be constrained with rules determined by the receiving party.

For example, consider a stock-exchange database and an interest in the price of IBM. Then, instead of polling the database at regular intervals with an SQL query or to trigger upon each update, we assume that the DBMS sent updates constrained by stream conditions. Possible stream conditions could be to sent new prices within five minutes of update, to redirect the stream if the receiving party does not accept the message, or to buffer a limited number for updates, i.e. send the last three prices.

Finally, their is no need to strongly relate the update scheme with the objects that can be retrieved from the database. It might even be more productive to clearly separate their role. A query scheme differs from the update scheme in objects being made available and the integrity rules are replaced by constraints over the query stream produced. Any overlap with the update scheme is to be considered accidental.

2.4   Transaction management is a contractual issue

In essence, transaction management is a rudimentary technique to establish a contract between user and DBMS. This contract assures atomicity, durability, isolation, and consistency for objects being managed. The focus on on-line-transaction management has led to a situation where these contractual primitives have been embedded deeply in the DBMS code, i.e. the contract deals with disk pages or individual records.

The limitations of this approach has already led to a plethora of proposed alternatives, i.e. sagas[5]. However, the perceived need for high performance - maintained by the TPC-wars - has neglected the inclusion of the primitives at the proper level of the architecture. It is hard to ignore transaction primitives when the application does not need this functionality and often impossible to refine.

For example, consider a simple bank account balance database. Even for a large bank this database can be kept in a relatively small main-memory database. To secure its content it has been known for years [6] that battery backed up RAM or SRAM ensures stability. Furthermore, the speed obtained in a main-memory system allows one to serialize processing the requests, while logging could be offloaded to the front-office, thereby reducing the points of total system failure. Nevertheless, the OLTP systems are still based on technology designed for databases equipped with a few hundred Kbyte DRAM and slow, small disks.

We conjuncture that future DBMS should recognize the contractual aspect from the outset and let the user model any contracts explicitly. The techniques to produce and maintain a sound contract can be encapsulated in a notary subsystem.

2.5 Respect the physical limitations of the platform

The last design choice concerns the DBMS software itself. Common practice is to built DBMS software with a general and traditional hardware platform in mind. The platform involves at least two levels in the memory hierarchy (disk+RAM), a single CPU embedded in an SMP node, a slow interconnect to the application (ODBC, TCP/IP). Refinement of the software is obtained by setting runtime and compilation parameters.

The net effect of this approach is a severe reduction in software production and maintenance cost. The down side is an overly complex software architecture, which is often not optimized for the platform concerned.

Given the trend to include database facilities in mobile systems, smart-cards, network computer, etc., make me believe that there is a need for a variety of DBMS engines that each respect the limitations of their platform. Their integration is obtained using a de-facto standard communication scheme, i.e. the Web.

3 Architectural overview

In this section we illustrate a possible architecture exploring some of the design choices. The system foreseen is illustrated in Figure 1. It consists of a large number of cells linked into a communication infrastructure. Each cell is a bounded container, i.e. a work-station or a mobile unit. Alternatively, a cell is a process with CPU and memory limitations running on a work-station. Our target is to enrich each cell such that it behaves as an autonomous DBMS.

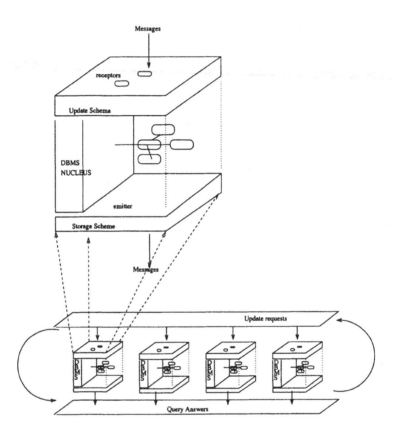

Fig. 1. The Cellular Architecture

3.1 Receptor and Emitter schemes

The general processing cycle of a cell is to accept messages, subsequently chance its internal state, and emit messages for other cells. A message is being accepted in two steps. First, the message is *structurally* checked against a collection of tree-structured patterns. This leads to a parse tree where leave nodes are equated with a lexical value and the tree itself provides for a structured name space to access the leaves. Second, a *semantic* check is performed using a predicate over the parse tree and information already stored in the cell.

Lets coin the term *receptor* for the definition of both components. A receptor bears a (locally) unique name and filters messages of interest. It ignores all that do not pass both subtests and leaves it to the environment to forward it to another candidate cell.

Once a message has been accepted it is interpreted by the cell nucleus. Commonly this results in moving part of the message to persistent store for future retrieval or updates of objects already stored. The internal representation is not essential for the external visible behavior. For the time being we assume that the parse tree are literary saved.

A cell emits messages to its environment using a message generator. This generator consists of two components: a pattern and a query expression. Lets coin the term *emitter* for their definition. The pattern defines the output message structure. It consists of literals and variables bound in the query expression. Once installed it starts querying the cell's historical state and emits an answer for each valid combination of variable bindings turning the query expression to truth.

Much like the receptor, an emitter is a permanent enhancement of a cell. Once installed it continues to produce messages when the internal state has been changed. By analogy, it behaves as a never ending traditional database query.

Example. Consider a cell to be configured as a database to manage a list of persons. Then a possible representation of the cell's update and query scheme is shown in Figure 2. In the spirit of Prolog, the identifiers starting with a capital

receptor	insert person:P(name:L,age:A)
	if $A > 0$, $P.A < 100$, string(L).
receptor	delete person(name:L)
	if string(L), person:P, P.name=L.
receptor	increaseAge person(name:N)
	if person:P(name:N,age:A)
	P.age is $A+1$.
emitter	accepted P
	if person:P.
emitter	q1 person(name:L,age:A)
	if person(name:L,age:A), $A < 21$.
emitter	q2 person(name:L,age:A)
	if person(name:L,age:A), $A >= Low$, $A <= High$.

Fig. 2. Person cell definition

letter are considered variables. The first receptor would unify with the message `insert person(name:"John",age:23)`. The semantic check can be read as a clause with a path naming scheme to access object components. The term P.A denotes the A component within the structure identified by P. The term `string(L)` relates to a builtin predicate that yields true if the argument belongs to the domain of strings. The effect of this receptor on the state space is determined by the built-in definition of the insert operator, i.e. assertion of a new fact.

The second receptor unifies with the message `delete person(name:"John")`. The semantic check involves a query over the cell state to look for knowledge about the person John in the persistent store. The term `person:P` is an existential binding of the variable P to a `person` object. The last receptor illustrates a possible route to encode state changes. It replaces the age component of John.

Querying the person cell involves definition of emitters. The first emitter generates a message whenever it detects a new person fact in the state space, e.g. `accepted person(name:"John",age:23)` would be sent as an acknowledgement of a successful insertion operation.

For example, often we are interested in a list of all known persons. Instead of introducing a new emitter each time we need this list, we might also change the state parameters maintained for the emitter itself. Namely, we reset its notion about what part of the state has been considered for emittance so far, e.g. by sending the message `reset accepted`.

The emitter q1 illustrates a simple query to find young persons. Once installed it starts checking the state for person objects qualifying the query condition. It leads to a stream of answers that can be differentiated form other queries using the emitter name.

Emitter q2 illustrates an emitter scheme or parameterized query. After receiving the message `q2(low:18,high:42)` an instance of q2 is constructed and behaves as an ordinary emitter.

3.2 Nucleus primitives

The `receptor` and `emitter` constructs are interface descriptors understood by the cell nucleus. Each results in an object that can be identified by a prefix match over its definition. For example, `receptor insert`, `receptor insert person`, and `receptor insert person(name)` all denote the insertion receptor in Figure 2. The pattern match for sub-structures should obey the order, but may be incomplete. Moreover, variables may be named differently. Thus, `insert person:L(age)` also denotes the insertion receptor.

To manage the receptors we need several nucleus primitives. The following partial messages are to be recognized:

- **destroy** R **if** C, which removes R from the cell interface as soon as the optional cell condition C is satisfied.
- **stop** R **if** C, put R temporarily in sleeping mode, ignoring all candidate messages, as soon as the optional cell condition C is satisfied.
- **awake** R **if** C, to re-activate R, as soon as the optional condition C is satisfied.
- **show** R, to emit the definition of R for inclusion in another cell.
- **reset** R **if** C, to reset the emitter R, as soon as the optional condition C is satisfied.

A cell will contains many global properties for controlling its behavior. Some will reflect the limitations imposed by the underlying hardware, e.g. Memory.size and Processor.type, others will keep track of the external state, for example Clock.month, or reflect aggregated information maintained Receptors.count. Properties are referenced by their name, which take the shape of a predefined variable. An actual implementation for the cell nucleus have to identify the minimal set.

3.3 Nucleus processing cycle

The nucleus maintains a virtual clock Now, which increments each time the cell accepts a message. Its value is a composite of the wall clock value, the cell identity, and a discriminative counter. It plays the role of a transaction identifier in ordinary systems and it is attached to all (partial) objects. A 'clock cycle' is finished when the action associated with the receptor (or emitter) has successfully been completed. It is up to the nucleus implementation to assure that concurrent execution of multiple actions are being serialized.

For example, emitters use the time line to generate answers as follows. Let Q be bound to an emitter then the property Q.now denotes the time stamp received upon installation. Q.current denotes the time stamp associated with the consolidated inspection of the state space. It is set to the origin of time upon installation or by receiving the reset Q message.

All objects with a time stamp less than Q.current have been considered candidates for emittance and the emitter looks for effects produced in the period (Q.current,Q.current+1). For each object introduced it tries to satisfy the query expression by looking for all variable bindings such that at least one binding is new. If Q.current = Q.now then we have explored the database up to the state the query was posed. In a traditional system it would mean that the query is finished. If Q.current < Now then the emitter is running behind the update stream. It remains dormant until new messages have been accepted.

The nucleus primitives in combination with the virtual clock can be used to implement a wide range of dynamic behavior. For example, we can stop accepting insertions of new persons until all queries are 'finished' using:

  stop   insert person
        if emitter:Q, Q.current<Now.
  awake insert person
        if not (emitter:Q, Q.current=Now).
or stop all receptors that have not been activated since last Sunday:
  stop R
        if receptor:R, R.now.day = "Sunday", R.now.daynr>= Now.daynr-7

3.4 Cell heritage

Another design choice for the cell implementation is to take into account the physical boundaries. This means that we should try to develop cell nuclei that are optimized for their target platform.

This design choice, however, raises a number of interesting management issues. How should a cell re-act when it has exhausted its resources ? How can we migrate the content to another cell without disrupting the complete system?

Let's explore the case that a cell runs out of persistent store. The base line for a nucleus implementation is to ignore any further attempt to insert new information into the cell. Ultimately this leaves the message handling system with an undeliverable message.

An alternative approach is to assume that spare cells are available. Then the cells should merely clone itself, occupying a spare cell and division of labour in such a way that the outer world is not aware that two cells now handle the task.

Cloning involves several steps. First, a spare cell should be identified and a copy of the nucleus code should be down loaded. Second, the persistent store should be broken into complementary pieces or partially replicated and distributed over both cells. Finally, the receptors and emitters should be cloned. A simple scheme would be to merely replicate them and leave it up to the communication infrastructure to assure that all messages are delivered to both cells.

In general it will not be possible to split a cell into completely autonomous and complementary cells. Often it would lead to a situation where either for validation of a receptor message or the construction of an emitter message that access is required to the content of the sibling cell. A possible solution could be to distribute the content of a cloning cell over two spare parts leaving a empty cell behind that merely controls forwarding of messages and control over distributed queries. But how this should be implemented is unknown.

For example, assume that the person cell is full and needs to be split. A possible division of labour would be to distribute the content over two cells based on the age property, shown in Figure 3. Such a divisor strengthens the predicate and correctly divides the space of messages.

The emitters could also be replicated over the clones, because they access a single object at a time. However, if we would install an emitter that relates two persons then the scheme breaks down.

emitter couples(M,F)
    if person:M, person:F, M!=F, M.age = F.age

Simple replication of the emitter is not sufficient. We also need an emitter that uses person objects stored in other cells. This leads to a more complicated variable binding term, which now also involves a reference to all clones. In essence this involves opening a query stream. A solution would be to clone as follows:

emitter couples(M,F)
    if personCell?person:M, person:F, M!=F, M.age = F.age

This emitter tries to bind a local person F with any person M in any cell recognized as a clone of personCell.

Another form of cloning would be triggered if we detect too many emitters or when they lag too far behind Now. Then, we need clones with copies of the emitters and access to the persistent store. Moreover, the cloning cell should assure that updates are propagated to replicas, or any new query is handled by all cells involved.

```
cell:personCell.1
receptor insert person:P(name:L,age:A)
         if A>0, P.A<50, string(L).
receptor delete person(name:L)
         if string(L), person:P, P.name=L.
receptor increaseAge person(name:N)
         if person:P(name:N,age:A)
         P.age is A+1.
cell:personCell.2
receptor insert person:P(name:L,age:A)
         if A>49, P.A<100, string(L).
receptor delete person(name:L)
         if string(L), person:P, P.name=L.
receptor increaseAge person(name:N)
         if person:P(name:N,age:A)
         P.age is A+1.
```

Fig. 3. Figure Cell division for cloning

3.5 Communication infrastructure

The cellular system is bound to be operational in a global environment over the Internet. Therefore, it makes sense to align the cell naming scheme with URLs and to include a separate protocol to handle the messages for the cellular system. The structure would become:

cds://*server.domain:port/user/path/cell message arguments*

This protocol delivers the *message* to a cds server located at *server.domain:port*. The cells addressed are located in the public readable directory identified by *user/path*. The directory *cell* contains the persistent versions of all cells of a given type identified by the directory name. Upon receipt of a request the cds server will forward the the message to any (or all) of the cells, possibly awakening them by turning them into runnable processes.

If no cell accepts the message then the protocol returns it to the originator with an error tag.

Example. Consider the cell link:

cds://cds.cwi.nl/person/friend emit P

A message arriving at the server cds.cwi.nl is forwarded to a cell identified as friend. If the target ignores the message then any friend clone is considered. After all friend cell clones we start checking the (clones of) person cells.

This scheme may be further refined to differentiate behavior according to the message kind being delivered. For example, emitter definitions could be broadcasted to all cells assuming the policy that an emitter definition is rejected if it can not potentially be answered. That is, the cell does not contain a receptor for the information needed. Alternatively, the target for a cell link accepts any message and based on a structural analysis decides how to forward it.

4 Summary

In this short paper we have reviewed some of the core assumptions underlying database technology and argued that there is still room for innovations. A possible architecture for a cellular database system has been sketched. Amongst the novelties explored are the notion of queries as DBMS enhancements that indefinitely emit answers when they become available; cloning has been proposed as the primary scheme to deal with the physical limitations; the message infrastructure has been aligned with the naming conventions on Internet.

Although this paper was intensionally a desktop study, I am looking forward to any serious attempt to implement a DBMS along the lines sketched.

References

1. P.M.G Apers, C.A. van den Berg, J. Flokstra, P.W.P.J. Grefen, M.L. Kersten, and A.N. Wilschut, *PRISMA/DB: A Parallel, Main-memory Relational DBMS*, IEEE KDE, special issue on Main-Memory DBMS. Dec, 1992.
2. Malcolm P. Atkinson, Franois Bancilhon, David J. DeWitt, Klaus R. Dittrich, David Maier, Stanley B. Zdonik: *The Object-Oriented Database System Manifesto*, In uilding an Object-Oriented Database System, The Story of O2. Morgan Kaufmann 1992, ISBN 1-55860-169-4
3. P. Boncz, W. Quak, and M. Kersten, *Monet and its geographical extensions* Proc. EDBT'96, Avignon (France), March 1996
4. P. Boncz, F. Kwakkel, M.L. Kersten *High performance support for O-O traversal in Monet* proc. BNCOD'96, Edingburgh (UK), July 1996.
5. Chrysanthis, Ramamritham *ACTA: The Saga Continues*, Invited book chapter, Database Transaction Models for Advanced Applications, Morgan, Kaufmann, A. Elmagarmid,Ed., 1992.
6. G.P. Copeland, T. Keller, R. Krishnamurthy, M. Smith, *The Case For Safe RAM*, Proc. VLDB 1989, Amsterdam, pp. 327-335.
7. Klaus R. Dittrich, Stella Gatziu, Andreas Geppert *The Active Database Management System Manifesto: A Rulebase of ADBMS Features* Proc. RIDS'95, pp. 3-20.
8. A.I. Wasserman, M.L. Kersten, D. Shewmake, P. Pircher, *Designing information systems within the User Software Engineering environm ent*, IEEE Transactions on Software Engineering, Feb. 1986.

BeeHive: Global Multimedia Database Support for Dependable, Real-Time Applications

John A. Stankovic, Sang H. Son, and Jörg Liebeherr

Department of Computer Science
University of Virginia
Charlottesville, VA 22903

Abstract. The confluence of computers, communications and databases is quickly creating a global virtual database where many applications require real-time access to both temporally accurate and multimedia data. We are developing a global virtual database, called BeeHive, which is enterprise specific and offers features along real-time, fault tolerance, quality of service for audio and video, and security dimensions. Support of all these features and tradeoffs between them will provide significant improvement in performance and functionality over browsers, browsers connected to databases, and, in general, today's distributed databases. We present a high level design for BeeHive and various novel component technologies that are to be incorporated into BeeHive.

1 Introduction

The Next Generation Internet (NGI) will provide an order of magnitude improvement in the computer/communication infrastructure. What is needed is a corresponding order of magnitude improvement at the application level. One way to achieve this improvement is through global virtual databases. Such databases will be enterprise specific and offer features along real-time, fault tolerance, quality of service for audio and video, and security dimensions. Support of all these features and tradeoffs between them will provide an order of magnitude improvement in performance and functionality over browsers, browsers connected to databases, and, in general, today's distributed databases. Such global virtual databases will not *only* be enterprise specific, but also interact (given proper protections) with the worldwide information base via wrappers. Such wrappers may be based on Java and Java Data Base Connectivity standards.

There are many research problems that must be solved to support global, real-time virtual databases. Solutions to these problems are needed both in terms of a distributed environment at the database level as well as real-time resource management below the database level. Included is the need to provide end-to-end guarantees to a diverse set of real-time and non-real-time applications over the current and next generation Internet. The collection of software services that support this vision is called BeeHive.

The BeeHive system that is currently being defined has many innovative components, including:

- real-time database support based on a new notion of *data deadlines*, (rather than just transaction deadlines),
- parallel and real-time recovery based on semantics of data and system operational mode (e.g., crisis mode),
- use of reflective information and a specification language to support adaptive fault tolerance, real-time performance and security,
- the idea of security rules embedded into objects together with the ability for these rules to utilize profiles of various types,
- composable fault tolerant objects that synergistically operate with the transaction properties of databases and with real-time logging and recovery,
- a new architecture and model of interaction between multimedia and transaction processing,
- a uniform task model for simultaneously supporting hard real-time control tasks and end-to-end multimedia processing, and
- new real-time QoS scheduling, resource management and renegotiation algorithms.

The BeeHive project builds upon these results and combines them into a novel design for a global virtual database.

In the remainder of this paper we discuss the high-level BeeHive system and sketch the design of a native BeeHive site showing how all the parts fit together. We also present technical details on the main functional ingredients of BeeHive which include Resource Management and QoS, Real-Time Databases, Adaptive Fault Tolerance, and Security. A brief description of the state of art is given. A summary of the work concludes the paper.

2 General BeeHive Design

2.1 An Overview of the Design

BeeHive is an application-focussed global virtual database system. For example, it could provide the database level support needed for information technology in the integrated battlefield. BeeHive is different than the World Wide Web and databases accessed on the Internet in many ways including BeeHive's emphasis on sensor data, use of time valid data, level of support for adaptive fault tolerance, support for real-time databases and security, and the special features that deal with crisis mode operation. Parts of the system can run on fixed secure hosts and other parts can be more dynamic such as for mobile computers or general processors on the Internet.

The BeeHive design is composed of native BeeHive sites, legacy sites ported to BeeHive, and interfaces to legacy systems outside of BeeHive (see Figure 1).

The native BeeHive sites comprise a federated distributed database model that implements a temporal data model, time cognizant database and QoS protocols, a specification model, a mapping from this specification to four APIs (the OS, network, fault tolerance and security APIs), and underlying novel object support. Any realistic application will include legacy databases. BeeHive

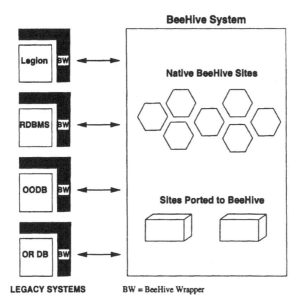

Fig. 1. BeeHive.

permits porting of these databases into the BeeHive virtual system by a combination of wrappers and changes to the underlying software of these systems. It is important to mention that BeeHive, while application focussed, is *not* isolated. BeeHive can interact with other virtual global databases, or Web browsers, or individual non-application specific databases via BeeHive wrappers. BeeHive will access these databases via downloaded Java applets that include standard SQL commands. In many situations, not only must information be identified and collected, but it must be analyzed. This analysis should be permitted to make use of the vast computer processing infrastructure that exists. For example, BeeHive will have a wrapper that can utilize a distributed computing environment, such as the Legion system [20], to provide significant processing power when needed.

2.2 Native BeeHive Design

The basic design of a native BeeHive site is depicted in Figure 2. At the application level, users can submit transactions, analysis programs, general programs, and access audio and video data. For each of these activities the user has a standard specification interface for real-time, QoS, fault tolerance, and security. At the application level, these requirements are specified in a high level manner. For example, a user might specify a deadline, full quality QoS display, a primary/backup fault tolerance requirement, and a confidentiality level of security. For transactions, users are operating with an object-oriented database invoking methods on the data. The data model includes timestamped data and data with validity intervals such as is needed for sensor data or troop position data. As transactions (or other programs) access objects, those objects become active and a mapping occurs between the high level requirements specification and the object API via the mapping module. This mapping module is primarily concerned with the interface to object wrappers and with end-to-end issues. A novel aspect of our work is that each object has semantic information (also called reflective information because it is information about the object itself) associated with it that makes it possible to simultaneously satisfy the requirements of time, QoS, fault tolerance, and security in an adaptive manner. For example, the information might include rules or policies and the action to take when the underlying system cannot guarantee the deadline or level of fault tolerance requested. This semantic information also includes code that makes calls to the resource management subsystem to satisfy or negotiate the resource requirements. The resource management subsystem further translates the requirements into resource specific APIs such as the APIs for the OS, the network, the fault tolerance support mechanisms, and the security subsystem. For example, given that a user has invoked a method on an object with a deadline and primary/backup requirement, the semantic information associated with the object makes a call to the resource manager requesting this service. The resource manager determines if it can allocate the primary and backup to (1) execute the method before its deadline and (2) inform the OS via the OS API on the modules' priority and resource needs.

In terms of this design, the main tasks to be undertaken include

- the full development of the high-level specification including how these requirements interact with each other,
- the implementation of real-time object-oriented database support,
- the design and implementation of our semantics enhanced objects,
- the design and implementation of the object-oriented wrappers,
- the development of the mapping module,
- the design and implementation of the resource management, fault tolerance, and security subsystems.

In the following sections, some of our ideas on resource management, real-time databases, adaptive fault tolerance, and security are described.

3   Resource Management and QoS

A critical component for the success of BeeHive is its ability to efficiently manage a vast amount of resources. BeeHive requires end-to-end resource management, including physical resources such as sensors, endsystems resources such as operating systems, and communications resources such as link bandwidth.

We assume that low-level resource management is available for single low-level system resources, such as operating systems and networks. For networks, resource reservation signaling is based on the RSVP [13] and UNI 4.0 [8] protocols for IP networks and ATM networks, respectively. Likewise, we assume that all operating systems are provided with a resource management entity.

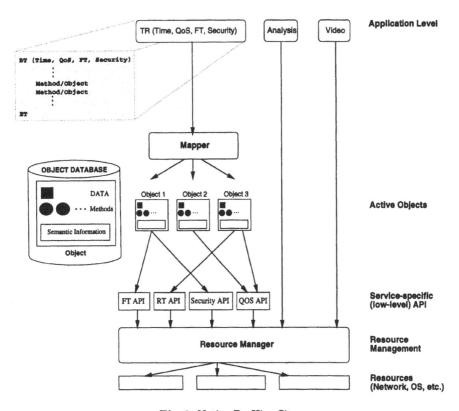

Fig. 2. Native BeeHive Site.

Based on these comparatively primitive resource management systems, Bee-Hive will implement a sophisticated end-to-end adaptive resource management system that supports applications with widely varying service requirements, such as requirements on timeliness, fault tolerance, and security. The resource management in BeeHive offers the following services:

- Provide service-specific application programming interfaces (APIs) that allow application programmers to specify the desired QoS without requiring knowledge of the underlying low-level resource management entities. The QoS can be a function of mode (normal or crisis mode).
- Map qualitative, application-specific service requirements into quantitative resource allocations.
- Dynamically manage network and systems resources so as to maximize resource utilization.

By providing service-specific APIs, we allow application programmers to specify the QoS requirements of an application in an application-specific fashion. The resource management entities of BeeHive are responsible for mapping the QoS requirements into actual resource needs. The advantage of this approach is

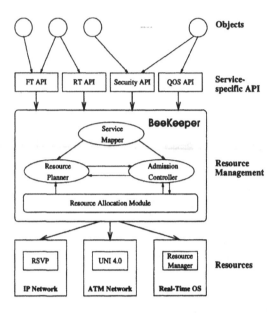

Fig. 3. Resource Management in BeeHive.

a significant increase of reusability. Specifically, an application need not be modified if the underlying resource infrastructure changes. (It may be convenient to think of our approach as "Resource Hiding").

To maximize resource utilization in BeeHive, we will enhance resource management with a planning component. The planning component keeps track of the dynamic behavior of resource usage. By maintaining information not only of the current state of resource utilization, but also of past and (predicted) future usage, the resource management scheme can adapt to the changing resource demands in the system especially during crisis.

In Figure 3 we illustrate the main components of the resource management system in BeeHive. These components will be discussed below.

Service-Specific Application Programming Interfaces

The application programming interface (API) provided by BeeHive must satisfy several constraints. On the one hand, the API must allow the application programmer to access the full functionality of the system without being burdened with internal details. On the other hand, the API must be simple enough as to provide a simple (and extensible) internal representation. The API of the resource management system in BeeHive is a trade-off between the requirements for application specificity and internal simplicity.

 - Since BeeHive operates in a heterogeneous distributed computing environment, application programmers should not be required to have knowledge of the underlying resource infrastructure on top of which the application is being executed.

- Rather than adopting a "one-size-fits-all" approach, we provide a set of different APIs. More specifically, we design a separate API for each of the value-added services provided by BeeHive. In this project, we will build four APIs for the following services:
  - Applications with Real-Time Requirements.
  - Applications with QoS Requirements.
  - Applications with Fault-Tolerance Requirements.
  - Applications with Security Requirements.

For example, the service-specific API allows application developers to specify the QoS requirements of a fault-tolerant application in terms of MTTF (Mean Time To Failure). The resource manager maps these service-specific QoS requests into actual resource requests. Of course, applications and/or individual tasks or transactions may require more than one or even all services. The BeeKeeper (described next) is responsible for tradeoffs between these services.

"BeeKeeper" - The Resource Manager of BeeHive

The resource manager of BeeHive, referred to as the "BeeKeeper", is the central entity of the resource management process. The main function of the BeeKeeper is the mapping of service-specific, possibly qualitative, QoS requirements into actual, quantitative, resource requests. The following are the main components of the BeeKeeper:

- The *Service Mapper* performs the mapping of qualitative resource requests into quantitative requests for physical resources. The service mapper generates a uniform internal representation of the multiple (service-dependent) QoS requests from applications. The uniform presentation is derived from a novel task model discussed below.
- The *Admission Controller* performs the tests that determine if BeeHive has sufficient resources to support the QoS requirements of a new application without compromising the QoS guarantees made to currently active applications.
- The *Resource Allocation Module* is responsible for managing the interface of BeeHive to underlying resource management systems of BeeHive components, i.e., the resource management entities of an ATM network, an RSVP managed IP network, or a real-time operating system, such as RT-Mach. It maintains a database on resources allocated to the BeeHive application.
- The *Resource Planner* attempts to globally optimize the use of resources. The Admission Controller of the BeeKeeper merely decides whether a new application is admitted or rejected. Obviously, such a binary admission control decision leads to a greedy and globally suboptimal resource allocation. (Note that all current resource allocation methods, e.g., for ATM networks or real-time operating systems, are greedy.) The Resource Planner is a module that enhances the admission control process in order to provide globally

optimal resource allocations. The Resource Planner prioritizes all current and incoming requests for resources. Based on the prioritization, it devises a resource allocation strategy.

The Resource Planner obtains from the Resource Allocation Module information on the state of current resource allocations. As much as possible, the Resource Planner should be provided with information on future resource usage. The Resource Planner processes this information and provides input to the Admission Controller.

In BeeHive, the Resource Planner of the BeeKeeper plays a central role for adaptive resource allocation. If an incoming request with high-priority cannot be accommodated, the Resource Planner initiates a reduction of the resources allocated to low-priority applications. If necessary, the Resource Planner will decide upon the preemption of low-priority applications.

Internal Uniform Task Model. An important part of resource management in BeeHive is a new task model which yields a uniform presentation of applications within the BeeKeeper. The model, referred to as *unified task model*, is flexible enough to express the stringent timeliness requirements of all applications that run in BeeHive. On the other hand, the scheme is sophisticated enough to cope with the complexity of multimedia tasks, such as variable bit rate compression of video streams. The unified task model will provide us with a single abstraction for reasoning about multimedia and real-time systems, thereby, overcoming the traditional separation of multimedia and real-time control systems.

Let a(t) denote the execution time necessary for a task to complete the workload that arrives for the task at time t. Let $A[t, t+\tau] = \int_{t,t+\tau} a(x)dx$ denote the execution time necessary to complete the workload that arrives to the system in the time interval $[t, t+\tau]$.

Then the workload that arrives for a task can be characterized by a so-called *task envelope* A^* which provides a time-invariant upper bound on A, that is, for all times $\tau \geq 0$ and $t \geq 0$ we have [15]:

$$A[t, t+\tau] \leq A^*(\tau) \tag{1}$$

A task envelope A^* should be *subadditive*, that is, it should satisfy

$$A^*(t_1) + A^*(t_2) \geq A^*(t_1 + t_2) \qquad \forall t_1, t_2 \geq 0 \tag{2}$$

If a task envelope A_1^* satisfies (1) but is not subadditive, it can be replaced by a subadditive envelope A_2^* such that $A_2^*(t) \leq A_1^*(t)$ for all $t \geq 0$. The notion of task envelopes is powerful enough to describe all hard real-time and soft-real time tasks.

The processing requirements of a task are described as follows. Let $S[t, t+\tau]$ denote the amount of service time that a processor can devote to processing one or more instances of the task in time interval $[t, t+\tau]$. With the task envelope A^* and a deadline for completing an instance of that task, say D, a task always meets its deadline if for all $\tau \geq D$ we have: $\min_\tau \{A^*(t-\tau) = S[0,t])\} \leq D$. We use $S^*(t) = A^*(t-D)$ to denote the *service envelope* of the task.

4 Real-Time Databases

In applications such as the integrated battlefield or agile manufacturing, the state of the environment *as perceived by the controlling information system* must be consistent with the actual state of the environment being controlled or within prescribed limits. Otherwise, the decisions of the controlling system may be wrong and their effects disastrous. Hence, the timely monitoring of the environment, the timely processing of the sensed information, and the timely derivation of needed data are essential. Data maintained by the controlling systems and utilized by its actions must be up-to-date and temporally correlated. This *temporal consistency* must be maintained through the timely scheduling of the actions that refresh the data.

In these applications, actions are triggered by the occurrence of events. An event triggers an action only if certain conditions hold. For instance, the occurrence of the event corresponding to a temperature reading would trigger an emergency reaction only if the temperature value is above a threshold value. The Event-Condition-Action (ECA) paradigm of active databases is convenient to enforce these constraints and also to trigger the necessary actions. Rules can be designed to trigger entry into specific modes; to trigger the necessary adaptive responses to time constraint violations – to effect recovery, to trigger actions if temporal data is (about to become) invalid; and to shed loads as well as adjust deadlines and other parameters, e.g., importance levels and QoS, of actions, when overloads occur [46], and to help support security. The ECA paradigm will be a core component of the BeeHive system.

Transactions that process data with validity intervals must use timely and relatively consistent data in order to achieve correct results. We have developed the ideas of data deadline and forced delay for processing transactions that use (sensor) data with temporal validity intervals. Data read by a transaction must be valid when the transaction completes, which leads to another constraint on completion time, in addition to a transaction's deadline. This constraint is referred to as *data-deadline*. Within the same transaction class, the scheduling algorithm should be aware of the *data-deadline* of a transaction, that is, the time after which the transaction will violate temporal consistency[1]. The scheduling algorithm should account for data-deadlines when it schedules transactions whenever a data-deadline is less than the corresponding transaction deadline. To do this, we have developed earliest data-deadline first (EDDF) and data-deadline based least slack first (DDLSF) policies. Since EDDF and DDLSF policies do not consider the *feasibility* of validity intervals of data objects that a transaction accesses, they are combined with the idea of *Forced-Wait*. With *Forced-Wait*, whenever a temporal data object is read by a transaction, the system checks if this transaction will commit before the validity of the data object expires. If the validity could expire before the commit then the transaction is made to wait until the data object is updated, else the transaction is allowed to continue.

---

[1] Note that a transaction can violate temporal consistency without missing its deadline.

Another important area in real-time database systems is recovery. As a basis for supporting real-time database recovery, we assume four-level memory hierarchy. The first level consists of main memory that is volatile. At the second level is non-volatile RAM (NV-RAM). The third level consists of the persistent disk storage subsystem, and at the fourth level is archival tape storage.

The motivation for the use of NV-RAM stems from the fact that maintaining large amounts of data in main memory can be very expensive while disk I/O times might be unacceptable in certain situations. For instance, writing to disk for the purpose of logging data touched by critical transactions and reading from disk to undo critical transactions might be too expensive. It is not difficult to conceive situations where writing to disk may result in missing deadlines, but by writing to NV-RAM, deadlines can be met. NV-RAM can be used purely as a disk cache where the data moved to NV-RAM later migrates to the disk or it can be used as a temporary stable storage where the data is stored for performance reasons and later may or may not migrate to the disk depending on the (durability) characteristics of the data.

Persistence of system data structures such as global lock tables, and rule bases that represent the dependencies between transactions could become potential bottlenecks in real-time databases. Making these system data structures persistent in NV-RAM results in better performance.

In our solution, the characteristics of a particular type of data will determine where data is placed in the four-level memory hierarchy, where the logs are maintained and how the system recovers from transaction aborts. Data is characterized by temporality, frequency of access, persistence, and criticality. We then tailor the data placement and logging and recovery techniques that are needed to the data characteristics. As an example, assume we have data which has a short time validity, high frequency of access, non-persistent, and is critical. Positions of flying aircraft are examples of such data. This kind of data will be placed in main memory. For space reasons, the data might temporarily migrate to NV-RAM if the validity is long enough for a NV-RAM write and read. No-steal buffer policy will be used and so there is no need to undo. In addition, given the short validity, redos will also not be needed or feasible. If some data has long validity, high frequency of access, persistent, and is critical (reactor temperatures in a chemical plant have this property), then this kind of data will be placed in main memory for performance reasons. No-steal buffer policy along with the force policy will be used where data is forced to NV-RAM and subsequently to disk. Similar tailored solutions exist for the other possibilities.

The frequency of access attribute dictates where one should place the data such that I/O costs are minimized. In traditional databases, disk pre-fetching is a technique that is used to minimize the I/O delay. In our context, an analog of this technique can be used, also to ensure that valid data is available when needed. Specifically, a similar technique, namely, *pre-triggering*, can be used to acquire temporal data that is going to be accessed, but is invalid or will become invalid by the time the data is needed. Instead of triggering a transaction to acquire the data just before it is needed, the transaction can be triggered earlier, at some opportune time.

5 Adaptive Fault Tolerance

Given the large and ever-growing size of databases and global virtual databases, faults may occur frequently and at the *wrong times*. For the system to be useful and to protect against common security breach points, we must have adaptive fault tolerance.

Our approach is to design adaptive and database centric solutions for non-malicious faults. Any system that deals with faults must first specify its fault hypotheses. In particular, we will consider the following fault hypotheses: processors may fail silently (multiple failures are possible); transient faults may occur due to power glitches, software bugs, race conditions; and timing faults can occur where data is out of date or not available in time. If the global virtual database can handle these faults and operate efficiently, then it should prove to be robust and useful under typical scenarios. With these fault tolerance mechanisms in place, it is possible to consider adding support for malicious faults at a future time, especially since our solutions (outlined below) will support adaptive fault tolerance. However, malicious faults are beyond the scope of work at this stage of the project.

In our solution we propose a service-oriented fault tolerance and support it with underlying model based on adaptive fault tolerance.

Service-Oriented FT: For service-oriented fault tolerance we consider how typical users operate with BeeHive and consider the fault tolerance aspects of these services. The services are:

- *Read Only Queries:* These can be dynamically requested by users or automatically triggered by the actions in the active database part of BeeHive. These queries can have soft deadlines and can retrieve data of all types including text, audio, video, etc.
- *Update Transactions:* These transactions can be user invoked or automatic. When permitted, they can update any type of data including temporal data.
- *Multimedia Playout and QoS:* When data that is retrieved is audio and video, the playout itself has time constraints, is large in volume, must be synchronized, can be degraded if necessary, etc.
- *Analysis Tools:* Retrieved data may be fed to analysis tools for further processing; this processing itself can be distributed.

The user-level fault tolerance interface includes features for each of the four service classes for each fault type. For example, the FT service for read-only queries allows queries to proceed when processors fail, be retried if transient faults occur, and can produce partial results prior to the deadline to avoid a timing fault. For multimedia playout, processing can be shifted to other processors when processors fail. A certain degree of transient faults is masked, and degraded service is used to avoid some timing faults. Similar fault tolerance services can be defined for the other combinations.

Support for Adaptive Fault Tolerance: Queries, update transactions, multimedia playout, and analysis tools may access any number of objects. In order to support these fault tolerant services, we propose an underlying system model based on adaptive (secure) fault tolerant (real-time) objects. Since fault tolerance can be expensive, we must be able to tailor the cost of fault tolerance to user's requirements. In our solution, each object in the system represents data and methods on that data and various types of semantic information that support adaptive (secure) fault tolerance in real-time. Briefly, this works as follows.

Input to an object can be, in addition to the parameters required for its functionality, the time requirement, the QoS requirement, the degree of fault tolerance, and the level of security. Inside the object and hidden from the users are control modules which attempt to meet the incoming requirements dynamically based on the request and the current state of the system. This is a form of admission control. For example, a user of an object may want to execute a method on a database object with a passive backup, have all outputs from the object encrypted and have results within three minutes. In such a case the control module inside the object dynamically interacts with the system schedulers, resource allocators, and encryption objects to perform admission control, make copies and encrypt messages. The admission control calling the schedulers decides whether this can all be done within three minutes. If not, its control strategies indicate how to produce some timely result based on the semantics of the object. In this way the user obtains the fault tolerance, security and time requirements desired on this invocation subject to the current system state. Another user or this same user at a different time may request different levels of service from this object and the system adapts to try and meet these requirements. Note that crisis mode may trigger changes to *sets of objects* based on the embedded tradeoff strategies.

One key research issue is the mapping of the service level fault tolerance request to the underlying objects. This research question is one of composition. That is, given the underlying object mechanisms that support adaptive fault tolerance how can objects be composed to meet the service level requirements. Similar mapping questions exist for fault tolerance, real-time, and security, and their interaction.

6 Security

Security is an integral part of the system and is one component in the integrated interface to our adaptive, fault tolerant, real-time, and secure objects. Our primary goal is to create a security architecture that is consistent with also meeting real-time, fault tolerance and QoS requirements. In the architecture, users can specify the level of security required and a secure mapping level takes this requirement and maps it to the underlying security API. This underlying API can change as results from our project or other projects become known. However, because of our novel underlying object paradigm, some novel security support techniques have been identified. In BeeHive, classes (in object oriented programming language terms) have security rules associated with them. Security rules can be inherited by subclasses or overridden depending on the security model in effect for that object. Rules can belong to each method or to the object as a whole. Each object can have its own security API which the mappping layer will utilize, but the rules themselves are hidden. The security rules can be if-then-else rules as well as utilize the notion of an *encrypted profile* to either look for patterns of illegal access or, alternatively, to certify a good pattern of access. Standard security features such as passwords, encryption, and bytecode verifiers can be part of this architecture. Legacy systems, subsystems, proprietary systems, etc. can be surrounded by a firewall which is an object wrapper with a particular security API.

7 Related Work

We are not aware of any efforts to design and build a system with the same capabilities as BeeHive, that is, a global virtual database with real-time, fault tolerance, and security properties in heterogeneous environments. However, there are several projects, past and present, that have addressed one or more of the issues of real-time databases, QoS at the network and OS levels, multimedia, fault tolerance, security, and distributed execution platforms. We briefly describe a few of these projects.

STRIP (STanford Real-Time Information Processor) [2] is a database designed for heterogeneous environments and provides support for value function scheduling and for temporal constraints on data. Its goals include high performance and ability to share data in open systems. It does not support any notion of performance guarantees or hard real-time constraints, and hence cannot be used for the applications we are envisioning in this project.

DeeDS (Distributed Active Real-Time Database System) [6] prototype is an event-triggered real-time database system, using dynamic scheduling of sets of transactions, being developed in Sweden. The reactive behavior is modeled using ECA rules. In the current prototype, they do not support temporal constraints of data and multimedia information.

To allow applications to utilize multiple remote databases in dynamic and heterogeneous environments, the notion of mediator was introduced and a prototype was implemented in the PENGUIN system [64]. A mediator is a software module that exploits encoded knowledge about certain sets or subsets of data to create information for a higher layer of applications. It mainly deals with the mismatch problem encountered in information representation in heterogeneous databases, but no real-time and fault-tolerance issues are pursued as in BeeHive.

While commercial database systems such as Oracle [31] or Sybase [30] allow for the storage of multimedia data, it is usually done as BLOBs. These systems are not integrated with real-time applications. Also developed in industry is the Mercuri project [21] where data from remote video cameras is transferred through an ATM network and displayed using X windows, but they provide only best effort services. The Presto project deals with providing session-based QoS guarantees to continuous multimedia database applications, and does not address the coexistence of control data with the continuous media data.

Projects such as Legion [36, 20] concentrate on distributed execution platforms but do not deal with multimedia databases and end-to-end QoS guarantees. By providing BeeHive wrappers to Legion we will be able to support Legion objects within BeeHive that satisfy QoS guarantees. Commercial systems with similar goals as Legion, however, focused exclusively on a client-server model, are OSF/DCE [40] and CORBA [63]. The CORBA standards and products based on them also do not have the functionality nor real-time properties that we are developing, although a real-time CORBA is emerging.

In recent years, considerable progress has been made in the areas of QoS support for operating systems, networks, and open distributed systems. However, no existing system can give end-to-end QoS assurances in a large-scale, dynamic, and heterogeneous distributed system. Note that none of the existing QoS network architectures support an integrated approach to QoS that contains the network as well as real-time applications.

The Tenet protocol suite [10] developed within the context of the BLANCA Gigabit testbed networks presented the first comprehensive service model for internetworks. The work resulted in the design of two transport protocols (CMTP, RMTP), a network protocol (RTIP), and a signaling protocol (RCAP) to support a diverse set of real-time services. The protocols of the Tenet Group have not been tailored towards hard real-time applications, and rather focused on support of multimedia data. The Tenet protocols do not provide a Middleware layer that can accommodate the needs of applications with special requirements for security or fault tolerance.

The Extended Integrated Reference Model (XRM) [34] that is being designed and implemented at Columbia University provides a resource management and control systems for multimedia applications over ATM networks. XRM is based on previous work on the Magnet-II testbed and shares with it the restriction to a small number of fixed QoS classes.

Several QoS standardization efforts are being made by several network communities. The ATM Forum recently completed a traffic management specification [7] which supports hard-real time applications via peak rate allocations in the CBR service class. All other ATM service classes only give probabilistic QoS guarantees. The IntServ working group of the IETF is working towards a complete QoS service architecture for the Internet, using RSVP [13] for signaling. The draft proposal for a *guaranteed service* definition will support deterministic end-to-end delays; However, an implementation is not yet available. Our work will take full advantage of the framework provided by ATM. Also, any output that comes from the IntServ group [49] at IETF will be applicable to our work.

The RT Mach project [35, 61] has built distributed real-time operating system services supported by a guaranteed end-to-end resource reservation paradigm.

The RT Mach paradigm is complemented by a functionally scalable microkernel along with a performance monitoring infrastructure. RT Mach is applicable to hard and soft real-time applications, but the services provided are not intended to scale to large geographical areas.

The Open Software's Foundation Research Institute is pursuing several efforts to build configurable real-time operating systems for modular and scalable high-performance computing systems. An important effort in respect to fault-tolerance is the CORDS [62] system. CORDS develops an extensible suite of protocols for fault isolation and fault management in support of dependable distributed real-time applications. The project is targeted at military embedded real-time applications and focuses on operating systems solutions, in particular IPC primitives.

The Globus [18] project is developing basic software infrastructure for computations that integrate geographically distributed computational and information resources. Globus creates a parallel programming environment that supports the dynamic identification and composition of resources available on large-scale internets, and provides mechanisms for authentication, authorization, and delegation of trust within environments of this scale. Globus emphasizes the importance of heterogeneity and security; however, it does not offer solutions for fault-tolerance and real-time.

BBN's Corbus [68] is a distributed, object-oriented system that facilitates the development of distributed applications. Corbus provides the middleware that closes the gap between QoS offered by real-time operating systems and networks and the communications researchers and object-oriented applications. Corbus is based on CORBA [63] and its object model.

8 Summary

We have described the design of BeeHive at a high level. We have identified novel component solutions that will appear in BeeHive. More detailed design is continuing an a prototype system is planned. Success of our approach will provide major gains in performance (and QoS), timeliness, fault tolerance, and security for global virtual database access and analysis. The key contributions would come from raising the distributed virtual system notions to the transaction and database levels while supporting real-time, fault tolerance, and security properties. In application terms, success will enable a high degree of confidence in the usability of a virtual database system where a user can obtain secure and timely access to *time valid data* even in the presence of faults. Users can also dynamically choose levels of service when suitable, or the system can set these service levels automatically. These capabilities will significantly enhance applications such as information dominance in the battlefield, automated manufacturing, or decision support systems.

However, since there are key research questions that must be resolved, there is risk involved with this approach. Fundamental research questions include:

- developing an overall *a priori* analysis on the performance and security properties of the system, given a collection of adaptive objects,
- developing efficient techniques for on-line dynamic composition of these new objects,
- analyzing interactions and tradeoffs among the myriad of choices available to the system,
- determining if the fault models are sufficient,
- creating time bounded resource management and admission control policies,
- determining if there is enough access to legacy systems to achieve the security, functionality, timeliness, and reliability required,
- determining how the system works in crisis mode, and
- determining how the system scales.

References

1. R. Abbott and H. Garcia-Molina, Scheduling Real-Time Transactions: A Performance Evaluation, *ACM Transactions on Database Systems*, Vol. 17, No. 3, pp. 513-560, September 1992.

2. B. Adelberg, B. Kao, and H. Garcia-Molina, An Overview of the STanford Real-time Information Processor, *ACM SIGMOD Record*, 25(1), 1996.

3. B. Adelberg, H. Garcia-Molina and B. Kao, Applying Update Streams in a Soft Real-Time Database System, *Proceedings of the 1995 ACM SIGMOD*, pp. 245 - 256, 1995.

4. B. Adelberg, H. Garcia-Molina and B. Kao, Database Support for Efficiently Maintaining Derived Data, Technical Report, Stanford University, 1995.

5. T. E. Anderson, D. E. Culler, and D. A. Patterson, A Case for NOW (Networks of Workstations), *IEEE Micro*, 15(1):54-64, February 1995.

6. S.F. Andler, J. Hansson, J. Eriksson, J. Mellin, M. Berndtsson, and B. Eftring, DeeDS: Towards a Distributed and Active Real-Time Database Systems, *ACM SIGMOD Record*, 15(1):38-40, March 1996.

7. ATM Forum, *ATM Traffic Management Specification 4.0*, April 1996.

8. ATM Forum, ATM User-Network Interface Specification, Version 4.0, 1996.

9. N. Audsley, A. Burns, M. Richardson and A. Wellings, A Database Model for Hard Real-Time Systems, Technical Report, Real-Time Systems Group, Univ. of York, U.K., July 1991.

10. A. Banerjea, D. Ferrari, B. A. Mah, M. Moran, D. C. Verma, and H. Zhang. The Tenet Real-Time Protocol Suite: Design, Implementation, and Experiences, *IEEE/ACM Transactions on Networking*, 4(1):1-10, February 1996.

11. A. Bondavalli, J. Stankovic, and L. Strigini, Adaptive Fault Tolerance for Real-Time Systems, *Third International Workshop on Responsive Computer Systems*, September 1993.

12. A. Bondavali, J. Stankovic, and L. Strigini, Adaptable Fault Tolerance for Real-Time Systems, *Responsive Computer Systems: Towards Integration of Fault Tolerance and Real-Time*, Kluwer, 1995, pp. 187-205.

13. R. Braden, L. Zhang, S. Berson, S. Herzog, and S. Jamin, Resource ReSerVation Protocol (RSVP) - Version 1 Functional Specification, Internet Draft, November 1996.

14. M. J. Carey, R. Jauhari and M. Livny, On Transaction Boundaries in Active Databases: A Performance Perspective, *IEEE Transactions on Knowledge and Data Engineering*, Vol. 3, No. 3, pp. 320-336, September 1991.

15. R. L. Cruz, A Calculus for Network Delay, Part I: Network Elements in Isolation, *IEEE Transactions on Information Theory*, 37(1):114–131, January 1991.

16. U. Dayal et. al., The HIPAC Project: Combining Active Databases and Timing Constraints, *SIGMOD Record*, Vol. 17, No. 1, pp. 51-70, March 1988.

17. M. Di Natale and J. Stankovic, Dynamic End-to-End Guarantees in Distributed Real-Time Systems, *Real-Time Systems Symposium*, Dec. 1994.

18. I. Foster and C. Kesselman, Globus: A metacomputing infrastructure toolkit, SIAM (to appear), 1997.

19. N. Gehani and K. Ramamritham, Real-Time Concurrent C: A Language for Programming Dynamic Real-Time Systems, *Real-Time Systems*, Vol. 3, No. 4, December 1991.

20. A. Grimshaw, W. Wulf, and the Legion Team, The Legion Vision of a Worldwide Virtual Computer, *CACM*, Vol. 40, No. 1, January 1997, pp. 39-45.

21. A. Guha, A. Pavan, J. Liu, A. Rastogi, and T. Steeves, Supporting Real-Time and Multimedia Applications on the Mercuri Testbed, *IEEE Journal on Selected Areas in Communications*, Vol. 13, No. 4, May 1995.

22. J.R. Haritsa, M.J. Carey and M. Livny, On Being Optimistic about Real-Time Constraints, *Proc. of 9th SIGACT-SIGMOD-SIGART Symposium on Principles of Database Systems*, April, 1990.

23. J.R. Haritsa, M.J. Carey and M. Livny, Earliest Deadline Scheduling for Real-Time Database Systems, *Proceedings of the Real-Time Systems Symposium*, pp. 232-242, December 1991.

24. J.R. Haritsa, M.J. Carey and M. Livny, Data Access Scheduling in Firm Real-Time Database Systems, *The Journal of Real-Time Systems*, Vol. 4, No. 3, pp. 203-241, 1992.

25. J. Huang, J.A. Stankovic, D. Towsley and K. Ramamritham, Experimental Evaluation of Real-Time Transaction Processing, *Real-Time Systems Symposium*, pp. 144-153, December 1989.

26. J. Huang, J.A. Stankovic, K. Ramamritham and D. Towsley, Experimental Evaluation of Real-Time Optimistic Concurrency Control Schemes, *Proceedings of the 17th Conference on Very Large Databases*, pp. 35-46, September 1991.

27. J. Huang, J.A. Stankovic, K. Ramamritham, D. Towsley and B. Purimetla, On Using Priority Inheritance in Real-Time Databases, **Special Issue** of *Real-Time Systems Journal*, Vol. 4. No. 3, September 1992.

28. M. Humphrey and J. Stankovic, CAISARTS: A Tool for Real-Time Scheduling Assistance, *IEEE Real-Time Technology and Applications Symposium*, June 1996.

29. B. Kao and H. Garcia Molina, Subtask Deadline Assignment for Complex Distributed Soft Real-Time Tasks, *Technical Report STAN-CS-93-1491*, Stanford University, Oct. 1993.

30. J. E. Kirkwood, *Sybase Architecture and Administration*, Prentice-Hall, 1993.

31. G. Koch and K. Loney, *Oracle: The Complete Reference*, Mc Graw-Hill, 1997.

32. T. Kuo and A. K. Mok, SSP: a Semantics-Based Protocol for Real-Time Data Access, *IEEE 14th Real-Time Systems Symposium* , December 1993.

33. T. Kuo and A. K. Mok, Real-Time Data Semantics and Similarity-Based Concurrency Control, *IEEE Transactions on Knowledge and Data Engineering*, 1996.

34. A. A. Lazar, S. Bhonsle, and K. S. Lim, A Binding Architecture for Multimedia Networks, In *Proceedings of COST-237 Conference on Multimedia Transport and Teleservices*, Vienna, Austria, 1994.

35. C. Lee, R. Rajkumar, and C. Mercer, Experiences with Processor Reservation and Dynamic QoS in Real-Time Mach, In *Proceedings of Multimedia Japan*, March 1996.

36. M. J. Lewis and A. Grimshaw, The Core Legion Object Model, In *Proceedings of the Fifth IEEE International Symposium on High Performance Distributed Computing*, August 1996.

37. J. Liebeherr, D. E. Wrege, and D. Ferrari, Exact Admission Control in Networks with Bounded Delay Services, *IEEE/ACM Transactions on Networking*, Vol. 4, No. 6, pp. 885-901, December 1996.

38. Y. Lin and S.H. Son, Concurrency Control in Real-Time Databases by Dynamic Adjustment of Serialization Order, *Proceedings of the Real-Time Systems Symposium*, pp. 104-112, December 1990.

39. M. Livny, *DeNet Users Guide*, version 1.5, Dept. Comp. Science, Univ. of Wisconsin, Madison, WI 1990.

40. H. W. Lockhart, *OSF DCE Guide to Developing Distributed Applications*, McGraw-Hill, New York, 1994.

41. E. McKenzie and R. Snodgrass, Evaluation of Relational Algebras Incorporating the Time Dimension in Databases, *ACM Computing Surveys*, Vol. 23, No. 4, pp. 501-543, December 1991.

42. D. Niehaus, K. Ramamritham, J. Stankovic, G. Wallace, C. Weems, W. Burleson, and J. Ko, The Spring Scheduling CO-Processor: Design, Use and Performance, *Real-Time Systems Symposium*, Dec. 1993.

43. H. Pang, M.J. Carey and M. Livny, Multiclass Query Scheduling in Real-Time Database Systems, *IEEE Transactions on Knowledge and Data Engineering*, Vol. 7, No. 4, August 1995.

44. B. Purimetla, R. M. Sivasankaran, J.Stankovic and K. Ramamritham, Network Services Databases - A Distributed Active Real-Time Database (DARTDB) Applications, *IEEE Workshop on Parallel and Distributed Real-time Systems*, April 1993.

45. K. Ramamritham, Real-Time Databases, *Distributed and Parallel Databases* 1(1993), pp. 199-226, 1993.

46. K. Ramamritham, Where Do Deadlines Come from and Where Do They Go? *Journal of Database Management*, Spring, 1996.

47. K. Ramamritham, J. Stankovic and P. Shiah, Efficient Scheduling Algorithms for Real-Time Multiprocessor Systems, *IEEE Transactions on Parallel and Distributed Systems*, 1(2):184-94, April 1990.

48. K. Ramamritham, J. Stankovic and W. Zhao, Distributed Scheduling of Tasks with Deadlines and Resource Requirements, *IEEE Transactions on Computers*, 38(8):1110-23, August 1989.

49. S. Shenker, C. Partridge, and R. Guerin, Specification of Guaranteed Quality of Service, IETF, Integrated Services WG, Internet Draft, August 1996.

50. R.M. Sivasankaran, J.A. Stankovic, D. Towsley, B. Purimetla and K. Ramamritham, Priority Assignment in Real-Time Active Databases, *The International Journal on Very Large Data Bases*, Vol. 5, No. 1, January 1996.

51. R. M. Sivasankaran, K. Ramamritham, J. A. Stankovic, and D. Towsley, Data Placement, Logging and Recovery in Real-Time Active Databases, *Workshop on Active Real-Time Database Systems*, Sweden, June 1995.

52. X. Song and J. W. S. Liu, How Well Can Data Temporal Consistency be Maintained? *IEEE Symposium on Computer-Aided Control Systems Design*, 1992.
53. X. Song, Data Temporal Consistency in Hard Real-Time Systems, Technical Report No. UIUCDCS-R-92-1753, 1992.
54. X. Song and J. W. S. Liu, Maintaining Temporal Consistency: Pessimistic vs. Optimistic Concurrency Control, *IEEE Transactions on Knowledge and Data Engineering*, Vol. 7, No. 5, pp. 786-796, October 1995.
55. J. Stankovic and K. Ramamritham, The Spring Kernel: A New Paradigm for Hard Real-Time Operating Systems, *IEEE Software*, 8(3):62-72, May 1991.
56. J. Stankovic, K. Ramamritham, and D. Towsley, Scheduling in Real-Time Transaction Systems, in *Foundations of Real-Time Computing: Scheduling and Resource Management*, edited by Andre van Tilborg and Gary Koob, Kluwer Academic Publishers, pp. 157-184, 1991.
57. J. Stankovic, SpringNet: A Scalable Architecture For High Performance, Predictable, Distributed, Real-Time Computing, Univ. of Massachusetts, Technical Report, 91-74, October 1991.
58. J. Stankovic, and K. Ramamritham, *Advances in Hard Real-Time Systems*, IEEE Computer Society Press, Washington, DC, September 1993.
59. J. Stankovic and K. Ramamritham, Reflective Real-Time Operating Systems, *Principles of Real-Time Systems*, Sang Son, editor, Prentice Hall, 1995.
60. J. Stankovic, Strategic Directions: Real-Time and Embedded Systems, *ACM Computing Surveys*, Vol. 28, No. 4, December 1996.
61. H. Tokuda, T. Nakajima and P. Rao, Real-Time Mach: Towards a Predictable Real-Time System, *Proc. Usenix Mach Workshop*, October 1990.
62. F. Travostino and E. Menze III, The CORDS Book, OSF Research Institute, September 1996.
63. S. Vinoski. CORBA: Integrating Diverse Applications Within Distributed Heterogeneous Environments, *IEEE Communications Magazine*, 14(2), February 1997.
64. G. Wiederhold, Mediators in the Architecture of Future Information Systems, *IEEE Computer*, Vol. 25, No. 3, March 1992, pp. 38-49.
65. D. E. Wrege, E. W. Knightly, H. Zhang, and J. Liebeherr, Deterministic Delay Bounds for VBR Video in Packet-Switching Networks: Fundamental Limits and Practical Tradeoffs, *IEEE/ACM Transactions on Networking*, 4(3):352-362, June 1996.
66. M. Xiong, J. Stankovic, K. Ramamritham, D. Towsley and R. M. Sivasankaran, Maintaining Temporal Consistency: Issues and Algorithms, *The First International Workshop on Real-Time Databases*, March, 1996.
67. M. Xiong, R. Sivasankaran, J. Stankovic, K. Ramamritham and D. Towsley, Scheduling Transactions with Temporal Constraints: Exploiting Data Semantics, *Real-Time Systems Symposium*, December 1996.
68. J. A. Zinky, D. E. Bakken, and R. Schantz, Overview of Quality of Service for Objects, In *Proceedings of the Fifth IEEE Dual Use Conference*, May 1995.

Paper Presentations

An Active Real-Time Database Model for Air Traffic Control Systems

Kwei-Jay Lin, Ching-Sang Peng and Tony Ng†

University of California, Irvine
Irvine, CA 92697, USA
{klin, cpeng}@ece.uci.edu

†Lockheed Martin Corporation
Rockville, MD 20850, USA
tony.ng@lmco.com

Abstract. The application of air traffic control systems is one of the more complex real-time applications that require timely responses as well as logical and temporal data integrities. An air traffic control system is highly safety-critical. In this paper, we propose a database model for the air traffic control system using the active database scheme to coordinate the interactions among external update transactions, time-triggered transactions and operator transactions. We define the system components, including a time-based trigger manager and a concurrency control manager with the implementation of semantic-based concurrency control protocols. The concurrency control utilizes the compatibility matrix technique with semantic-based operations that can be carefully designed to enhance the temporal correctness in terms of external consistency and data deadlines.

1 Introduction

Real-time database systems (RTDB) must be designed to meet the timing constraints of transactions and to allow critical real-world information to be used actively and timely. There are two issues involved: firstly, there must be a data flow path from real world to transactions with a tight and bounded end-to-end delay; secondly, the system must be able to react quickly when certain conditions are true. Many applications fit into this category, including avionics systems, target tracking systems, and air traffic control systems. In these systems, data are collected from the real-world through some devices (e.g. sensors and radars) periodically. Transactions operate on these data according to some resource sharing (e.g. CPU, data locks) protocols. Since real-time data are valid only for a short time interval, RTDB must provide an acceptable level of performance to keep the data in RTDB always valid. The concept of *external consistency* was introduced [Lin89] to define the timely reflection of the physical world in a database. To maintain or guarantee external consistency brings new challenges to real-time database designs.

In this paper we investigate an active database model for databases used in air traffic control (ATC) systems. An air traffic control system receives one or more streams of surveillance target data from radars. The raw data are processed to form tracks and displayed on workstation monitors. In addition, the target and track database is also used to detect tactical alerts, i.e. situations where two aircrafts are getting too close to each other or an aircraft is getting too close to a restricted airspace. The alert detection must be based on the most current data which are constantly being updated. The arbitration between updates and alerts presents a unique problem for concurrency control.

We have proposed a semantic-based concurrency control protocol in our earlier work [PL96, PLN97]. The protocol allows cooperative transactions to meet both external and logical consistency criteria. One of the guidelines is that real-time transactions should always utilize the most current data to make correct decisions. Sometimes, a transaction may have to be aborted if a newly received data value is in conflict with an old value being used in the transaction. We use the object-oriented database model and define objects that corresponds to external sensors in ATC. The semantic-based concurrency control protocol defines a method compatibility matrix (CM) for each data object. A transaction using these objects issues a sequence of method calls each of which is examined by the objects. If the transaction sending the method call has a high external consistency requirement, objects may provide a more temporally correct (but possibly non-serializable) execution.

In our model, we use active database rules to trigger certain lock requests when the conditions are satisfied. The triggered transaction will prevent an update transaction from receiving the lock and/or from aborting ongoing transactions that have read older data. We can also use the active database model to implement the "data deadline" concept which prevents some old data from being used when they have almost expired their lifetime. To do that, we use the timer in the trigger manager to initiate an on-hold lock which puts all read operations in a delayed mode. The hold lock will be released when the new value arrives. We also study the *data similarity* protocol [KM93] to avoid unnecessary transaction aborts.

Our work in this paper is different from many previous work on active real-time databases in that we utilize the active database model to enhance the real-time capability of a real-time database. In other words, our focus in this paper is not to improve the real-time performance of active databases. Rather, our goal is to enhance the real-time correctness of databases by adopting active database mechanisms. The rest of this paper is organized as follows. In Section 2, related work on real-time and active databases is presented. Section 3 defines our active object model and the semantic concurrency control protocol. Section 4 shows the scenario of a real-time air traffic control system. The system performance model used in our study is presented in Section 5. We conclude the paper in Section 7.

2 Background and Motivation

2.1 Real-time databases

Many transaction management protocols coordinate concurrent transactions executions to ensure serializability [BHG87], which is usually regarded as the notion of correctness for interleaved transaction schedules. Most of today's DBMS's use the two phase locking protocol (2PL) [EGLT76] to guarantee the serializability of transactions.

For real-time systems with resource sharing, Sha et al. [SRL90] propose the priority ceiling protocol (PCP) to solve the priority inversion problem in a system scheduled by the rate monotonic scheduling algorithm. A sufficient schedulability condition has been derived to help design hard real-time applications that need to access shared resource in critical sections. In [CL91], Chen and Lin address the same bounded blocking issue under the Earliest Deadline First (EDF) scheduling algorithm using a protocol called DPCP. Baker [Bak91] extends PCP to handle multiunit resources as well as dynamic priority schemes such as EDF. The protocol, stack resource policy (SRP), uses a shared stack to avoid unnecessary context switches. Since the PCP algorithm itself does not guarantee serializability, another integrated scheduling and concurrency control algorithm, the convex ceiling protocol (CCP) has been proposed in [NL93]. All of these work provide important foundations for real-time systems with static resource access behaviors.

One of the earlier work on the concurrency control protocol that exploits the semantics of non-real-time database transactions was done by Garcia-Molina [GM83]. Transactions are classified into various semantic types and there is a compatibility set associated with each semantic type. A compatibility set for an atomic step determines the atomic steps that can be interleaved with it. In [BR92], a state-independent, parameter-dependent commutativity matrix is used to enhance the concurrency. A higher degree of concurrency among transactions is achieved through the concept of recoverability. Another correctness criteria called *orderability* is proposed in [AAS93]. As long as user transactions observe the same consistency assertions in different execution histories, these histories are considered equivalent. A semantic-based concurrency control protocol designed for open nested OODB is presented in [MRW+93]. The concurrency allowed among object methods are pre-defined and the number of lock conflicts is reduced. No real-time constraint is considered in all above work.

In many applications, external object values do not change rapidly with time. In other words, the values reported by periodic sensors are often similar between consecutive periods. To exploit this semantics of real-time data objects, Kuo and Mok [KM93] propose a real-time data access protocol called the similarity stack protocol (SSP). The correctness of schedules is justified by the concept of *similarity* which allows different but temporally adjacent data to be used interchangeably in a computation without adversely affecting the outcome. DiPippo and Wolfe describe a real-time concurrency control technique that supports logical and temporal consistency [DW93] based on user-defined compatibility functions.

Their model is very powerful since it allows any consistency constraint (temporal and logical), imprecision bound (defined in the context of Epsilon Serializability [Pu91]), and even the object state to be checked in the compatibility functions. As a result, it suffers from high complexity and overhead.

In [Lin89], external consistency is distinguished from internal consistency. It has been suggested that external consistency is sometimes more desirable or critical than serializability. Song and Liu [SL95] further refine the concept into data age and dispersion. They studied the performance of maintaining temporal consistency under pessimistic and optimistic concurrency control protocols. Adelberg et al. [AGMK95] investigate scheduling protocols in program trading systems to import external views as update streams. Their simulation studies the relationship between different scheduling methods and data staleness. The concurrency control issues have not been addressed in their work. Xiong et al. [XRST96] suggests that all data values should be defined with "data deadlines" which are when those values will become out-of-date. Therefore, any transaction using those data should try to finish its execution before the data deadlines or the result is no longer valid.

2.2 Active Databases

Conventional databases (including conventional real-time databases) are *passive*; they only execute transactions explicitly submitted by a user or an application program. In many (real-time) applications, it is important to monitor the execution environment and initiate certain system operations immediately. Active database systems enhance conventional database systems with ECA rules to allow for reactive behavior in responding to certain events, including timing events. The general form of an ECA rule is defined by

> **on** event
> **if** condition
> **then** action.

This allows rules to be triggered by events that meet certain conditions. Rules are defined and stored in the database and evaluated by rule managers, subject to concurrency control, recovery control, as well as task scheduling protocols.

Most previous work on active databases studies how rules should be specified, how efficient events may be detected and, most importantly, how rules are checked and fired (e.g., [CKAK93, DHL90, DPG91, GD94, GJS92, HLM88]). For example, the performance model of an active DBMS was developed by Carey et al. and was used to study various performance issues in active database systems [CJL91]. Recently, the topic of active real-time database systems has received much interest due to the requirement of meeting real-time constraints in active database systems that support time-critical applications. One of the first projects to study real-time issues in active databases is the HIPAC (High Performance ACtive Database System) project [DBB+88, DBB+89]. In their work, the concept of contingency plans is defined as alternate actions to be invoked

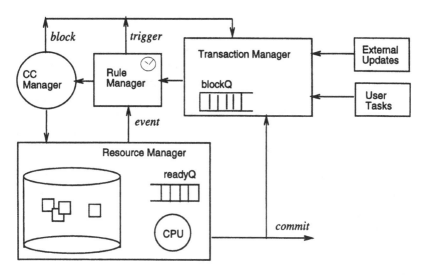

Fig. 1. Components of Active Object

whenever the system determines that it cannot complete an action within its deadline. The concept is similar to the work of *Imprecise Computation* except it is under the active database environment which makes it more powerful. More current work on active, real-time databases has been reported in ARTDB'95.

3 Active Real-Time Databases

3.1 The Active Object Model

An OODB consists of many data objects. Each object has some internal states that are protected by the object abstraction. The only way the object state can be accessed from transactions is to invoke the methods defined by the object. Each transaction in the system invokes one or more methods defined in objects. A set of objects could be accessed in a transaction execution. At any time, more than one transaction may request and execute methods in the same object. The concurrency control mechanism enables each object to grant *locks* to a transaction according to the method it is requesting or executing. A method will be executed only after the transaction gets the proper lock(s). Herein we will use the name of the method as the name of the corresponding lock.

Each object has a transaction manager to accept update transactions and user transactions. Before execution, all transactions must acquire the needed locks from the concurrency control manager. Transactions then must wait for the resources (CPU and data) to start executions. Once they are finished, transactions either commit or suspend until their next periods. In the active object model, each object contains a rule manager (Figure 1). The rule manager is responsible for monitoring the object state and its execution environment. If a specific event occurs and the condition defined in the corresponding rule is satisfied, the rule manager will generate an internal transaction to conduct the action. Therefore, an object may receive method calls from both external transactions and internal transactions generated by the rule manager. Some transactions have real-time constraints defined. The timing constraint will be used in system scheduling and concurrency control protocols. In our proposal, the rule manager may change the semantics of the method calls from transactions. In other words, lock requests submitted from transactions to the concurrency control manager are checked by the rule manager first. If certain condition is satisfied, a different type of the request may be resubmitted for the transaction.

Depending on the semantics, many different types of methods [PL96] can be defined in an object. For example, the following is a list of read/write operations with different semantics :

- R_{ex}: Exclusive read operation.
- R_{up}: Read operation to access the most recent external value.
- R_{ab}: Read operation with conditional abort.
- W_{ex}: Exclusive write operation.
- W_{up}: External update which writes the most recent object value.
- W_{ab}: Write operation with conditional abort.

R_{ex} and W_{ex} maintain a strict serializability as in conventional databases. R_{up}, however, allows a transaction to access objects which are being updated by concurrent W_{up}'s. A transaction holding a R_{ab} lock will be aborted if a conflict happens due to another transaction's request for W_{up} or W_{ex}. It thus enhances the external consistency when the object receives a new value. Similarly, an object can invoke different types of write operations. For some systems, external objects can be distinguished from derived objects in a database [PL96]. Write operations thus have different requirements on data consistency and integrity. W_{up} is used to update the values of external objects and will not be blocked by any concurrent R_{up}'s. W_{ab} can be used to give scheduling preferences to conflicting reads or writes if the value to be recorded does not make too much difference to the system operations. For example, when an aircraft is in an isolated air space with no danger of flying path conflicts with any other aircraft, the recording of its current position can be given a low priority, especially when it is on a steady course.

Note that an object designer should select appropriate operation types for the object according to the desired semantics. Not all above operation types need to be defined in each object.

3.2 Compatibility Matrix and Correctness Criteria

Suppose an object has n methods defined. A compatibility matrix (CM) can be defined for that object by an $n \times n$ table. The CM model has been reported in [PL96]. We give an overview here for the completeness of the paper.

Each entry in CM (Table 1) is represented by CM (i,j) where i and j are the method indexes for row and column, respectively. CM (a,b) will be checked when a transaction requests a semantic lock for method a while another transaction has acquired method b for the same object. The possible values in CM(a,b) are $\sqrt{}$ (grant lock to a), X (block the lock request), and $\triangle$ (abort b and grant lock to a). If CM (a, b) is compatible (not "X"), a can be scheduled for execution as long as some CPU time is available. Otherwise, a's execution will be delayed. It is also possible to associate some special operation with an entry, like to restart a (b), or to promote the priority of a or b as defined in the Priority Inheritance Protocol [SRL90].

CM is an extension of the conventional read/write table enhanced with more transaction semantics. The entries between (R_{ex}, W_{ex}) and (W_{ex}, W_{ex}) are exactly the same as their values would be in any traditional lock-based concurrency control protocol to preserve serializability. Similarly, (R_{ex}, W_{up}) and (W_{up}, W_{up}) are defined to be not compatible. An on-going transaction with a semantic lock R_{ab} of an external object will be aborted by a newly arrived update transaction, i.e. CM (W_{up}, R_{ab}) = '$\triangle$'. The reason is that the transaction always wants to read the most up-to-date data to avoid decisions that is based on some old, out-of-date information. On the other hand, CM (R_{ab}, W_{up}) is incompatible since the read should let the update to finish first to provide the newest data.

	R_{ex}	R_{con}	R_{ab}	W_{up}
R_{ex}	$\sqrt{}$	$\sqrt{}$	$\sqrt{}$	X
R_{con}	$\sqrt{}$	$\sqrt{}$	$\sqrt{}$	$\sqrt{}$
R_{ab}	$\sqrt{}$	$\sqrt{}$	$\sqrt{}$	X
W_{up}	X	$\sqrt{}$	$\triangle$	X

Table 1. An Example Compatibility Matrix

R_{up}, on the other hand, relaxes the serializability to allow a higher degree of concurrency. An R_{up} method can read the object even when a W_{up} is still being held. Although this may compromise the serializability, the responsiveness is enhanced. R_{up} is compatible with any other semantic lock request and vice versa.

3.3 The Rule Manager

For many update operations, the new values to be entered are similar to their old values in the database. We can improve the object performance by exploring the data similarity. The idea is that a recent update in progress could be aborted so that a reader transaction can get the required read lock to start execution sooner if the value to be updated is similar to the value in the system. Since the values are similar, aborting the update in progress does not sacrifice the correctness of the system operations.

The decision to be made here is what lock type should be given to an update transaction. From the update transaction's point of view, it is sending another value to the system. Whether the current value is similar to the last value sent is irrelevant to its operations. Therefore, the transaction will always request the same lock type W_{up} to the object. On the other hand, an active object is to manage its state and to provide the best (real-time and throughput) performance possible. If an update can be delayed or aborted to improve the object's performance, it is up to the object itself to ensure that happens. Therefore, we decide to adopt the active object mechanism to decide which lock type is to be requested for an update transaction, using the following rule:

$$
\begin{aligned}
&on \quad request\_lock(W_{up}, value) \\
&if \quad is\_similar(value) \ and \ is\_overload() \\
&then \ request\_lock(W_{ab})
\end{aligned}
$$

In this rule, when a request to have a W_{up} lock on the object with the value *value* is received by the object, the rule manager will check to see if the new value is similar to the old value. If so, and if the system is now overloaded, the rule manager will request W_{ab} for the transaction. Otherwise, the request to lock will be submitted unchanged and the CM is checked to see if the lock can be granted.

Another scenario where an active object may improve the object performance is to prevent an old, out-of-date object value from being read if a new value is expected to arrive soon and the old value is expected to be different from the new one. This is the *forced wait* policy defined in [XRST96]. This is implemented in the following rule:

$$
\begin{aligned}
&on \quad data\_deadline() \\
&if \quad is\_irregular() \\
&then \ request\_lock(W_{hd})
\end{aligned}
$$

In this rule, the data_deadline event is triggered by a timer which is set by the object itself. When a value has reached its data deadline, the object will request a write_hold W_{hd} lock to hold the data from being read by any transaction. The W_{hd} lock is incompatible with any read lock but can be aborted by any update. The *is_irregular()* condition is set when the previous two updates have a value difference larger than a threshold. To allow the data deadline event to always trigger a write_hold lock, the object can set the threshold value to 0.

The former scenario (data similarity) discussed in this section usually applies to objects that are being updated very frequently. Due to their frequency, the values usually do not change too much and therefore can skip some updates without affecting the object integrity. The latter scenario (data deadline), on the other hand, applies to those objects that are updated infrequently. Therefore, each object version may present a very different value and should be adopted by an on-going read transaction even if the value is not quite there yet. We do not expect any object to adopt both rules at the same time since they are contradictory to each other.

3.4 Examples on Transaction Interactions

In this section, we show some examples to show how the semantic-based concurrency control protocol is used. Suppose there are two objects x and y in a RTDB. Assume that object x has a CM as in Table 1 and there are three transactions as follows:

$$T_1 = f(x) \quad : requests \ R_{ab} \ for \ Object \ x$$
$$T_2 = g(x) \quad : requests \ W_{up} \ for \ Object \ x \ (periodically)$$
$$T_3 = h(x, y) : requests \ R_{up} \ for \ Object \ x$$

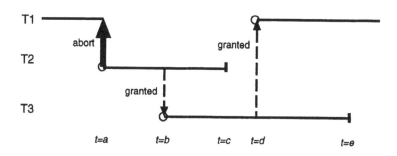

Fig. 2. Example History

Suppose transaction T_1 is started before time $t = a$ and has acquired R_{ab} on object x. In the first scenario (Figure 2), transaction T_2 with a W_{up} request arrives at time $t = a$. Since CM (W_{up}, R_{ab}) has a value $\triangle$, T_1 is aborted. While T_2 is in execution, T_3 requests an R_{up} at $t = b$. The lock is granted according to CM(R_{up}, W_{up}). Therefore, T_3 can start execution right away[1]. At time $t = c$, T_2 finishes execution and releases the W_{up}. At time $t = d$, T_1 is started again and acquires the R_{ab} lock since CM (R_{ab}, R_{up}) = "$\sqrt{}$". Finally, R_{up} is released after T_3 commits at time $t = e$.

In the second scenario, again suppose transaction T_1 is started before time $t = a$ and has acquired R_{ab} on object x. When transaction T_2 arrives at time $t = a$ with a W_{up} request, the rule manager decides that the value is similar to the last update. Therefore a W_{ab} is requested instead. Since CM (W_{ab}, R_{ab}) has a value of X, T_2 is blocked. When T_3 requests an R_{up} at $t = b$, the lock is granted according to CM(R_{up}, R_{ab}). Eventually, both T_1 and T_3 finish their executions and release their locks.

Clearly, the advantage of providing these alternatives is to allow cooperative transactions to utilize more up-to-date data. In the first scenario, T_1 is forced to

---

[1] This paper is concerned only with transaction-level locks. We assume that there are memory-level locks to make sure the read and write accesses to the same memory locations are serialized so that a read operation does not read a partially written result.

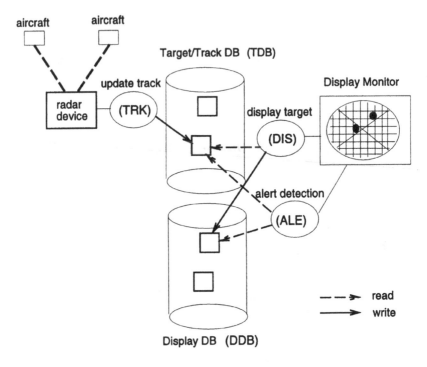

Fig. 3. ATC Databases

read more up-to-date data from x while T_3 is allowed to get the value of object x earlier than in traditional CC protocols. In the second scenario, T_2 is delayed since the value to be entered does not contribute to the effectiveness of the system significantly. The semantic-based concurrency control protocol provides a simple mechanism to either force or relax the serializability property based on the object semantics and the execution context.

4 Air Traffic Control System

4.1 System Model

The real-time database scenario used in an air traffic control system has been introduced in [PLN97]. The scenario has two databases as shown in Figure 3. One is the target and track database (TDB) and the other is the display database (DDB). For each detected target (i.e. aircraft), a "track" is created and maintained. Each track is stored as an object in TDB while the corresponding display record is a derived object stored in DDB. There is a stream of external update transactions (TRK) that update the TDB. A collection of display transactions (DIS) read TDB database to put the targets on display as well as to store the objects in DDB. Moreover, tactical alert detection transactions (ALE) will read the TDB and correlated into DDB in order to determine if there is an alert. If an alert is detected, ALE displays the alert in a special format (e.g. flashing) on some specific monitors.

Each TRK is a periodic job with a period defined by the radar scan frequency. An instance of TRK on a particular track will arrive at the system periodically. Furthermore, since it is extremely dynamic, a target stays within the detecting range for a certain time interval called *life time*. The completion of a TRK task in each period triggers a DIS which visually displays the updated geometric information. Similarly, the completion of DIS in each period activates an ALE to detect the alert situations. When a TRK job first arrives, it creates a new track object with a new identification number. That identification number will be used consistently in both TDB and DDB for TRK's and DIS's. The track will be dropped by the system after the target is out of the detecting range.

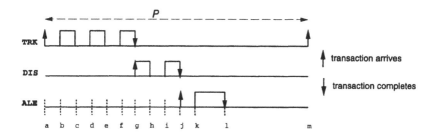

Fig. 4. TRK, DIS and ALE Activations

Figure 4 shows the transaction dependencies among TRK, DIS and ALE. The figure shows an example execution flow of those transactions. TRK is ready at time a and starts execution at time b by the scheduler. During execution, it is preempted (c and e) and then resumed (d and f). The transaction completes at time g and triggers a DIS execution immediately. The DIS is run to completion at time j. An ALE is ready at the same time (j), but not executed until time k. ALE executes without interruption and finishes at time l.

Timing Constraints The transaction scheduler uses the Earliest Deadline First (EDF) [LL73] policy. Previous work shows that EDF minimizes the number of transactions missing deadlines in most situations [AGM88]. Rate monotonic scheduling (RM) is not appropriate for our air traffic control model because DIS and ALE are not periodic tasks but triggered by other transactions. In addition, the RM schedule favors high frequency TRKs which will result in a high missing deadline percentage for low frequency TRKs during high loads.

Each TRK has a firm deadline which is the end of period P. Any incomplete TRK after its deadline will be aborted. Each DIS has a soft deadline D ($D \leq P$) relative to the time when the triggering TRK arrives. This time interval D is for system safety concern so that the operator can quickly see the target displayed on the monitor screen. An ALE also has a soft deadline which is the end of the period for the most recent TRK. Assume a TRK arrives at time $t = a$ in Figure 4, it is assigned an effective deadline $d = a + D - T^{DIS}$ where T^{DIS} is the estimated DIS execution time. This formula takes into consideration that DIS is triggered after TRK finishes. If T^{DIS} is exact, d is the latest starting time for the DIS to meet its soft deadline. As soon as the TRK finishes, a DIS is triggered with a deadline $a + D$. When DIS completes, an ALE transaction is triggered with a deadline $t = a + P$.

There is another type of deadline called *data deadline*, denoted by D_d. The data deadline of each track object means that the contents are no longer valid after the data deadline expires. The assignment of the data deadline is based on the nature of the environment and has nothing to do with the transaction deadline. However, we assume $D_d \leq P$ in our periodic model.

4.2 Concurrency Control Issues

	R_{ex}	W_{ex}
R_{ex}	$\checkmark$	X
W_{ex}	X	X

Table 2. The Compatibility Matrix for DDB Object

There are two types of possible read/write conflicts for an external TDB object, namely TRK-DIS and TRK-ALE. A conflict happens when a previously triggered DIS or ALE past its soft deadline unfinished. Since TRK has a firm deadline, a TRK-TRK conflict is avoided by automatically aborting the old TRK. Likewise, because of the deadline assignment scheme and active triggering properties, DIS-DIS and DIS-ALE conflicts over a DDB object do not happen. The CM table for a DDB object using the traditional read/write semantics is defined in Table 2. In the following, we discuss the definitions of CM for a TDB object with different semantics.

	R_{ab}	R_{ex}	W_{up}
R_{ab}	$\checkmark$	$\checkmark$	$\triangle$
R_{ex}	$\checkmark$	$\checkmark$	X
W_{up}	X	X	X

Table 3. The Compatibility Matrix for TDB Object

Table 3 shows the compatibility matrix for a TDB object. A TRK transaction needs a W_{up} lock to update a track object. A DIS transaction requests a R_{ab} lock for that track object and a W_{ex} lock for the derived display object. As explained in Section 3, the entry CM (R_{ab}, W_{up}) is set to be "$\triangle$" so that the newly arrived TRK can be executed without delay. An ALE also requests a R_{ab} lock for the track object and a R_{ex} lock of the derived display object.

Several design issues must be considered to enhance performance, especially when the system is suffering abnormally high workloads. First of all, even though the most recent TRK is always desirable, we may not want to sacrifice the display refresh rate too much so that the operator does not have a good picture about the current aircraft positions. The refreshing rate could suffer for two reasons : (1) a DIS transaction could be aborted in consecutive periods due to the high load. (2) since a DIS is triggered by a TRK, a TRK abort (cannot complete before the next update arrives) also delays the display refresh.

To handle the above problem, each track object keeps track of its execution history so that each TRK abort is recorded. Similarly, each display object logs the DIS abort. A newly arrived TRK transaction can abort a DIS in progress only if the sum the of previous abort count for both TRK and DIS is less than a predefined threshold. The system lock manager will upgrade the read lock on display object x from R_{ab} to R_{ex} so DIS may not be aborted by TRK. By doing this, we can avoid unbounded DIS aborts and the chain reaction for unbounded ALE aborts.

Likewise, since the alert warning display allows the operator to detect the danger in addition to watching targets on display, a certain level of ALE performance should be maintained even during high system loads. Therefore, if an ALE detects an alert, then the system mode will be changed and the lock on the track object will be automatically upgrade to R_{ex}. In other words, the system will favor TRK if there is a conflict between TRK and ALE provided that the detection transaction has not discovered an alert yet. Once an alert is detected, the system will try to complete a warning display no matter where the most current position of the object is at.

	R_{ab}	R_{ex}	W_{up}	W_{ab}
R_{ab}	$\checkmark$	$\checkmark$	X	$\triangle$
R_{ex}	$\checkmark$	$\checkmark$	X	$\triangle$
W_{up}	$\triangle$	X	X	$\triangle$
W_{ab}	X	X	X	X

Table 4. The TDB Compatibility Matrix with Similarity

Implementing Similarity To integrate the idea of data similarity with the concurrency control, a semantic lock , W_{ab}, can be introduced. A value comparison procedure is invoked every time a TRK requests the W_{up} lock. If it is similar to the content of the current active data, a W_{ab} lock will be granted instead. W_{ab} can be aborted if there is a conflict with read operations requested by DIS or ALE. The related entries are marked in Table 4, where the TRK holding a W_{ab} has the lowest priority compared to R_{ex}, R_{ab} and W_{up}.

The data similarity provides the system flexibility to deal with a high load. The most recent update could be aborted if the value is similar to the value in the previous period and a DIS has already started to read it. Thus, DIS could finish earlier without abort. At the same time, the system outcome is still considered correct or acceptable. How to define *similarity*, however, is application-dependent.

	R_{ab}	R_{ex}	W_{hd}	W_{up}
R_{ab}	√	√	◯	X
R_{ex}	√	√	◯	X
W_{hd}	√	√	X	X
W_{up}	△	X	△	X

Table 5. The TDB Compatibility Matrix with Forced Wait

Implementing Forced Wait In this scenario, data deadline explicitly imposes temporal constraint on a track object in TDB read by DIS and ALE transactions. A transaction commits in time using expired TDB data is useless or even detrimental. To develop such notion within concurrency control, CM can support forced wait policy to meet the data deadline requirement of the track data as shown in Table 5. As we have discussed earlier, the data deadline for a track object will trigger an W_{hd} lock to stop all new read requests until a new update place a new value in the system. In the new CM, W_{hd} is compatible with all read operations but not with another W_{hd}. On the other hand, W_{hd} will be aborted by a new update with the W_{up} lock request. The read operations (R_{ex}, R_{ab}) are incompatible with write operations (W_{ex}, W_{hd}). That is, a read lock won't be granted if at least one of the write locks has been set. However, instead of blocking the transaction requesting that read operation, we introduce another matrix symbol '◯' that will abort the requesting transaction. Since in our model, a blocked DIS or ALE is going to be aborted by the next TRK arrival anyway.

5 Simulation Model

In our simulation, the arrival of new periodic target transactions forms an exponential distribution with mean inter-arrival time equals to $\frac{1}{\lambda_1}$. The period specification is chosen from different preset classes P_i ($i = 1, 2$) with an equal probability. The life time is uniformly distributed between C_{min} and C_{max}. According to the Little's Law, when the simulated system is stable, there are about $\lambda_1 * \frac{(C_{min}+C_{max})}{2}$ targets existing simultaneously within the detectable range.

The execution times of TRK, DIS, and ALE transactions are determined by the following distribution functions:

$$T_{exec}^{TRK} = Uniform(U_{min}, U_{max}) \tag{1}$$

$$T_{exec}^{DIS} = Uniform(D_{min}, D_{max}) \tag{2}$$

$$T_{exec}^{ALE} = Uniform(T_{min}, T_{max}) \quad (no\ alert) \tag{3}$$

$$T_{exec}^{ALE'} = Uniform(TD_{min}, TD_{max}) \quad (with\ alert) \tag{4}$$

To determine whether or not an alert actually happens in each TRK update period, a probability parameter Pro_{alert} is defined. In addition, another parameter Pro_{cont_alert} specifies the conditional probability that an alert situation continues from the previous period. Equations (3) and (4) are then used to decide the execution time for ALE's. Note that the exact execution time required is assumed to be unknown to the scheduler thus not used in making scheduling decisions.

The deadline assignment scheme follows the definitions in Section 4.3. The scheduling deadline assignment for TRK is

$$d^{TRK} = t + D_{rel} - \frac{D_{min} + D_{max}}{2}$$

where t is the TRK arrival time and D_{rel} is the soft deadline for DIS.

In addition to TRK, DIS, and ALE transactions, there are local background tasks such as record logging and system housekeeping. We use two sporadic tasks to simulate local tasks. The minimum inter-arrival time is *dist*. Parameter λ_2 and λ_3 are used to generate the additional exponentially distributed inter-arrival times. The execution time of each local task instance, T_{exec}^{local}, is uniformly distributed between l_{min} and l_{max}. Finally, the deadline is determined by a slack factor as follows:

$$D^{local} = t + SF_1 * T_{exec}^{local}$$

where t is the local task arrival time and SF_1 is the slack factor.

As mentioned in Section 3.3, an internally triggered event INT is used to set/rest the W_{hd} lock to implement the forced wait policy. We use a transaction to simulate the overhead that is represented by parameter O_1 or O_2, where O_1 is the time to set/reset the lock and O_2 is the time required to check the *irregularity* condition (determined probabilistically by Pro_{irr}). The internally triggered transaction is assigned an immediate deadline to enable its execution immediately.

The simulation model is shown in Figure 5. We use the same system parameters and loads in both baseline and experimental models, the baseline model uses the conventional two phase lock (2PL) and the experimental models adopt the semantic-based concurrency control policies (S2PL, S2PL-S, and S2PL-FW). In the baseline model, TRK requests a write lock upon entering the system. If the

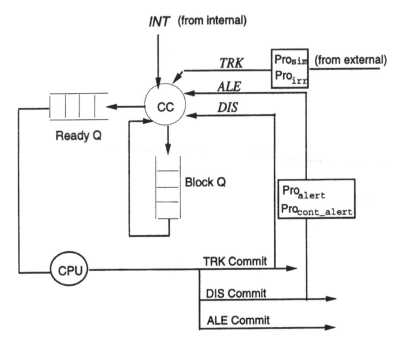

Fig. 5. RTDB Simulation Model

lock is granted, it is put into the ready queue ("ReadyQ" in Figure 5) . Otherwise it goes into a blocking queue ("BlockQ" in Figure 5). A DIS needs to get a read lock for the track record in TDB and a write lock in DDB, and an ALE requires read locks in both TDB and DDB. The system ready queue is a priority queue based on transaction deadlines. Once a transaction in the blocking queue gets all the locks it needs, that transaction could be moved from the blocking queue to the ready queue. Since the system is priority driven by using EDF, a higher priority transaction can preempt the transaction in execution if there is no data locking conflict. A preempted transaction still holds the lock(s) it has and is put back to the ready queue. Because only update transactions have firm deadlines, transaction abort happens when the current system time exceeds the transaction deadline, regardless of whether it is currently in the ready queue or the blocking queue.

The experimental model follows the transaction model described in Section 3. The concurrency control unit is responsible for managing the semantic-locks of objects in TDB and DDB. Upon each transaction request, the S2PL protocol will examine CM to determine whether to grant the lock or not. As in 2PL, a transaction must get all the locks before it can be dispatched. The concurrency control unit maintains the TRK abort history of each track object as well as the DIS abort history of each display object. A semantic lock promotion will take place (from R_{ab} to R_{ex}) when the abort threshold has been reached. The threshold value is set to be 2 which means that if there was a TRK or DIS abort in the previous period, the current DIS must be able to finish its execution. Also, the detection status of a TDB object will be set if the related ALE transaction has run for more than T_{max} time unit and there is an alert happening currently. As a result, the R_{ab} will be upgraded to R_{ex} on that track object. Note that under this assumption, it is possible that an on-going ALE transaction which will eventually detect a tactical alert situation could be aborted by the next TRK instance if the ALE transaction is still in an early execution stage.

To simulate semantic-based concurrency control with similarity policy (S2PL-S), a probability variable Pro_{sim} is defined to specify how likely the most recent TRK update value is similar to the previous one. The corresponding CM will be used (Table 4) for TDB objects. For semantic-based concurrency control with forced wait policy (S2PL-FW), Table 5 will be used.

Parameter	Meaning	Value
λ_1	new target arrival rate	0.075 - 0.10/sec
C_{min}	min. life time	500 sec
C_{max}	max. life time	1000 sec
U_{min}	min. execution time for TRK	0.005 sec
U_{max}	max. execution time for TRK	0.01 sec
D_{min}	min. execution time for DIS	0.05 sec
D_{max}	max. execution time for DIS	0.075 sec
T_{min}	min. execution time for ALE (w/o alert)	0.008 sec
T_{max}	max. execution time for ALE (w/o alert)	0.01 sec
TD_{min}	min. execution time for ALE (w/ alert)	0.06 sec
TD_{max}	max. execution time for ALE (w/ alert)	0.08 sec
D_{rel}	relative deadline for a display transaction	2 sec
Pro_{alert}	prob. of detecting tactical alert in a period	0.002
Pro_{cont_alert}	prob. of continuous alert situation	0.3
Pro_{sim}	prob. TRK contains similar data	0.3
Pro_{irr}	prob. current TRK update is irregular	0.3
P_i	period defined for external devices	4, 10 sec
D_d	data deadline for TDB track	2.5 sec
O_1	overhead to set/reset W_{hd}	0.001 sec
O_2	overhead to check if regular	0.0005 sec
λ_2	local task-1 arrival rate	0.5/sec
λ_3	local task-2 arrival rate	1.0/sec
$dist$	minimum distance between two consecutive local tasks	2 sec
l_{min}	min. execution time required for a local task	0.1 sec
l_{max}	max. execution time required for a local task	0.5 sec
SF_1	slack factor for deadline assignment for local task-1	4
SF_2	slack factor for deadline assignment for local task-2	3

Table 6. System Parameters and Baseline Values

Table 6 shows all the parameters for the baseline model. We will present and discuss the simulation results in next section.

6 Simulation Result

In this section, we present the simulation result for comparing different concurrency control protocols described in Section 4.2. The performance metrics are first specified, followed by the analysis of simulation result.

6.1 Performance Measurement

A real-time database designed for the air traffic control system must be able to handle unexpectedly heavy load caused by scenarios like severe weather or ground facility failures. The following are the performance metrics measured in our experiments.

1. TRK_{comp} : Update transaction completion ratio. It is the percentage of the completed TRK out of the total TRK arrivals.
2. DIS_{meet} : Percentage of completed DIS 's meeting their soft deadlines. DIS_{dmeet} is the percentage of completed DIS's meeting data deadlines.
3. Age_{age} : Average Age of all completed DIS, where Age is defined as the normalized data age used by a DIS. That is, if the the completion time of a DIS is t', and the track data (with update period P) arrived at the system at time t, then

$$Age = \frac{t' - t}{P}$$

4. Ref_{avg} : Average Ref of all completed DIS, where Ref is defined as the normalized refresh rate for a DIS as follow. Suppose $t(n)$ is the nth DIS completion time.

$$Ref = \frac{t(n) - t(n-1)}{P}$$

5. Res_{avg} : Average Res of all completed ALE, where Res is defined as the normalized response time for an ALE which detects an alert. Suppose an ALE detects an alert finishes at time t', the track data (with TRK period P) used for detection is ready at time t,

$$Res = \frac{t' - t}{P}$$

In our simulation, there are two different classes of TRK's with period equal to 4 and 10 seconds respectively. The simulation result are analyzed for each class independently.

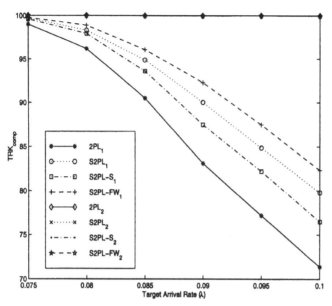

Fig. 6. Effects of λ on TRK completion ratio

6.2 Simulation Result

Figure 6 shows the TRK completion ratio. As the aircraft arrival rate increases, TRK_{comp} decreases. A higher arrival rate generates more transactions in the system and causes some TRKs to miss deadlines even when the CPU is not fully utilized. The completion ratio drops to below 70% when $\lambda = 0.1$ for class 1 but above 99% at all time for class 2. In Figure 6, S2PL-FW has the highest TRK_{comp} values over other protocols due to two factors: Firstly, some DIS's and ALE's can be forced to release locks earlier so that the conflicting TRK's can finish by their firm deadlines. Secondly, internally triggered INT may abort some DIS's and ALE's as well. For S2PL-S, a TRK can be aborted by an on-going DIS or ALE. TRK aborts intuitively should decrease the TRK completion ratio. However, since TRK aborts also avoid subsequent triggering of DIS and ALE, it eliminates some possible conflicting situations and actually helps later TRK instances to finish earlier. As a result, the TRK_{comp} values of S2PL-S are between those of S2PL and 2PL.

Figures 7 to 10 show the performance of DIS transactions. Like TRK_{comp}, DIS_{meet} decreases as the system load increases (Figure 7). There are approximately 80% of the DIS's finish before deadlines when λ is 0.075, but only less than 10 percent of DIS's meeting soft deadlines when λ reaches 0.1. In Figure 7, we see that 2PL has the least number of DIS transactions meeting their deadlines. All semantic approaches improve the performance, especially S2PL-FW. This is probably because the transaction manager in S2PL-FW aborts a DIS once its data deadline expires. S2PL and S2PL-S perform pretty similar to each other because they use essentially the same strategy except that a long running

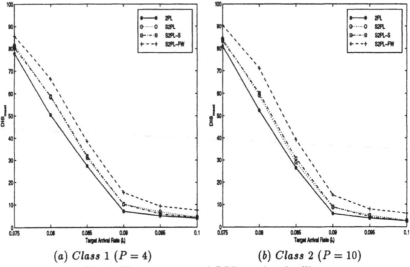

(a) *Class* 1 ($P = 4$)   (b) *Class* 2 ($P = 10$)

Fig. 7. The percentage of *DIS* meeting deadlines

DIS has no chance to finish after a new TRK arrives in S2PL but can continue the execution in S2PL-S, as long as the most current update is similar to the previous one. However, this effect somehow is offset by the fact that the R_{ab} lock of DIS can be upgraded to R_{ex}, which allows DIS to run to its completion in both cases.

In Figure 8, the performance of DIS meeting data deadlines is shown. As expected, S2PL-FW is the best protocol since it takes the extra data constraint into scheduling considerations. It is followed by S2PL, S2PL-S and 2PL, in that order. Again, 2PL tries to finish every DIS as well as ALE thus has the worst performance. In comparison, the semantic approaches prevent delayed DIS or ALE from proceeding and reduce the percentage of completed DIS's missing data deadlines.

The average ages of all completed DIS's are shown in Figure 9. Since a heavier system load results in a longer waiting time for TRKs, DIS reads more stale data as λ gets larger. It is seen that DIS can get more up-to-date external information using the semantic-based concurrency control. The improvement is significant for both classes. In our measurement, we update the data ready time of a track to the most recent TRK arrival time even when the TRK is aborted by the similarity protocol. S2PL-S benefits from this measurement and has a smaller Age_{avg} value for class 1, where the lock contention is high. For class 2, S2PL-FW performs better since the early abort of DIS (or ALE) helps the next triggered DIS (or ALE) get fresher track data.

In Figure 10, the average refresh rate gets larger when λ increases, meaning that the screen refresh frequency slows down under a heavier load. Since 2PL tries to finish every DIS, the refresh rate increases slowly as the load increases.

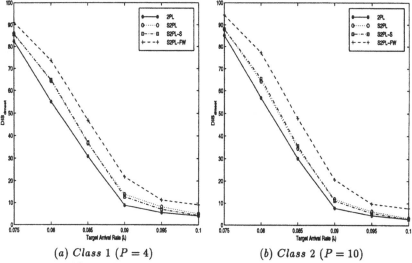

(a) *Class* 1 $(P = 4)$ (b) *Class* 2 $(P = 10)$

Fig. 8. The percentage of DIS meeting data deadlines

Among the four protocols, S2PL has the highest Ref_{avg}, even worse than S2PL-FW. In other words, the early aborts of DIS's in S2PL-FW do not increase the Ref value by too much since the next triggered DIS might start earlier too. Similarly, in S2PL-S, even though TRK might be aborted due to its similarity, the conflicting DIS has already been late which does not particularly lengthen the interval before the DIS completion. Compared to S2PL, S2PL-S has less DIS aborts than S2PL does. Consequently, the refresh rate is lower.

To evaluate the performance of ALE transactions, Res_{avg} comparisons is presented in Figure 11. The ALE response time is affected by many factors such as DIS response time and alert detecting ratio. Since the semantic-based approaches can upgrade read lock for ALE transactions, the response time is usually better than that of 2PL. In Figure 11 (a), S2PL-S produces higher Res_{avg} values than 2PL does. This reflects that the late DIS execution plus ALE abort (by TRK) out-weigh the benefit from upgrading the lock. For S2PL-FW, a completed DIS normally has a shorter response time which in turn results in a shorter response time for ALE.

7 Conclusions

In this paper, we study the performance of semantic-based concurrency control protocols for the air traffic control database system using the idea from active databases to enhance the data validity. Air traffic control system is a complex real-time application that requires a careful design. From our experiments, it can be seen that semantic concurrency control protocols may enhance the performance of air traffic control transactions. The concurrency control protocols

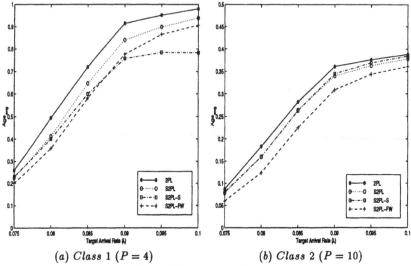

(a) *Class* 1 ($P = 4$)   (b) *Class* 2 ($P = 10$)

Fig. 9. The average data age

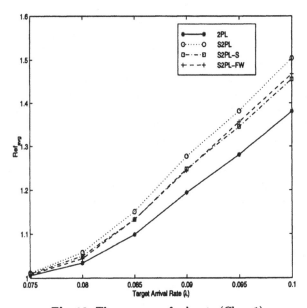

Fig. 10. The average refresh rate (Class 1)

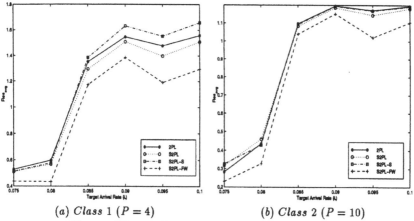

(a) *Class* 1 $(P = 4)$ (b) *Class* 2 $(P = 10)$

Fig. 11. Effects of λ on the average ALE response time

studied in this paper utilize the real-time data semantics and the active database scheme to make systems more responsive to real-time workloads. We believe that this is a promising approach for designing real-time database systems.

References

[AAS93]   D. Agrawal, A. E. Abbadi, and A. K. Singh. Consistency and Orderability: Semantics-Based Correctness Criteria for Databases. *ACM Transactions on Database Systems*, 18(3):460–486, 1993.

[AGM88]   R. Abbott and H. Garcia-Molina. Scheduling Real-Time Transactions: A Performance Study. In *VLDB Conference*, pages 1–12, September 1988.

[AGMK95] B. Adelberg, H. Garcia-Molina, and B. Kao. Applying Update Streams in a Soft Real-Time Database System. *ACM SIGMOD*, 1995.

[Bak91]   T. P. Baker. Stack-Based Scheduling of Realtime Processes. *Real-Time Systems*, 3(1):67–99, March 1991.

[BHG87]   Bernstein, Hadzilacos, and Goodman. *Concurrency Control and Recovery in Database Systems*. Addison-Wesley, 1987.

[BR92]   B. R. Badrinath and K. Ramamritham. Semantics-Based Concurrency Control: Beyond Commutativity. *ACM Transactions on Database Systems*, 17(1):163–199, March 1992.

[CJL91]   M.J. Carey, R. Jauhari, and M. Livny. On Transaction Boundaries in Active Databases: A Performance Perspective. *IEEE Transactions on Knowledge and Data Engineering*, 3(3):320–336, 1991.

[CKAK93] S. Chakravarthy, V. Krishnaprasad, E. Abwar, and S.K. Kim. Anatomy of a composite event detector. Technical Report Technical Report UF-CIS-TR-93-039, CIS Department, University of Florida, 1993.

[CL91]   M. Chen and K. J. Lin. A Priority Ceiling Protocol for Multiple Instance Resources. In *Real-Time Systems Symposium*, pages 140–149, December 1991.

[DBB+88] U. Dayal, B. Blaustein, A. Buchmann, U. Chakravarthy, M. Hsu, R. Ledin, D. McCarthy, A. Rosenthal, S. Sarin, M.J. Carey, M. Livny, and R. Jauhari. The HiPAC Project: Combining Active Database and Timing Constraints. *ACM SIGMOD Record*, 17(1):51–70, 1988.

[DBB+89] U. Dayal, B. Blaustein, A. Buchmann, U. Chakravathy, M. Hsu, R. Ledin, D. McCarthy, A. Rosenthal, and S.Sarin. HiPAC. A Research Project In Active, Time-Constrained Database Management. Technical Report Technical Report XAIT-89-02, Xerox Advanced Information Technology, Cambridge, 1989.

[DHL90] U. Dayal, M. Hsu, and R. Ladin. Organizing Long-Running Activities with Triggers and Transactions. In *ACM SIGMOD Conference*, 1990.

[DPG91] O. Diaz, N. Paton, and P. Gray. Rule Management in Object-Oriented Databases: A Uniform Approach. In *International Conference on Very Large Data Bases*, pages 317–326, 1991.

[DW93] L. B. C. DiPippo and V. F. Wolfe. Object-Based Semantic Real-Time Concurrency Control. In *Real-Time Systems Symposium*, pages 87–96, December 1993.

[EGLT76] K. P. Eswaran, J. N. Gray, R. A. Lorie, and I. L. Traiger. The Notions of Consistency and Predicate Locks in a Database System. *Communications of the ACM*, pages 624–633, 1976.

[GD94] S. Gatziu and K.R. Dittrich. Detecting Composite Events in Active Database Systems Using Petri-Nets. In *International Workshop on Research Issues in Data Engineering*, 1994.

[GJS92] N. Gehani, H.V. Jagadish, and O. Shumeh. Composite Event Specification in Active Databases: Model and Implementation. In *International Conference on Very Large Data Bases*, 1992.

[GM83] H. Garcia-Molina. Using Semantic Knowledge for Transaction Processing in a Distributed Database. *ACM Transactions on Database Systems*, 8(2):186–213, 1983.

[HLM88] M. Hsu, R. Ladin, and D. McCarthy. An Execution Model for Active Database Management Systems. In *International Conference on Data and Knowledge Bases*, pages 171–179, 1988.

[KM93] T. W. Kuo and A. K. Mok. SSP: a Semantics-Based Protocol for Real-Time Data Access. In *Real-Time Systems Symposium*, pages 76–86, December 1993.

[Lin89] K. J. Lin. Consistency Issues in Real-Time Database Systems. In *Proceedings of the 22nd Annual Hawaii International Conference on System Sciences*, pages 654–661, January 1989.

[LL73] C. L. Liu and J. W. Layland. Scheduling Algorithms for Multiprogramming in a Hard Real-Time Environment. *Journal of ACM*, 20(1):46–61, January 1973.

[MRW+93] P. Muth, T. C. Rakow, G. Weikum, P. Brossler, and C. Hasse. Semantic Concurrency Control in Object-Oriented Database Systems. In *9th International Conference on Data Engineering*, 1993.

[NL93] H. Nakazato and K. J. Lin. Concurrency Control Algorithms for Real-Time Systems. *Microprocessing and Microprogramming*, pages 647–654, 1993.

[PL96] C. S. Peng and K. J. Lin. A Semantic-Based Concurrency Control Protocol for Real-Time Transactions. In *Second IEEE Real-Time Technology and Applications Symposium*, Boston, Massachusetts, June 1996.

[PLN97]   C. S. Peng, K. J. Lin, and T. P. Ng. A Performance Study of the Semantic-Based Concurrency Control Protocol in Air Traffic Control systems. In *Second Int. Real-Time Database Workshop*, Burlington, Vermont, September 1997.

[Pu91]   C. Pu. Generalized Transaction Processing With Epesilon-Serializability. In *Proc. of 1991 International Workshop on High Performance Transaction Systems*, 1991.

[SL95]   X. Song and J. Liu. Maintaining Temporal Consistency : Pessimistic vs Optimistic Concurrency Control. *IEEE Transactions on Knowledge and Data Engineering*, pages 787–796, October 1995.

[SRL90]   Lui Sha, R. Rajkumar, and J. Lehoczky. Priority Inheritance Protocols: An Approach to Real-Time Synchronization. *IEEE Transactions on Computers*, 39(9):1175–1185, September 1990.

[XRST96]   M. Xiong, K. Ramamritham R. Sivasankaran, J. A. Stankovic, and D. Towsley. Scheduling Transactions with Temporal Constraints: Exploiting Data Semantics. In *Real-Time Systems Symposium*, pages 240–251, December 1996.

Performance Issues in Processing Active Real-Time Transactions*

Özgür Ulusoy

Department of Computer Engineering and Information Science, Bilkent University,
Bilkent, Ankara 06533, TURKEY
e-mail: oulusoy@bilkent.edu.tr

Abstract. An active real-time database system (ARTDBS) is designed
to provide timely response to the critical situations that are defined on
database states. Several studies have already addressed various issues
in ARTDBSs. The distinctive features of our work are to describe a
detailed performance model of a distributed ARTDBS and investigate
various performance issues in time-cognizant transaction processing in
ARTDBSs.

1 Introduction

Real-time database systems are designed to provide timely response to the transactions of data-intensive applications. Each transaction processed in a real-time
database system is associated with a timing constraint typically in the form of
a deadline. The research on real-time database systems has focused on development and evaluation of time-cognizant scheduling techniques that aim to maximize the fraction of satisfied timing constraints while maintaining consistency of
the underlying database (e.g., Abbott and Garcia-Molina 1992, Bestavros and
Braoudakis 1996, Chen and Lin 1990, Datta et al. 1996a, Haritsa et al. 1992,
Hong et al. 1993, Huang et al. 1992, Lam and Hung 1995, Lee and Son 1995,
Ulusoy and Belford 1993).

Active database systems, on the other hand, extend conventional database
systems with the ability to specify and implement reactive behavior which is
typically specified in terms of event-condition-action (ECA) rules. The general
form of an ECA rule is: on *event* if *condition* do *action*. The semantics of such
a rule is that when an event occurs, the corresponding condition is checked,
and if the condition is satisfied, then a specified action is executed (Dayal et al.
1988a). Therefore, an active database system has to monitor events of interest
and detect their occurrences. The semantics of rule execution can be specified
in a transaction framework. A transaction which triggers rules can be called a
triggering transaction, and the transaction which executes the triggered rule can
be called the *triggered transaction*. Most of the work on active databases has
concentrated on rule specification, efficient event detection and rule execution

* This research is supported by the NATO Collaborative Research Grant CRG 960648.

(e.g., Chakravarthy et al. 1993, Dayal et al. 1990, Diaz et al. 1991, Gatziu and Dittrich 1994, Gehani et al. 1992, Hsu et al. 1988).

Active real-time database systems (ARTDBSs) field has emerged as a result of the requirement to apply real-time scheduling techniques to rule execution in active database systems that support time-critical applications. Some examples of such application areas are command and control systems, automated manufacturing, air-traffic control, intelligent network services, and cooperative distributed navigation systems (Sivasankaran et al. 1996). Few studies, that are briefly described in the next section, have addressed various problems that might arise in integrating the concepts from real-time scheduling algorithms and active database systems.

In our work, we investigate various performance issues in time-cognizant transaction processing in distributed ARTDBSs. We describe a performance model designed for studying the performance of various components of a distributed ARTDBS, and present the results of experiments conducted to be able to address the performance issues in executing transactions under various types of active workload. The performance metric used in the evaluations is the fraction of transactions that miss their deadlines. Two different transaction-processing architectures, that we call *distributed transaction* and *mobile data*, are employed in the experiments. In the distributed transaction architecture, a transaction executes a cohort at each site that stores one or more data pages required by the transaction. The mobile data architecture, on the other hand, is based on transmitting data pages to wherever they are needed. We also consider different types of semantics in controlling the concurrent execution of triggering and triggered transactions. Besides conducting experiments with the assumption that the triggering and triggered transactions share the locks, we also describe a nested transaction execution scheme that aims to exploit the nested structure of rule execution to improve the performance.

The next section summarizes the related work. Section 3 provides a description of a simulation model of an ARTDBS which was used in obtaining the performance results we report in Section 4. We describe a nested execution model for the active workload in Section 5. The conclusions of our work are summarized in the last section.

2   Related Work

A detailed performance model of an active DBMS was described by Carey et al. for studying various performance issues in active database systems (Carey et al. 1991). The authors investigated the performance impact of different transaction boundary semantics without addressing any real-time issues for transactions.

Involvement of timing constraints in active databases was first considered in the HiPAC (High Performance ACtive Database System) project (Chakravarthy et al. 1989, Dayal et al. 1988b). Three basic concepts explored in this project are active database management, timing constraints, and contingency plans. *Contingency plans* are defined as alternate actions that can be invoked whenever the system determines that it cannot complete an action within its deadline. A knowledge model was developed for the project that provides primitives for defining condition-action rules and timing constraints, control mechanisms for efficient rule searching, and support for the execution model primitives. The execution model introduces a generalized transaction model that provides correct execution of specified actions and user transactions together in a timely manner.

The problem of assigning priorities to transactions in ARTDBSs was studied by Purimetla et al. (1994, 1996). Three priority assignment policies, that use different amount of semantic information about transactions, were proposed, and the performance of the policies was evaluated using an ARTDBS simulator. The same research group also developed some strategies for data placement, logging, and recovery to achive efficient transaction processing in ARTDBSs (Sivasankaran et al. 1995). It was shown that exploiting the characteristics of data for transaction processing, placing the data at the appropriate level of the memory hierarchy, and performing logging and recovery of data appropriate for each type of data is crucial to attain high performance in ARTDBSs.

Branding and Buchmann (1995) identified 'network management' as one of the applications that require both active and real-time database support. Their primary work was development of an ARTDBS for this application and seamless integration of the ARTDBS's execution model with the underlying operating system primitives.

Berndtsson and Hansson (1995) characterized the basic features of active and real-time database systems, and addressed several issues that need to be considered while combining those features. In a recent work, Datta and Son (1996b) studied various concurrency control methods in ARTDBSs, and proposed a number of new strategies. Performance of the proposed concurrency control strategies was investigated through simulation experiments.

3   A Distributed Active Real-Time Database System Model

We have extended the performance model of a distributed real-time database system that we used in an earlier work (Ulusoy 1995), by adding a **Rule Manager** to handle triggering transactions. In the distributed system model, a number of data sites are interconnected by a local communication network. Each site contains a **Transaction Generator**, a **Transaction Manager**, a **Rule Manager**, a **Message Server**, a **Resource Manager**, a **Scheduler**, and a **Buffer Manager**.

The **Transaction Generator** is responsible for generating the workload for each data site. The arrivals at a data site are assumed to be independent of the arrivals at the other sites. Each transaction in the system is distinguished by a globally unique transaction id. The id of a transaction is made up of two parts: a transaction number which is unique at the originating site of the transaction and the id of the originating site which is unique in the system.

The **Transaction Manager** is responsible for modeling the execution of transactions. It accepts transactions from the **Transaction Generator** and the **Rule Manager**. Each transaction is characterized by a real-time constraint in the form of a deadline. The transaction deadlines are *soft*; i.e., each transaction is executed to completion even if it misses its deadline. The **Transaction Manager** at the originating site of a transaction assigns a real-time priority to the transaction based on the *Earliest Deadline First* priority assignment policy; i.e., a transaction with an earlier deadline has higher priority than a transaction with a later deadline. If any two transactions originated from the same site carry the same deadline, a scheduling decision between those two transactions prefers the one that has arrived earlier. To guarantee the global uniqueness of the priorities, the id of the originating site is appended to the priority of each transaction. The **Transaction Manager** is responsible for the implementation of any of the transaction-processing architectures described in Section 4.1. For each operation of the executing transaction, the **Transaction Manager** communicates with the **Scheduler** to see whether the operation leads to any conflict with the operations of the other transactions.

Access requests for data pages are ordered by the **Scheduler** on the basis of the concurrency control protocol executed. The protocol we use in our experiments is the *High-Priority* concurrency control protocol which resolves data conflicts always in favor of high-priority transactions (Abbott and Garcia-Molina 1992). At the time of a data lock conflict, if the lock-holding transaction has higher priority than the priority of the transaction that is requesting the lock, the latter transaction is blocked. Otherwise, the lock-holding transaction is aborted and the lock is granted to the high priority lock-requesting transaction. Assuming that no two transactions have the same priority, this protocol is deadlock-free since a high priority transaction is never blocked by a lower priority transaction. Concurrency control is implemented at a page granularity.

There is no globally shared memory in the system, and all sites communicate via message exchanges over the communication network. A **Message Server** at each site is responsible for sending/receiving messages to/from other sites. Reliability and recovery issues were not addressed in this paper. We assumed a reliable system, in which no site failures or communication network failures occur. Also, we did not simulate in detail the operation of the underlying communication network. It was just considered as a switching element between sites with a certain service rate.

IO and CPU services at each site are provided by the **Resource Manager**. IO service is required for reading or updating data pages, while CPU service is necessary for processing data pages, performing various page access control operations (e.g. conflict check, locking, etc.) and processing communication messages. Both CPU and IO queues are organized on the basis of real-time priorities, and preemptive-resume priority scheduling is used by the CPU's at each site. The CPU can be released by a transaction either due to a preemption, or when the transaction commits or it is blocked/aborted due to a data conflict, or when it needs an IO or communication service.

Data transfer between disk and main memory is provided by the **Buffer Manager**. The *Least Recently Used (LRU)* page replacement strategy is used in the management of memory buffers.

3.1 Handling the Active Workload

The **Transaction Manager** informs the **Rule Manager** of each page update. Each successful update operation which changes the database state is considered as an *event*. The **Rule Manager** is responsible to check if any *action* is triggered when an event message is raised by the **Transaction Manager**. Upon getting an event message, the **Rule Manager** models the *condition evaluation*. Satisfaction of a condition can lead to the triggering of one or more of the immediate, deferred, and detached actions of the rule. Condition evaluation is performed probabilistically, using a separate probability value for each of the immediate, deferred, and detached coupling modes (see Table 1). A subtransaction corresponding to each triggered action is submitted to the **Transaction Manager**.

A detached subtransaction submitted to the **Transaction Manager** is treated as a new transaction and it is executed independent of the triggering transaction. Immediate and deferred subtransactions, on the other hand, are executed as a part of the parent transaction which has triggered them. They are executed with the same real-time priority as their parent. Some more sophisticated priority assignment policies for subtransactions were proposed in the literature (e.g., Purimetla et al. 1994, Sivasankaran et al. 1996); however, those policies require some a priori knowledge about transactions like their estimated execution times. Our system does not assume the knowledge of execution time of transactions. The subtransactions might access remote as well as local data pages, and their access requests are scheduled in the same way as the parent transactions (according to the rules associated with one of the two transaction-processing architectures described in Section 4.1). We assume that immediate and deferred subtransactions do not trigger further subtransactions; i.e., there is no cascading rule firings.

When an immediate subtransaction is submitted to the **Transaction Manager**, the execution of the parent transaction is suspended until the completion of the immediate subtransaction. All the deferred subtransactions triggered by a transaction are started to execute when their parent completes its operations. We assume that all the immediate and deferred subtransactions triggered by a transaction share the locks. Therefore, although the deferred subtransactions of a transaction are executed concurrently with the same priority, deadlock is still not possible with the High-Priority concurrency control protocol because the subtransactions do not block each other. When all the deferred subtransactions of a transaction complete their execution, the locks of the subtransactions and the parent transaction are released.

3.2 Configuration and Workload Parameters

The list of parameters described in Table 1 was used in specifying the configuration and workload of the distributed ARTDBS. It is assumed that each site has one CPU and one disk.

CONFIGURATION PARAMETERS	
NrOfSites	Number of sites
DBSize	Size of the database in pages
MemSize	Number of pages that can be held in memory
PageSize	Page size in bytes
CPURate	Instruction rate of CPU at each site (MIPS)
DiskAccessTime	Average disk access time
DiskOverheadInst	CPU overhead for performing disk I/O
NetworkBandwidth	Network Bandwidth
ControlMsgSize	Control message size in bytes
FixedMsgInst	Fixed number of instructions to process a message
PerByteMsgInst	Additional number of instructions per message byte
TRANSACTION PARAMETERS	
ArrivalRate	Average arrival rate of transactions at each site
TransSize	Average number of pages accessed by each transaction
SubTransSize	Average number of pages accessed by each subtransaction
RemoteAccessRate	Probability of accessing a page with a remote origin
StartTransInst	Number of instructions to initialize a transaction
EndTransInst	Number of instructions to terminate a transaction
ProcessPageInst	Number of CPU instructions to process a page
WriteProb	Probability of writing to a page
ImmediateProb	Probability of triggering an immediate subtransaction following an update
DeferredProb	Probability of triggering a deferred subtransaction following an update
DetachedProb	Probability of triggering a detached subtransaction following an update
SlackRate	Average rate of slack time of a transaction to its processing time

Table 1. Distributed ARTDBS Model Parameters

The time spent at each disk access is chosen uniformly from the range 0.5 * *DiskAccessTime* through 1.5 * *DiskAccessTime*. The CPU spends *DiskOverheadInst* instructions for each I/O operation. A control message is a non-data message like commit, abort, lock-request, lock-grant messages etc., and the size of such messages is specified by *ControlMsgSize*.

The average transaction arrival rate at each of the sites is determined by the parameter *ArrivalRate*. Arrivals are assumed to be Poisson. The slack time of a transaction specifies the maximum length of time the transaction can be delayed and still satisfy its deadline. It is detailed in the Appendix how the **Transaction Generator** involves the parameter *SlackRate* in assigning deadline to transactions.

4 Performance Experiments

The default parameter values used in each of the experiments are presented in Table 2. All data sites in the system are assumed identical and operate under the same parameter values. The settings used for configuration and transaction parameters were basicly taken from our earlier experiments (Ulusoy 1995). It was intended by those settings to provide a transaction load and data contention high enough to bring out the differences between various alternative execution environments for distributed ARTDBSs. The default values used for the resource-related parameters can be accepted as reasonable approximations to what can be expected from today's systems.

CONFIGURATION PARAMETERS	
NrOfSites	10
DBSize	2500 pages
MemSize	20% of the *DBSize*
PageSize	4,096 bytes
CPURate	50 MIPS
DiskAccessTime	20 msec
DiskOverheadInst	5,000 instructions
NetworkBandwidth	10 Mbps (e.g., Ethernet) or 100 Mbps (e.g., FDDI)
ControlMsgSize	256 bytes
FixedMsgInst	20,000 instructions
PerByteMsgInst	10,000 instructions per 4 Kbytes
TRANSACTION PARAMETERS	
ArrivalRate	1 transaction per second
TransSize	10 pages
SubTransSize	4 pages
RemoteAccessRate	0.5
StartTransInst	30,000 instructions
EndTransInst	40,000 instructions
ProcessPageInst	30,000 instructions
WriteProb	0.5
ImmediateProb	0.5
DeferredProb	0.5
DetachedProb	0.5
SlackRate	10

Table 2. Distributed ARTDBS Model Parameter Values

The performance metric we used in our evaluations is *miss_ratio*, which determines the fraction of transactions that miss their deadlines. For each experiment, the final results were evaluated as averages over 20 independent runs. Each run continued until 1000 transactions were executed at each data site. 90% confidence intervals were obtained for the performance results. The width of the confidence interval of each data point is within 4% of the point estimate. In displayed graphs, only the mean values of the performance results are plotted.

4.1 Transaction Processing Architectures

We consider two different architectures for processing ARTDBS transactions: *distributed transaction* and *mobile data*. Both architectures described in the following subsections assume that there exists exactly one copy of each data page in the system.

Distributed Transaction (DT) Architecture Each transaction exists in the form of a master process that executes at the originating site of the transaction and a collection of cohort processes that execute at various sites where the required data pages reside. This architecture (also called *function shipping* or *database-call shipping*) was already studied for traditional distributed database management systems by a number of researchers (e.g., Kohler and Jeng 1986, Garcia-Molina and Abbott 1987, Carey and Livny 1988). In our system, the priority of a transaction is carried by all of the cohorts of the transaction to be used in scheduling cohorts' executions. The **Transaction Manager** is responsible for the creation of the master process for each transaction. The master process coordinates the execution of cohorts through communicating with the **Transaction Manager** of each cohort's site. There can be at most one cohort of a transaction at each data site. If there exists any local data in the access list of the transaction, one cohort will be executed locally. For each operation of the transaction, a global data dictionary is referred to find out which data site stores the data page referenced by the operation. A cohort process is initiated at that site (if it does not exist already) by the master process by sending an 'initiate cohort' message to that site. If a cohort of the transaction already exists at that site, it is just activated to perform the operation. Before accessing a data page, the cohort needs to obtain a lock on the page. In the case of a lock conflict (i.e., the lock has already been obtained by another cohort), if the lock-holding cohort has higher priority than the priority of the cohort that is requesting the lock, the latter cohort is blocked. Otherwise, the lock-holding cohort is aborted and the lock is granted to the high priority lock-requesting cohort.

For the atomic commitment of the distributed transactions, we use the centralized *two-phase commit* protocol. The blocking delay of two-phase commit (i.e., the delay experienced at both the master process site and each of the cohort process sites while waiting for messages from each other) is explicitly simulated in conducting the performance experiments.

Mobile Data (MD) Architecture This architecture is characterized by the movement of data pages among the sites. With this approach each transaction is executed at a single site (the site it has been originated). Whenever a remote data page is needed by a transaction, the page is transferred to the site of the transaction. Besides the global data dictionary which shows the origin of each data page in the system, each data site also maintains a relocation table to keep track of the pages transferred from/to that site. More specifically, for each data page P whose origin is site S_i and the current location is site S_j, a record is maintained in the relocation table of each of the sites S_i and S_j. The record in the relocation table of S_i shows that P has been sent to S_j, and the record in the relocation table of S_j shows that P has been transferred from S_i.

For each operation of a transaction T executed at site S_i, the data dictionary of S_i is referred to to find out the origin of the required data page P. If page P has been originated at site S_i but currently being resided at another site, a request message is sent to that site. If P has a remote origin, say site S_j, and its current location is not S_i, then a request message is sent to S_j. The message includes the id of transaction T, its priority, the id of originating site S_i, and the id of the requested data page P. If P has been shipped to another site S_k, the request message is forwarded to S_k.

Similar to DT, access to a data page is controlled on the basis of the High-Priority protocol. Transaction T can obtain a lock on a page only if either the page is not being accessed by any other transaction or T's priority is higher than the priority of the transaction currently accessing the page [2]. If the lock is granted, the reply message contains both the grant and the requested page; otherwise, the message will cause the transaction to become blocked until the requested lock becomes available. When the execution of a transaction finishes successfully, it can be committed locally. All updates performed by the transaction are stored on the local disk.

It is ensured by this transaction-processing architecture that the current location of a data page can always be found out by communicating with the originating site of that page. Whenever a data page P with originating site S_i is transmitted to site S_j, the relocation tables at both sites are updated to keep track of the relocation information. A record is inserted into the relocation table of S_i to store the current location of P (i.e., S_j). The corresponding record inserted into the relocation table of S_j stores the origin of P (i.e., S_i). If page P later needs to be transmitted to another site S_k, the related record is removed from the relocation table of S_j and the id of originating site S_i is sent to S_k within the message containing data page P. Upon receiving that message, a new record is inserted into the relocation table of S_k. Another message from site S_j is sent to site S_i containing the new location of P so that the related record of the relocation table of S_i can be updated appropriately. This architecture is also called *I/O shipping* in traditional database literature.

Summary of Results Obtained without any Triggering Transactions
When we evaluated the two different transaction-processing architectures in a

---

[2] This leads to a priority abort; the low priority transaction currently accessing the page is aborted.

distributed real-time database system environment without any active capabilities (i.e., in the absence of triggering transactions), we obtained the following
results (Ulusoy 1995): The relative performance of the architectures is primarily
determined by the resource requirements of transactions processed under each
of the architectures. With a slow network, the overhead of messages for each
transaction did not show much difference under two different architectures. Although the average message volume with MD was much higher, DT was not able
to outperform MD because the cost of transferring a message is primarily due to
the CPU time to initiate sending/receiving the message and not the transmission
time; and DT was characterized by the larger number of messages (compared to
MD) issued for each transaction. When a fast network was used, on the other
hand, the average volume of messages did not have much influence on the performance, and MD demonstrated superior performance. MD was also observed
to produce less I/O delay in storing the updated pages on stable storage. With
MD, the pages with a remote origin that are updated by a transaction can be
consecutively placed on the local disk preventing the delay of separate seek time
for each stored page.

4.2   Results Obtained with an Active Workload

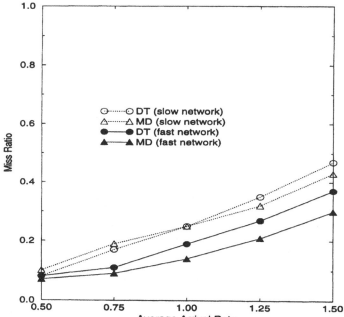

Fig. 1. Real-time performance in terms of the fraction of missed deadlines as a function
of transaction load.

Impact of Transaction Load This experiment was conducted to observe the performance of the system under different levels of transaction load. Average transaction arrival rate at a site (i.e., *ArrivalRate*) was varied from 0.5 to 1.5 transactions per second in steps of 0.25. This range of *ArrivalRate* values corresponds to an average CPU utilization of about .93 to .55 at each data site.

It can be observed from Figure 1 that as the transaction load is increased, more transactions miss their deadlines. Obviously, the increasing load leads to more data and resource conflicts among transactions, and therefore more blockings and priority aborts are experienced. The involvement of active workload does not change the general conclusions obtained for performance of the transaction-processing architectures. The discussion provided in Section 4.1.3 for the relative performance results of architectures is applicable here as well. When a slow network is employed (i.e., *NetworkBandwidth* = 10 Mbps), the performance results obtained with DT and MD are comparable to each other. With a fast network (i.e., *NetworkBandwidth* = 100 Mbps), MD is the clear winner, especially under high levels of transaction load.

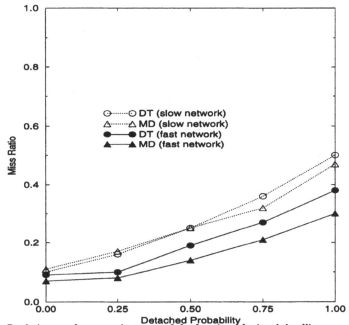

Fig. 2. Real-time performance in terms of the fraction of missed deadlines as a function of the probability of triggering detached subtransactions.

Impact of Triggering Probabilities In this experiment, we examined the system behavior while the probability of triggering a subtransaction was varied for each of the three coupling modes: detached, immediate, and deferred.

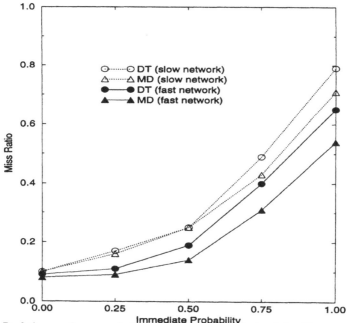

Fig. 3. Real-time performance in terms of the fraction of missed deadlines as a function of the probability of triggering immediate subtransactions.

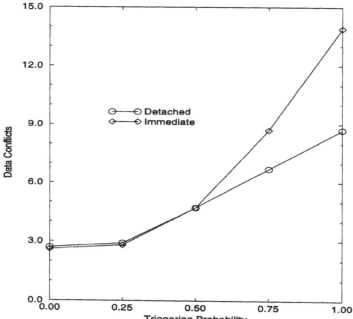

Fig. 4. Average number of data conflicts experienced by a transaction as a function of the probability of triggering detached/immediate subtransactions.

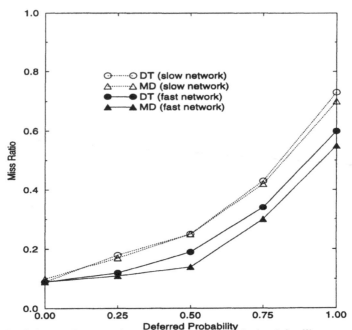

Fig. 5. Real-time performance in terms of the fraction of missed deadlines as a function of the probability of triggering deferred subtransactions.

While evaluating the performance impact of a coupling mode, the parameter values used to determine the probabilities of the other coupling modes were kept constant at 0.5.

We first varied the probability of triggering a detached subtransaction following each page update (i.e., *DetachedProb*) from 0.0 to 1.0. The overall shapes of the curves presented in Figure 2 remain the same as those in Figure 1. This is not surprising as detached subtransactions are treated as new submissions (i.e., they are executed independent of their triggering transactions), and therefore increasing the number of detached subtransactions can be considered as another way of increasing the transaction load in the system. However, this argument is not applicable to the other coupling modes. As the subtransactions created in immediate or deferred modes are executed as a part of the triggering transaction, increasing the number of such subtransactions has an implication of increasing the average length of transactions, rather than directly increasing the transaction load. Figure 3 displays the *miss_ratio* results obtained by varying the amount of immediate subtransactions. For the small number of triggered subtransactions (i.e., when the triggering probability is less than 0.5), the trends observed with varying probabilities of detached and immediate subtransactions are similar. However, when the system is characterized by a high volume of triggered subtransactions, an increase in the number of immediate subtransactions leads to a much sharper increase in the number of missed deadlines compared to that observed with the increase in the number of detached subtransactions.

We contribute this result to the fact that extending the lifetime of transactions by involving some extra operations has more crucial effects on the real-time performance than executing those operations in the form of separate transactions. Figure 4 presents the average number of data conflicts experienced by a transaction as a function of the probability of both immediate and detached coupling modes. The results presented were obtained with DT and a fast network. Similar trends were observed with the other alternative configurations. A data conflict results in either transaction abort or blocking, and in any case the execution of a transaction is delayed. With both DT and MD architectures, increasing the number of immediate subtransactions has more adverse effects on the real-time performance compared to the effects of detached subtransactions; and this observation is more apparent with DT architecture. The difference between the performances of DT and MD becomes more pronounced as the amount of immediate subtransactions increases. Data conflict aborts, that are experienced more with the immediate coupling mode, lead to much more message overhead with DT than that with MD. When a cohort of a transaction is aborted, the DT architecture requires the master process of the transaction send control messages to the sites executing the cohorts of the transaction to notify them about the abort decision. Also, when the aborted transaction is restarted, the master process should again communicate with the other sites to perform remote accesses although it might already have communicated with them before being aborted. With MD, on the other hand, a restarted transaction can find the previously accessed data pages in local buffers, thus it does not require to generate new request messages.

The performance results we obtained by varying the probability of triggering deferred subtransactions on each data update are displayed in Figure 5. Similar to immediate subtransactions, deferred subtransactions are also executed as a part of the triggering transaction. Therefore, the rapid increase in the number of missed deadlines is again a result of increasing the size of transactions by involving more deferred subtransactions. However, as a difference from the results obtained by varying the number of immediate subtransactions, we have a little bit better results for DT architecture. The performance results of DT and MD are closer to each other compared to those presented in Figure 3. This result is due to the fact that while the deferred subtransactions of a transaction are started to execute at the end of the transactions, there is a chance with DT architecture to execute some of those subtransactions in parallel if they are accessing data pages stored at different sites.

The large number of deadline misses experienced with immediate and deferred subtransactions confirms the observation of Branding and Buchmann (1995) that immediate and deferred coupling modes have some negative properties to be supported by real-time database systems.

Impact of Subtransaction Length Figure 6 provides the performance results obtained under different levels of data contention by varying the length of (i.e., number of data pages accessed by) each type of subtransactions. While

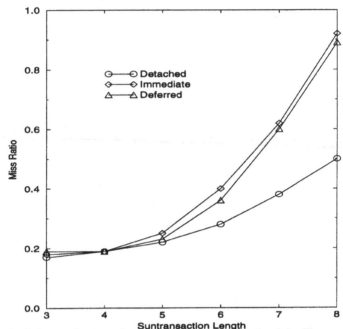

Fig. 6. Real-time performance in terms of the fraction of missed deadlines as a function of the length of a subtransaction triggered in a specific coupling mode.

conducting the experiment for different lengths of the subtransactions (i.e., *Sub-TransSize*) of a coupling mode, the length of subtransactions triggered in other coupling modes was set to 4 pages . The results were obtained by employing DT architecture with a fast network. For small lengths of subtransactions, the performance results obtained for different coupling modes are about the same. The difference between the performance results starts to appear when the length of a subtransaction triggered in a coupling mode is increased beyond 4. This difference becomes more pronounced with each additional data page accessed by a subtransaction. The real-time performance of the system is affected much more negatively when the size of immediate or deferred subtransactions is increased, compared to the performance degradation observed by increasing the detached subtransaction size. This result is due to, as explained in the preceding section, executing immediate and deferred subtransactions as a part of the triggering transaction. Data contention increases much faster when the lifetime of triggering transactions, which are larger than detached subtransactions, is extended further, compared to the increase in data contention due to increasing the size of detached subtransactions.

5   Adapting a Nested Transaction Model

In this section, we describe a nested transaction execution model that can be adapted to our ARTDBS. This model enables us to execute immediate subtransactions concurrently with their triggering transactions; in other words, a triggering transaction need not to be suspended during the execution of its immediate subtransactions. In this case, we do not assume that immediate and deferred subtransactions triggered by a transaction share the locks. Again, a transaction and its subtransactions[3] are associated with the same priority, and a subtransaction does not trigger further subtransactions. The locking rules proposed by Harder and Rothermel (1993) for nested transactions can be adapted to our system as follows: Besides holding a lock, a transaction can *retain* a lock. When a subtransaction commits, the triggering parent transaction inherits the locks of the subtransaction and retains them. A retained lock does not give the right to its owner to access the locked page, rather it indicates that only the subtransactions of the retainer or the retainer itself can potentially acquire the lock.

When a subtransaction S requests a lock, the following protocol is executed:

> **if** (there exists any (sub)transaction S' that holds the lock)
>   **if** (priority(S) > priority(S'))
> S' is aborted;
>   The lock is granted to S;
>   **else**
> S is blocked;
> **else if** (there exists any transaction T that retains the lock
>   and is not the parent of S)
>   **if** (priority(S) > priority(T))
> T is aborted;
>   The lock is granted to S;
>   **else**
> S is blocked;
> **else**
>   The lock is granted to S;

The lock request of a transaction is handled similarly; the only difference is that the phrase "and is not the parent of S" should be replaced by "and is not the lock-requesting transaction itself".

When a subtransaction is aborted, its parent transaction is also aborted only if it retains at least one of the locks that have been held by the aborted subtransaction. All the locks that have been retained/held by an aborted (sub)transaction are released.

We are planning to repeat the experiments of the preceding section by involving the nested locking protocol described above to investigate how the performance trends can be affected by the nested execution.

---

[3] For the remainder of this section, we use the term subtransaction to denote either immediate or deferred subtransaction. We again assume that a detached subtransaction and its triggering transaction has no dependency, and they are executed as independent transactions.

6 Conclusions

An active real-time database system (ARTDBS) executes actions of rules subject to some timing constraints. In this paper, by modeling the semantics of rule execution in the form of a transaction, we provided a performance analysis of various transaction execution strategies in a distributed ARTDBS environment. Using a detailed ARTDBS simulation model, we conducted a series of experiments to investigate various performance issues involved in processing distributed transactions. The performance metric we used in evaluations is the fraction of transactions that violate their timing constraints.

In our ARTDBS model, transactions arrive at each site from an external source. Each data update operation of a transaction is considered as an event of a rule. Each event leads to a condition evaluation which is performed probabilistically. Satisfaction of a condition can lead to the triggering of one or more of the immediate, deferred, and detached actions of the rule. A separate probability value is used for each of the immediate, deferred, and detached coupling modes. On behalf of each triggered action, a subtransaction is created. Immediate and deferred subtransactions are executed as a part of the parent transaction which has triggered them, while detached subtransactions are executed independent of the triggering transaction. When an immediate subtransaction is started to execute, the execution of the parent transaction is suspended until the completion of the immediate subtransaction. All the deferred subtransactions triggered by a transaction are started to execute when their parent completes its operations. It is assumed that all the immediate and deferred subtransactions triggered by a transaction share the locks.

We considered two different transaction-processing architectures in our experiments. The first one, which is called distributed transaction (DT), distributes the execution of each transaction onto the sites that store the data pages required by the transaction. The other architecture, called mobile data (MD), moves the remote data pages requested by a transaction to the site of the transaction. Both architectures consider the timing constraints of transactions in scheduling accesses to data and hardware resources. The main drawback of DT is the large number of messages required to control the execution of a distributed transaction, while the primary overhead of MD is the large-sized messages carrying data pages between sites.

Main results of our experiments can be summarized as follows. Increasing the probability of triggering immediate/deferred subtransactions led to a steep increase in the number of missed deadlines. The negative impact of detached subtransactions on the real-time performance was not that crucial. Since detached subtransactions are executed independent of their triggering transactions, increasing the number of detached subtransactions effectively corresponds to increasing the transaction load in the system. The direct effect of increasing the number of immediate or deferred subtransactions, on the other hand, is an increase in the average length of triggering transactions. Extending the lifetime of transactions by triggering such subtransactions was observed to result in much more data conflicts (and therefore more priority aborts and blockings) compared to increasing the transaction load by triggering detached subtransactions.

The performance results obtained with MD were more satisfactory in general, compared to those obtained with DT, under various types of active workload. When a fast network was employed, MD was observed to be the clear performance winner. Data conflict aborts lead to much more message overhead with DT than with MD. The difference between the performances of DT and MD became more pronounced as the amount of immediate subtransactions was increased. However, the performances of DT and MD were comparable to each other under a high volume of deferred subtransactions. The deferred subtransactions triggered by a transaction have a chance to be executed in parallel with DT, if they access data pages stored at different sites.

Increasing the size of immediate and deferred subtransactions also caused a steep degradation in real-time performance due to rapidly increasing data and resource contention among larger-sized transactions.

In order to reduce the negative impact of immediate and deferred subtransactions on the real-time performance, we described a nested transaction execution model for the active workload. In that model, immediate and deferred subtransactions triggered by a transaction do not share the locks any more. The locks are managed on the basis of a nested locking protocol. Also, a triggering transaction needs not to be suspended during the execution of its immediate subtransactions. As a future work, we are planning to conduct some new experiments involving the proposed nested execution model in order to see how the performance impact of immediate and deferred subtransactions can change.

References

Abbott, R., Garcia-Molina, H.: Scheduling Real-Time Transactions: A Performance Evaluation. ACM Transactions on Database Systems 17 (1992) 513–560

Berndtsson, M., Hansson, J.: Issues in Active Real-Time Databases. International Workshop on Active and Real-Time Database Systems (1995) 142–157

Bestavros, A., Braoudakis, S.: Value-Cognizant Speculative Concurrency Control for Real-Time Databases. Information Systems 21 (1996) 75–102

Branding, H., Buchmann, A.: On Providing Soft and Hard Real-Time Capabilities in an Active DBMS. International Workshop on Active and Real-Time Database Systems (1995) 158–169

Carey, M.J., Livny, M.: Distributed Concurrency Control Performance: A Study of Algorithms, Distribution, and Replication. International Conference on Very Large Data Bases (1988) 13–25

Carey, M.J., Jauhari, R., Livny, M.: On Transaction Boundaries in Active Databases: A Performance Perspective. IEEE Transactions on Knowledge and Data Engineering 3 (1991) 320–336

Chakravarthy, S. et al.: HiPAC: A Research Project In Active, Time-Constrained Database Management. Technical Report XAIT-89-02, Xerox Advanced Information Technology, Cambridge (1989)

Chakravarthy, S., Krishnaprasad, V., Abwar, E., Kim, S.K.: Anatomy of a composite event detector. Technical Report UF-CIS-TR-93-039, CIS Department, University of Florida (1993)

Chen, M., Lin, K.J.: Dynamic Priority Ceilings: A Concurrency Control Protocol for Real-Time Systems. Real-Time Systems 2 (1990) 325–346

Datta A. et al.: Multiclass Transaction Scheduling and Overload Management in Firm Real-Time Database Systems. Information Systems 21 (1996) 29–54

Datta, A., Son, S.H.: A Study of Concurrency Control in Real-Time Active Database Systems. Technical Report, Department of MIS, University of Arizona (1996)

Dayal, U., Buchmann, A., McCarthy, D.: Rules are Objects too: A Knowledge Model for an Active, Object-Oriented Database System. Workshop on Object-Oriented Database Systems (1988)

Dayal U. et al.: The HiPAC Project: Combining Active Database and Timing Constraints. ACM SIGMOD Record 17 (1988) 51–70

Dayal U., Hsu, M., Ladin, R.: Organizing Long-Running Activities with Triggers and Transactions. ACM SIGMOD Conference (1990)

Diaz, O., Paton, N., Gray, P.: Rule Management in Object-Oriented Databases: A Uniform Approach. International Conference on Very Large Data Bases (1991) 317–326

Garcia-Molina, H., Abbott, R.K.: Reliable Distributed Database Management. Proceedings of the IEEE 75 (1987) 601–620

Gatziu, S., Dittrich, K.R.: Detecting Composite Events in Active Database Systems Using Petri Nets. International Workshop on Research Issues in Data Engineering (1994)

Gehani, N., Jagadish, H.V., Shumeli, O.: Composite Event Specification in Active Databases: Model and Implementation. International Conference on Very Large Data Bases (1992)

Harder, T., Rothermel, K.: Concurrency Control Issues in Nested Transactions. VLDB Journal 2 (1993) 39–74

Haritsa, J.R., Carey, M.J., Livny, M.: Data Access Scheduling in Firm Real-Time Database Systems. Real-Time Systems 4 (1992) 203–241

Hong, D., Johnson, T., Chakravarthy, S.: Real-Time Transaction Scheduling: A Cost Conscious Approach. ACM SIGMOD Conference (1993) 197–206

Huang, J., Stankovic, J.A., Ramamritham, K., Towsley, D., Purimetla, B.: Priority Inheritance in Soft Real-Time Databases. Real-Time Systems 4 (1992) 243–268

Hsu, M., Ladin, R., McCarthy, D.: An Execution Model for Active Database Management Systems. International Conference on Data and Knowledge Bases (1988) 171–179

Kohler, W.H., Jeng, B.H.: Performance Evaluation of Integrated Concurrency Control and Recovery Algorithms Using a Distributed Transaction Testbed. International Conference on Distributed Computing Systems (1986) 130–139

Lam, K.Y., Hung, S.L.: Concurrency Control for Time-Constrained Transactions in Distributed Database Systems. The Computer Journal 38 (1995) 704–716

Lee, J., Son, S.H.: Concurrency Control Algorithms for Real-Time Database Systems. Performance of Concurrency Control Algorithms in Centralized Database Systems, V. Kumar (ed.), Prentice-Hall, Englewood Cliffs, NJ (1995)

Purimetla, B., Sivasankaran, R.M., Stankovic, J.A., Ramamritham, K., Towsley, D.: Priority Assignment in Real-Time Active Databases. Conference on Parallel and Distributed Information Systems (1994)

Sivasankaran, R.M., Ramamritham, K., Stankovic, J.A., Towsley, D.: Data Placement, Logging and Recovery in Real-Time Active Databases. International Workshop on Active and Real-Time Database Systems (1995) 226–241

Sivasankaran, R.M., Stankovic, J.A., Towsley, D., Purimetla, B., Ramamritham, K.: Priority Assignment in Real-Time Active Databases. The VLDB Journal **5** (1996) 19–34

Ulusoy, Ö., Belford, G.G.: Real-Time Transaction Scheduling in Database Systems. Information Systems **18** (1993) 559–580

Ulusoy, Ö.: A Study of Two Transaction Processing Architectures for Distributed Real-Time Database Systems. Journal of Systems and Software **31** (1995) 97–108

APPENDIX
Deadline Calculation

In our system, the **Transaction Generator** chooses the slack time of a transaction randomly from an exponential distribution with a mean of *SlackRate* times the estimated minimum processing time of the transaction. Although the **Transaction Generator** uses the estimation of transaction processing times in assigning deadlines, we assume that the system itself lacks the knowledge of processing time information.

The deadline D_T of a transaction T is determined by the following formula:

$$D_T = A_T + PT_T + S_T$$

where

$$S_T = expon(SlackRate * PT_T)$$

A_T, PT_T, and S_T denote the arrival time, estimated minimum processing time, and slack time of transaction T, respectively.

The estimated minimum processing time formula actually determines the processing time of a transaction under an ideal execution environment in which the system is unloaded (i.e., no data and resource conflicts occur among transactions), and the transaction does not require any data page that is remotely placed. To satisfy the deadline, the delay that will be experienced by the transaction due to conflicts and remote accesses should not exceed the slack time included in the deadline formula.

$$PT_T = PT_{T-Parent} + PT_{T-Children}$$

where $PT_{T-Parent}$ denotes the processing time spent due to the operations of T itself, and $PT_{T-Children}$ denotes the processing time due to the operations of immediate and deferred subtransactions triggered by T.

$$PT_{T-Parent} = CPU\_delay_{T-Parent} + IO\_delay_{T-Parent}$$

$$CPU\_delay_{T-Parent} = \frac{10^{-3}}{CPURate} * (StartTransInst + (1 + WriteProb)$$

$$*TransSize * ProcessPageInst + EndTransInst)$$

$$IO\_delay_{T-Parent} = [(1 - \frac{MemSize}{DBSize})*TransSize*(\frac{DiskOverheadInst}{CPURate}*10^{-3} + DiskAccessTime)]$$

$$+[WriteProb * TransSize * (\frac{DiskOverheadInst}{CPURate} * 10^{-3} + DiskAccessTime)]$$

The expression contained in the second pair of square brackets corresponds to the delay experienced while writing updated pages back into the disk. The unit of both $CPU\_delay_{T-Parent}$ and $IO\_delay_{T-Parent}$ is milliseconds.

The computation of $PT_{T-Children}$ involves the probabilities of triggering immediate and deferred subtransactions.

$$PT_{T-Children} = TransSize * WriteProb * (ImmediateProb + DeferredProb)$$

$$*(CPU\_delay_{T-Children} + IO\_delay_{T-Children})$$

The computations of $CPU\_delay_{T-Children}$ and $IO\_delay_{T-Children}$ are similar to those of $CPU\_delay_{T-Parent}$ and $IO\_delay_{T-Parent}$, respectively, except that $TransSize$ is replaced by $SubTransSize$ in both formulas.

In determining the deadline of a transaction, detached subtransactions that could be triggered by the transaction are not considered since such subtransactions are treated as independent transactions.

Scheduling of Triggered Transactions in Distributed Real-Time Active Databases

Kam-yiu Lam[1], Gary C.K. Law[2] and Victor C.S. Lee[3]

Department of Computer Science
City University of Hong Kong
83 Tat Chee Avenue, Kowloon
HONG KONG
email: cskylam@cityu.edu.hk
fax: 852-2788-8614
tel: 852-2788-9807

Abstract. A Distributed Real-time Active Database System reacts to the critical events occurred in the external environment by triggering of transactions. In this paper, the priority and deadline assignment to triggered transactions under two coupling modes, the deferred and immediate, in a DRTADBS is discussed. A new approach, the data state dependent (DSD) is proposed to assign criticality to the triggered transactions, respectively. In the DSD approach, the criticality of a triggered transaction is defined according to the state of the temporal data object which is responsible for its triggering. The objective of the DSD approach is to increase the number of commit achieved by the triggered transactions especially the more critical ones. The performance of these two approaches under the two coupling modes has been investigated. The results show that the DSD approach is more effective under the immediate coupling mode than under the deferred coupling mode due to the late creation of the triggered transactions under the deferred coupling mode.

1 Introduction

In recent years, there is a strong move toward integrating Real-time Database Systems [15] [25] with Active Database Systems [21] with an attempt to provide a better solution to their potential applications [5] [10], e.g., the applications which have to react to the changes in the external environment in real-time manner. The new area is called Real-time Active Database System (RTADBS) [12]. If the database is distributed in different sites, the system is called Distributed Real-time Active Database System (DRTADBS) [3] [7]. The scheduling of transactions in a DRTADBS is complicated by the distributed nature of the transactions, the additional overhead for the management of distributed data objects and the unpredictability of the system workload due to triggering of transactions. Some common applications of DRTADBS are international program stock trading systems and battlefield management systems.

In a DRTADBS, transactions that are dynamically created by other transactions in react to the changes (or the occurrences of critical events) in the external environment are called triggered transactions. For example in a program stock trading system, applications create transactions to access the database and check for trading opportunities. Once the conditions are satisfied, e.g., the price of a particular stock is lower than a certain value, an action will be triggered (in form of transaction) for buying or selling of the stocks.

The transactions, which have triggered other transactions, are called triggering transactions. The relationship between the triggering and the triggered transactions (e.g., the creation time of the triggered transaction and the commit dependency between them) is defined by the coupling mode. Different coupling modes have been proposed to cater for the requirements of different applications [8] [22]. Some examples are deferred, immediate and detached coupling modes. In the deferred and immediate coupling modes, the triggered transactions are defined to be dependent on the triggering transactions. The triggered transaction is a part of the triggering transaction (its sub-transaction). If a triggering transaction is aborted, its triggered transaction will be aborted as well. If the triggered transaction misses the deadline of the triggering transaction, it will also be aborted.

Comparing with the transactions, which have not triggered transaction (we call them non- triggering transactions), the triggered transactions are more critical. Failing to commit the triggered transactions is highly undesirable as they represent the reactions to the critical events occurred in the external environment. If the events are beneficial (e.g., in the program stock trading systems), it represents a serious loss in opportunities. If the events are harmful, it represents that some unattended risk is coming (e.g., in the missile tracking systems). The consequence can be catastrophic. Thus, how to maximize the number commit of the triggered transactions, especially the more important ones, for a given sequence of events occurred in the external environment is an important issue in the design of a DRTADBS.

Due to the high complexity of a DRTADBS and the unpredictability introduced from triggering of transactions, a number of factors can cause the abort of the triggered transactions. Although some recent work has been done on scheduling transactions which dynamically trigger other transactions, most of them are concentrated on meeting the deadlines of the triggering transactions which lengths are suddenly increased as the result of the triggering [9] [16] [19]. They have ignored the impact of the temporal data objects, especially the temporal data objects which are responsible for the triggering (we call them triggering data objects), on the timing constraints and criticality of the transactions. The timing constraints on the transactions due to temporal data objects has been discussed in [18] [23] [24]. In [24], a forced wait method is suggested to reduce the number of transaction aborts due to the access of invalid temporal data objects. However, the impact of triggering data object on the criticality of the transactions has not been addressed.

In this paper, we discuss how to assign priorities and deadlines to triggered transactions with the objective to maximize the number of commit of triggered transactions especially the more important ones. New approaches, called data state dependent (DSD) and transaction-data deadline (TDD) are suggested. The remaining parts of the paper are organized as follows. Section 2 discusses the mechanisms to trigger transactions under the deferred and the immediate coupling modes. Section 3 discusses the effect of the scheduling of triggering transactions on the scheduling of the triggered transactions. Section 4 introduces our approaches to deadline and priority assignments. Section 5 is the performance study of our approaches under different workload and environment. The Conclusions of the paper is in Section 6.

2 Triggering of Transactions in DRTADBS

A DRTADBS has to monitor the status of the external environment. In the other words, the system has to keep an updated view of the external environment [2]. So, some of the data objects in the database, called temporal data objects, are used to record the status of the associated objects in the external environment. Each temporal data object is associated with a temporal constraint to define its validity. The data object is invalid if the value recorded in the temporal data object may be significantly deviated from the actual status of the associated object in the external environment. The consistency between the value recorded in the temporal data objects and the actual status of the associated objects in the external environment is called absolute consistency. The period that the valued recorded in temporal data object is validated is called absolute validity interval (avi) [11] [17].

Since events are occurring in the external environment, the status of the objects is also changing dynamically. Absolute consistency has to be maintained by timely installation of the update transactions which capture the up-to-date status of the objects in the external environment. Each update transaction is responsible to update one temporal data object. If an update transaction cannot be installed before the temporal data object becomes invalid, the absolute consistency will be violated. When these data objects are accessed by transactions, the transactions have to be restarted or even aborted .

Transactions are created by applications to access the database. They may read some temporal data objects to check the conditions which are predicates on the state of the database. In addition to observe the absolute consistency, they also have to observe relative consistency which is defined on the relative ages of the temporal data objects accessed by a transaction [11]. It is relative inconsistent if the temporal data objects accessed by a transactions are representing the views at a very different time span. In this case, the transaction has to be restarted or aborted.

In accessing a temporal data object, the conditions for triggering of transaction will be checked. If any one of the defined conditions is satisfied, a triggered transaction will be created according to the specified coupling mode. In the following, we will consider two coupling modes, the deferred and the immediate in which the dependency between the triggering and triggered transactions is greater as the triggered transactions are sub-transactions of the triggering transactions. The scheduling problem is more difficult as more constraints have to be satisfied before a triggered transaction is allowed to commit.

Under the deferred coupling mode, the creation and the execution of a triggered transaction is started only after the completion of the triggering transaction even though the conditions are satisfied in the course of execution of the triggering transaction as shown in Figure 1.

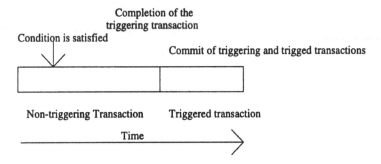

Fig. 1. Triggering of Transaction under the Deferred Coupling Mode

In a DRTADBS, the time required to process an operation is unpredictable. It is affected by the location of the required data object and the distribution of workload in the system. Thus, the waiting time of a triggered transaction may be very long under the deferred coupling mode.

Under the immediate coupling mode, once the conditions are satisfied, the triggered transaction will be created and executed "immediately" (Figure 2). At the same time, the execution of the triggering transaction will be suspended until the completion of the triggered transaction. Thus, the processing order of the remaining part of the triggering transaction and the triggered transaction is just the opposite of that under the deferred coupling mode.

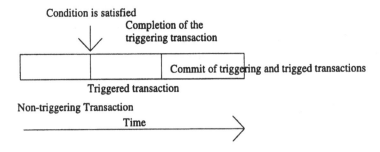

Fig. 2. Triggering of Transaction under the Immediate Coupling Mode

Since the triggered transaction is dependent on the triggering transaction, the triggered transaction cannot commit even though it is completed. It has to wait until the commit of the triggering transaction. Similar to the situation under the deferred coupling mode, the delay is unpredictable and is dependent on the scheduling of the triggering transaction.

3   Scheduling of the Triggering Transactions

The precedence and dependency relationships between the triggering and the triggered transactions as defined by the coupling modes (e.g., the deferred and the immediate coupling modes) make the scheduling of the triggered transactions highly affected by the scheduling of the triggering transactions. If the triggering transaction is completed earlier, it is more possible for the triggered transaction to be completed because much slack time is left. Otherwise, the triggered transaction may not be able to be completed due to short slack time. This in turn depends on the scheduling of the triggering transaction.

Triggering of transaction is an unpredictable event. None can forecast when the conditions will be satisfied. Therefore, none can predict which transaction will trigger a transaction and when it will trigger the transaction until at the time of triggering. It is because triggering of transaction is resulted from the state of the database which is highly dynamic. Thus, the system cannot anticipate the additional resource requirements of a triggered transaction by scheduling the triggering transaction first (at that time, the system still recognizes it as a non-triggering transaction). If the system schedules the triggering transactions in the same way as the non-triggering transactions, the probability to commit the triggered transactions will be affected as the transaction length of a non-triggering transaction is usually shorter compared with the sum of the length of the triggering and triggered transactions. Consequently, the slack time available for the triggered transaction (and the triggering transaction under the immediate coupling mode) is also shorter. This is especially true when the triggering is occurred at the later stage of the transaction. Suppose there are two transactions T_1 and T_2. They have the same criticality but the priority of T_1 is higher than T_2 due to a closer deadline. The system schedules T_1 before T_2. When T_2 triggers a transaction, $T_{2,1}$, the slack for $T_{2,1}$ to complete may be very short as the system does not know in advance that T_2 will trigger a transaction and has not pre-allocated extra slack time for the execution of $T_{2,1}$. As a result, $T_{2,1}$ is likely to be aborted due to deadline missing.

Triggered transactions increase the system workload and affect the schedulability of the system. If a large number of triggered transactions are created in a short period of time, the system will be suffered from a transient overloading. The most affected ones are the triggered transactions as their scheduling is dependent on the scheduling of the triggering transactions.

Although some sub-transaction priority assignment policies have been suggested to solve the scheduling problem due to triggering of transactions [16] [19], these policies have two major problems. Firstly, deadlock is possible as they dynamically adjusted the priority of the transactions based on their remaining slack times. Resolving deadlock in a distributed environment is highly expensive and difficult. They should be avoided by adopting some deadlock free approaches. Secondly, they have assumed that the criticality of different transactions (different kinds of triggered and triggering transactions) are the same. This is not true in most cases (a detail explanation is given in Section 4.2.)

4 Scheduling of Triggered Transactions

Although to commit a triggered transaction is highly important to the usefulness of a DRTADBS, not much work has been addressed on how to assign deadlines and priorities to the triggered transactions. Mostly, they are considered as a part of the triggering transactions. However, due to the access of temporal data objects, the deadline and criticality of a triggered transaction may be different from that of its triggering transaction. In this Section, we introduce two approaches to assign deadlines and priorities to the triggered transactions according to the current status of the temporal data objects.

4.1 Assigning Deadlines to Triggered Transactions

Due to the access of temporal data objects, the timing constraints on the triggered transactions may become tighter as they have to commit before any of their accessed temporal data objects becomes invalid. If a triggered transaction is dependent on the triggering transaction (as under the deferred and immediate coupling modes), its completion time (deadline) is constrained by :

1. the deadline of the triggering transaction; and
2. the temporal constraints of the accessed temporal data objects (to observe the absolute consistency).

The second constraints are called the data deadlines. Missing the deadline of the triggering transaction will abort the triggered transaction as it is defined to be dependent on the triggering transaction. Missing the data deadlines also causes the abort of the triggered transaction as the values in the temporal data objects are no longer valid. Thus, the deadline of a triggered transaction can be defined as:

$$\text{Deadline}_{tt} = \min(\text{Deadline}_t, \text{Temporal}_D)$$

where
> Deadline_t is the deadline of the triggering transaction and
> Temporal_D is the earliest data deadline among the temporal data objects accessed by the transaction.

We call this approach for assigning the deadline to a triggered transaction as transaction-data deadline (TDD) approach. Whenever a transaction accesses a temporal data object, its deadline will compare with the data deadline of the temporal data object. If the data deadline is closer, its deadline will be replaced by the data deadline. With the TDD approach, any abort due to missing the data deadlines can be identified earlier so that the amount of resources wasted on those transactions which would be aborted can be minimized. This can also improve the schedulability of the whole system especially when the system workload is heavy.

4.2 Assigning Priority to Triggered Transactions

Not only the timing constraint of the triggered transaction is different from the triggering transaction, their criticality may not be the same. The creation of a triggered transaction implies that some specific attention has to be paid to the current system status because some interesting or important event has occurred, e.g., missile is coming. Therefore, the importance of the triggered transactions are usually much higher than the non-triggering transactions. Thus, higher criticality should be assigned to the triggered transactions.

Example 1: Consider a navigation system of robot in which detection transactions are created periodically to check whether there are any obstacle in front of the robot. Once it has found that there is an obstacle in its way, a reaction transaction will be triggered to stop the robot or to change its moving direction. The criticality of the detection transactions should be lower than the criticality of the reaction transactions as the existence of any reaction transactions implies that a risk is coming. On the other hand, missing the deadlines of the detection transactions is less serious as the detection transactions will find nothing in front of the robot in most of the cases. To reflect the higher importance, higher criticality, and thus higher priorities, should be assigned to the triggered transactions comparing with the non- triggering transactions.

No only the criticality of the triggered transactions may be higher than the non-triggering transactions, the criticality amongst the triggered transactions may be different. It is because the generation of triggered transactions is the result of satisfaction of some triggering conditions which importance may be different. The triggered transaction in connection with an important condition should be assigned to a higher criticality.

Example 2: In a program stock trading system, the condition to buy the stock X and Y is when their prices are lower than $10. Assuming that the new price of stock X is $9, thus a buy transaction, B1, is triggered. At the same time, the price of stock Y is $2. Thus, another buy transaction B2 is triggered to buy stock Y. To the system users, B2 is more critical than B1 as completing it can yield more profit. In this scenario, B2 should be given a higher criticality.

This example shows that the criticality of a triggered transaction is affected by the current status of the triggering data object. Thus, in assigning criticality to a triggered transaction, both the criticality of the triggering transaction and the criticality resulted from the triggering data object have to be considered. We call this approach as the data state dependent (DSD) approach such as :

$$\text{Criticality}_{tt} = \alpha \ \text{Criticality}_t + \beta \times \text{DataState}_D$$

where a and b are the weighting factors. Criticality_t is the original criticality of the triggering transaction and DataState_D is a function which defines the criticality for the triggering data object. It is based on the current state of the triggering data object, D, and the condition for triggering. Referring to the above example on the program stock trading system, the DataState_D can be defined as the difference between the price of the stock set in the condition for triggering and the current price of the stock. A higher criticality will be assigned to the one which is triggered from a greater difference in stock prices.

The priority of a triggered transaction is a function of its deadline and criticality. In order to support the scheduling of triggered transactions with different criticality, the system is defined to have multiple priority levels. By the use of DataState_D, a triggered transaction can be assigned to different priority levels based on its criticality. It is expected that by promoting the triggered transactions which have higher criticality to a higher priority level, they will have a higher probability to commit even with a shorter slack time.

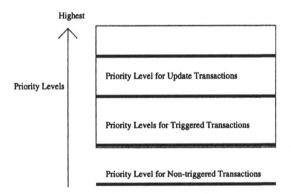

Fig. 3. Assigning Priorities to Triggered Transactions

How to raise up the criticality (and priority) of a triggered transaction is dependent on the semantic of the transaction and the condition for triggering. However, simply promoting the triggered transactions to a higher priority level may not be able to improve their performance effectively. It is affected by a number of factors such as the length of the triggered transactions, the data deadlines of the temporal data objects and the workload of the update transactions. The avi of the temporal data objects and the length of the triggered transactions determine the tightness of the timing constraint of a triggered transaction.

The workload of the update transactions affects the scheduling of the triggered transactions. In Figure 3, there exists multiple priority levels in the system. The non-triggering transactions are assigned to the lowest level. Since the update transactions are important to maintain the absolute consistency of the temporal data objects, they are assigned to the priorities higher than the non-triggering transactions. The probability to commit a triggered transaction is then dependent on where is the priority of a triggered transaction relative to the update transactions. If its priority is lower than the update transactions, they still have a high chance to miss their deadlines if the workload of update transactions is heavy.

4.3 Effect of Coupling Modes on Triggering

The effect of the TDD and the DSD approaches on the performance of the triggered transactions can be very different under different coupling modes. Under the deferred coupling mode, the creation of the triggered transactions are delayed until the completion of the triggering transactions. So, they are more affected by the scheduling of the triggering transactions. The effectiveness of promoting the triggered transactions to a higher priority level may be small if the remaining time for the execution of the triggered transactions is short. In case the remaining time is less than the required execution time of the triggered transaction, it will be useless to schedule the triggered transactions even though they are promoted to the highest priority level.

Under the immediate coupling mode, priority promotion can be much more effective especially if the triggering occurs at the early stage of a transaction. Since the triggering transactions are still in the middle of execution, there remains much slack time for the execution of the triggered transactions as compared with the deferred coupling mode. However, the commit of a triggered transaction requires the completion of its triggering transaction. It has to wait for the triggering transaction even though it has been completed. If the priority of the triggering transaction remains low, it is still possible for the triggered transaction to miss its deadline because of waiting for the completion of the triggering transaction.

Another more serious problem under the immediate coupling mode is that deadlock is possible if it is combined with some blocking based real-time concurrency control protocols such as High Priority Two Phase Locking (H2PL) [1]. Suppose there are two transactions, T_t and T_l with priorities, P_t and P_l, respectively. After T_t accesses a temporal data object such that the conditions to trigger a transaction T_{tt} (with priority P_{tt}) are satisfied. The priorities order of these three transactions is $P_{tt} > P_l > P_t$. The triggered transaction T_{tt} may block T_l if T_l requests a lock after T_{tt}. After the completion of T_{tt}, T_t resumes its execution. Since P_t is lower than P_l. It is possible that T_t is blocked by T_l if it requests a lock holding by T_l. This is a deadlock even the original concurrency control protocol is deadlock free. In order to avoid the deadlock and to reduce the probability of missing deadlines of triggered transactions while they are waiting for the completion of their triggering transactions, the priorities of the resumed triggering transactions are set to be the priorities of the triggered transactions after the completion of triggered transactions.

5 Performance Evaluation

5.1 Simulation Model

A simulation model has been implemented to investigate the performance of the DSD and TDD approaches under different system environment and coupling modes. Figure 4 depicts the DRTADBS model consisting of a number of sites, fully-connected in a point-to-point network. Each communication link is modeled as a delay center, i.e., constant message delay. Each site is a local database system consisting of two transaction generators, a scheduler, a CPU, a ready queue, a local database, a communication interface, and a block queue.

Database Site

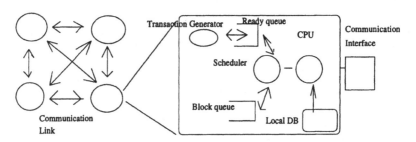

Fig. 4. The DRTADBS Model

The local database consists of two types of data objects: temporal and static data objects. Static data objects are for storing static information which does not change frequently with time such as the stock number of a particular stock in a stock market. Temporal data objects store dynamic information reflecting the current status of the associated objects in the external environment. For each temporal data object, an absolute validity interval, avi is defined for checking its validity. The temporal data objects are also constrained by relative validity intervals (rvi) for checking the relative consistency. Since main memory databases can better support real-time applications, it is assumed that the database is residing in the main memory.

One of the transaction generator generates update transactions periodically. They are single operation transactions. A time stamp of the current time is assigned to each update transaction to indicate under which snapshot the value is taken. When an update transaction is installed, the time-stamp will be recorded into the time-stamp of the temporal data object. A temporal data object is absolute consistent if the sum of its time-stamp and avi is greater than the current time. If the time-stamp of the data objects accessed by a transaction is greater than the rvi, then the transaction has violated the relative consistency. A transaction has to be restarted if it is absolute or relative inconsistent. Basically, the update transactions do not have deadlines. However, it is important to install the update as soon as possible in order to maintain the validity of the temporal data objects. Thus, they are assigned to the higher priority level.

Another transaction generator creates user transactions following a Poisson distribution. Each user transaction is defined with a deadline and a priority based on its deadline and criticality. It is assumed that all user transactions are of the same criticality upon their generation. Thus, a user transaction with a closer deadline will be assigned to a higher priority.

A user transaction is modeled as a sequence of database operations. The processing of the operations requires CPU computations and the access of data objects (some of them may be temporal data objects).To simply the model, it is assumed that each operation will access one data object. If the required data object of an operation is resided in a remote site (different from the site where the transaction is generated), it will be transmitted to the remote site through the communication networks, and be processed there.

When a user transaction accesses a temporal data object, a transaction will be triggered if certain conditions are satisfied. The probability to trigger a transaction is defined by Trigger_Probability. The triggered transaction is also modeled as a sequence of operations. Dependent on the status of the temporal data objects, the criticality and deadlines of the triggering and the triggered transactions will be reassigned if the DSD and the TDD approaches are used. To simplify the analysis and without loss of generality, we define two levels of criticality for the triggered transactions (high and low). When a triggered transaction is created, the probability to have a high criticality is High_Priority. Otherwise, it has a low criticality. Thus, we can classify the committed transactions into three classes :

1. Class H : the triggered transactions with high criticality;
2. Class L : the triggered transactions with low criticality (although it is low, it is still higher than the non-triggering transactions); and
3. Class N : the user transactions which have not triggered any transaction

The transactions (the update, user, triggering and triggered transactions) queue in the ready queue for the CPU according to their priorities. The scheduling of the CPU is performed by the scheduler. It selects the transaction at the head of the ready queue (the one with the highest priority) to use the CPU when it is free.

In order to maintain the data consistency (internal consistency), a concurrency control protocol [4] is adopted to manage the access of the data objects by transactions. It is assumed that the high priority two phase locking (H2PL) [1] is used in which each data object is associated with a lock. Before accessing a data object, a transaction has to seize the lock associated with the data object. If the lock is already seized by a higher priority transaction, the lock requesting transaction has to be blocked in the block queue until the lock holding transaction releases the locks. Otherwise, the lock holding transaction will be forced to release the lock and be restarted. Then, the lock requesting transaction can seize the lock and continue its execution.

When all operations of a user transaction has been completed, before it enters the commitment stage, the relative consistency of all its accessed temporal data objects will be checked. It will be allowed to enter the commitment stage only if all the relative consistent constraints have been satisfied. Otherwise, it has to be restarted. In the commitment stage, it performs a commit protocol to ensure the transaction atomicity. It is assumed that the two phase commit is used [4]. Permanent updates of the data objects will be performed if the final decision is commit. If the decision is abort, all the effect to be applied to the database by the transaction will be cleared. Finally, the transaction releases all its seized locks upon its commit or at the time of abort.

It is assumed that all transactions, except the update transactions, are firm real-time [1] [25]. Before a transaction is granted to use the CPU, its deadline will be checked. If it has missed its deadline, it will be aborted immediately.

5.2 Model Parameters and Performance Measures

The simulator is built using OPNET [14], a proprietary graphical simulation package. The structure of the simulation model follows the system model described in the last Sub-section with the following characteristics. The end-to-end deadline of a transaction (T) is generated according to the following formula :

$$Deadline = ar(T) + pex(T) \times (1 + SF) + T_{comm} \times N_{transit}$$

where

SF : the slack factor which is a random variable uniformly chosen from a range;

ar(T) : the arrival time of transaction T;

$N_{transit}$: the number of transit across the networks required in order to access the data objects in a transaction;

T_{comm} : the communication delay;

pex(T) : the predicted execution time of T. It is defined as :

$$pex(T) = (T_{lock} + T_{process} + T_{update}) \times N_{oper}$$

where

N_{oper} : the number of operations in a transaction;

T_{lock} : the CPU time required to set a lock;

$T_{process}$: the CPU time required to process an operation; and

T_{update} : the CPU time to update a data object.

In most of the previous studies on real-time database systems, the missing rate is used as the primary performance measure [1] [20]. They indicate the probability of missing deadline of the transactions. However, they are not suitable for DRTADBS in which it is not possible to determine the number of triggered transactions as their creations are system dependent. In a DRTADBS, the most important performance objective is how well the system can respond to the changes in the external environment. This can be measured in terms of the number of commit of triggered transactions for a given set of events occurred in the external environment. To the system users, it is more preferable to have a larger number of commit of triggered transaction in a given period of time even though the missing rate is higher. Thus, in our experiments, the primary performance measure is the commit rate (CR) which is the number of committed transactions per unit time.

In the simulation model, a small database (200 data objects per site) is used to create a high data contention environment. The small database also allows us to study the effect of hot-spots, in which a small part of the database is accessed frequently by most of the transactions. Table 1 summarizes the model parameters and their baseline values. In the baseline setting, the amount of workload for the update transactions is 15%. In the model, streams of update transactions are defined to maintain the validity of the temporal data objects. Their periods are defined based on the avi of the temporal data objects. To simplify the model, it is assumed that all the temporal data objects have the same avi and rvi. The period of an update stream, for each temporal data object, is defined to be twice of the avi in the baseline setting.

System
- CPU Scheduling : High Priority First
- Concurrency Control : High Priority Two Phase Locking (HP2PL)
- Time to Lock a Data Object (T_{lock}) : 2 msec
- Time to Process an Operation $(T_{process})$: 34 msec
- Time to Update a Data Object (T_{update}) : 6 msec
- Communication Delay (T_{comm}) : 100 msec

Transaction
- Mean User Transaction Arrival Rate :
  - 0.2 - 1.4 transactions per sec (uniform distribution)
- Transaction size (N_{oper}) :
  - 3 - 20 operations (uniform distribution)
- Triggered Length Ratio (TL) : 0.2 of the triggering transaction
- Slack Factor (SF) : 2.5 - 13.75 (uniform distribution)

Update
- Period of each update stream (P_{update}) : 2 seconds
- Absolute Validity Interval (avi) : 4 seconds
- Relative Validity Interval (rvi) : 4 seconds

Database
- Number of database sites : 4
- Number of data objects / site : 200 data objects
- Fraction of temporal data objects $(TempFac)$: 0.25
- Probability of Being a Triggering Data Object $(TriggerProbability)$: 0.6
- Probability of Being a Triggering Data Object
  - with High Priority $(HighProbability)$: 0.5

5.3 Results Analysis and Discussions

Each simulation reports the results for a simulation length of 2400sec. About 10,000 user transactions are generated in the system with four sites when the arrival rate is 1 user trans/sec. In the experiments, the impact of different factors on the performance of the system with the application of the DSD and the TDD approaches have been studied. It is compared with the system using the deadline and criticality of the triggering transaction for the scheduling of the triggered transaction. We call this approach as the Single Priority Level (SPL).

Figure 5 depicts the commit rate (CR) of the three classes of transactions with and without the DSD under the deferred coupling mode when the arrival rate of the user transactions is increased from 0.2 to 2.0 transactions per second. Although the CR of all the three classes of transactions increase with the arrival rate, the rates of increase are different. The CRs of Class H and Class L become flat starting from medium workload whereas the CR of Class N transactions, which do not triggered any transaction, continue to increase steadily. It is because under a higher workload (due to increased arrival rate), the triggered transactions (Class H and Class L transactions) have higher probability to abort due to deadline missing as the remaining slack time for their execution decreases with an increase in system workload. The CRs of Class L and Class H are almost the same in the SPL case. Since the priorities of the triggered transactions in these two classes inherit the same priorities as their triggering transactions, they should attain a similar performance.

Surprisingly, as shown in Figure 5, the DSD approach helps little to improve the performance of the Class H and Class L transactions. Compared with the CRs in the SPL case, the differences are insignificant. Although the priorities of Class H transactions are promoted, their probability to commit is similar to the SPL case where there is no priority promotion. It is because, under the deferred coupling mode, the creation of the triggered transactions is delayed until the completion of the triggering transactions. At the start time of the triggered transaction, the remaining slack time may be very short. To promote the priorities of the triggered transactions may be too late to save them from missing their deadlines.

Under the immediate coupling mode, the improvement is much significant when the DSD approach is applied as shown in Figure 6. It is because the creation of the triggered transaction is earlier. To promote the priorities of the triggered transactions and the triggering transactions can make them to have higher probability to complete before their deadlines. However, the CRs of the Class L and Class N transactions are reduced as their priorities are lower than the priorities of the Class H transactions. They have to wait longer for the CPU and have higher chances to be restarted due to lock conflict with Class H transactions. The drop is more significant in the Class N transactions as their priorities are the lowest.

As can be seen in Figure 7, the performance of Class H and Class L transactions decreases as the length of the triggered transactions increases. If the length is increased, the triggered transactions have a higher probability to miss their deadlines as the result of tightened time constraints. The amount of slack time is determined at the creation of their triggering transactions. At that moment, there is no prior knowledge of the length of the triggered transactions or even whether there is any triggering will occur. As a result, the longer is the length of the triggered transactions, it is more likely for them to miss their deadlines and the CRs decrease subsequently. Class N transactions are less affected by the increased length of the triggered transactions because they do not triggered any transaction. Consistent with the results in Figure 6 and Figure 7, the improvement with the application of DSD is only significant under the immediate coupling mode as shown in Figure 8. The performance of the Class H and Class L transactions is very similar under the deferred mode even with the application of the DSD approach due to the late start time of the triggered transactions.

Figures 9 and 10 show the CRs with different avi values. The performance of all classes improves as the avi increases. It is reasonable because a wider avi means that the validity of the temporal data objects can last for a longer time. In the other words, it is less likely for a transaction to access an invalid temporal data object or that the temporal data object accessed by a transaction becomes invalid at the time of commit. As a result, number of restarts and number of aborts due to temporal inconsistency are reduced. Consequently, the CR increases. Since the Class N transactions may or may not access temporal data objects and the data deadlines are not a big problem to them. Thus, the impact of this factor is less significant. The large improvement of the Class H transactions under the immediate coupling mode shows that the avi is a bound to their performance. To loosen the avi helps those triggered transactions which meet the deadlines to commit without violating the temporal consistency.

Figures 11 to 14 give the CRs with different update transaction rates. There are two sides to interpret this factor. If the update rate is low, given a fixed avi value, the temporal consistency of the data objects may not be able to be maintained. This will lead to an increase in the number of restarts and aborts. If the update rate is high, the temporal consistency can be maintained but it may be very expensive. Part of the resources in the system will be drawn by them and lead to the degradation of the performance of the other user transactions as the priority of the update transactions is set to be high. So, for some applications, it may be desirable to have a low update rate in spite of the possibility of temporal inconsistency.

Figures 11 and 12 give the performance when the priority of update transactions is set to be the highest. When the update rate is low (0.25 update per second), temporal inconsistency must exist even though all updates can be installed once they are generated. So, the CRs are low. When the update rate is increased to 0.5 update per second, the temporal consistency can be maintained if all updates can be installed once they are generated. The CRs increased to larger values. However, further increase of the update rate helps little to improve the performance. It is reasonable because the highest priority of the update transactions allow them to install the updates into the database efficiently. So, when the update rate is further increased, deterrent effect due to the large volume of workload generated by the update transactions can be observed. The CRs of all classes drop slightly.

Figures 13 and 14 gives the performance when the priority of the update transactions is set to be higher than the priority of the non-triggering transactions but lower than the priority of the triggered transactions. In general, the performance and the analysis are very similar to Figures 11 and 12. But there are two points to note. When the update rate is 0.75 update per second, the CRs of Class L and Class H are increased comparing with the CRs when the update rate is 0.5 update per second. Since the priorities of the update transactions are lower than the priorities of the triggered transactions, the increase of update rate can now help to improve the degree of temporal consistency in the database. Compared with the case when the priority of the update transactions is the highest, the extent of increase is much significant. It is because the triggered transactions are now scheduled before the updates. They have a higher probability to meet their timing constraints. Consistent with the results in previous figures, the improvement with DSD is much more significant under the immediate coupling mode.

Figure 15 depicts the CRs of the three classes of transactions when both the DSD and the TDD approaches are applied under the deferred coupling mode. The CRs of all the three classes of transactions are improved due to early abort of missed deadline transactions with the use of the TDD approach. Similar to the previous results, the performance of Class H and Class L transactions is similar even though their priorities are different. On the contrary, further improvement can be obtained under the immediate coupling mode when both the DSD and the TDD approaches are applied as shown in Figure 16. All classes are benefit from early abort of missed deadline transactions. In this case, the performance of the Class L transactions is improved compared with the case when only the DSD is applied as shown in Figure 6.

6 Conclusions

Two fundamental requirements of a Distributed Real-time Active Database System is to process the time-constrained transactions so that they can be committed before their deadlines and to react to the occurrences of critical events in the external environment by the creation of triggered transactions to be the event handlers. However, in most of the previous studies, the importance of the triggered transactions has been ignored. Mostly, they are considered as a part of the triggering transactions. The same deadline and criticality will be inherited from the triggering transactions for the scheduling of the triggered transactions. However, if we examine the implication of triggering in real life applications, triggered transactions represent very important actions to the critical events. Committing them is highly important and desirable.

Central to the importance of a triggered transaction is the status of the temporal data object which is responsible for the triggering. Thus, in this paper, we have suggested a new approach, the DSD to assign priorities to the triggered transactions based on the status of the temporal data objects which are responsible for the triggering. Different status implies different importance and the triggered transactions created for a more important condition is given a higher criticality and thus a higher priority.

In the DSD approach, the triggered transactions are assigned with higher priorities. However, it may not be able to effectively increase their probability of commitment since it is highly affected by the coupling mode used for the triggering. Under the deferred coupling mode, the scheduling is affected by the scheduling of the triggering transaction to a great extend, even with the use of the DSD, the performance of the triggered transactions seems to be about the same. The DSD approach is much more effective under the immediate coupling mode as the triggered transactions are created earlier. Thus, one way to increase the performance of the triggered transactions under the deferred coupling mode is to applied the DSD approach at the time on the triggering transactions even though the generation of the triggered transaction is at their completion. In this way, the slack time for the triggered transaction can be much increased. The use of the TDD approach can improve the system performance under both coupling modes. However, the degree of improvement is affected by the avi of the temporal data objects, the relative priorities and workload of the update transactions and the length of the triggered transactions.

References

1. R. Abbott, and H. Garcia-Molina, "Scheduling Real-time Transactions: A Performance Evaluation", ACM Transactions on Database Systems, Volume 17, Number 3, pp. 513-560, 1992.
2. B. Adelberg, H. Garcia-Molina and B. Kao, "Applying Update Stream in a Soft Real-time Database System", in Proceedings of the 1995 ACM SIGMOD Conference, California, pp. 245-256, 1995.
3. S. F. Andler, J. Hansson, J.Eriksson, J. Mellin, M. Berndtsson, B. Eftring, "DeeDS Towards a Distributed and Active Real-Time Database System", SIGMOD Record, volume. 25, number 1, pp.38-40, 1996.
4. P.A. Bernstein, V. Hadzilacos and N. Goodman, Concurrency Control and Recovery in Database Systems, Addison-Wesley, Reading, Mass, 1987.
5. M. Berndtsson, J. Hansson, "Workshop Report : The First International Workshop on Active and Real- Time Database Systems", SIGMOD Record, volume 25, number 1, pp. 64-66, March 1996.
6. H. Branding, Alejandro P. Buchmann, "On Providing Soft and Hard Real-Time Capabilities in an Active DBMS", Proceedings of the First International Workshop on Active and Real-time Database Systems, Sweden, May 1995.
7. A. Buchmann, H. Branding, T Kudrass and J. Zimmermann, "Reach : A real-time, active and heterogeneous mediator system", IEEE Quarterly Bulletin on Data Engineering, volume 14, number 1, pp. 44-47, December 1992.
8. A. Buchmann, J. Zimmermann, J.A. Blakeley and D.L. Wells, "Building an Integrated Active OODBMS: Requirements, Architecture, and Design Decisions", In Proceedings of International Conference on Data Engineering, 1995.

9. Y.W. Chen and L. Gruenwald, "Effects of Deadline Propagation on Scheduling Nested Transactions in Distributed Real-time Database Systems", Information Systems, Volume 21, Number 1, pp. 103-124, 1996.

10. International Workshop on Database: Active and Real-time, U.S.A., November 1996.

11. Y.K. Kim and S.H. Son, "Predictability and Consistency in Real-time Database Systems", Advances in Real-time Systems, Edited by S.H. Son, Prentice Hall, 1994.

12. Henry F. Korth, Nandit Soparkar, Abraham Silberschatz, "Trigger Real-Time Databases with Consistency Constraints", in Proceedings of the 16 VLDB Conference, Brisbane, pp.71 - 82, 1990.

13. Victor C.S. Lee, Kam-yiu Lam, Sheung-lun Hung, "Impact of High Speed Network on Performance of Distributed Real-time Systems", Journal of System Architecture, volume 42, number 6-7, pp.531-546, 1996.

14. OPNET Modeling Manual, Release 2.5, MIL 3, Inc., Washington, DC, 1996.

15. G. Ozsoyoglu and R. Snodgrass, "Temporal and Real-time Database: A Survey", IEEE Transactions on Knowledge and Data Engineering, Volume 7, Number 4, pp. 513-532, 1995.

16. B. Purimetla, R.M. Sivasankaran, J. Stankovic, K. Ramamritham and D. Towsley, "Priority Assignment in Real-time Active Databases", In Proceedings of the 3rd International Conference on Parallel and Distributed Information Systems, 1994.

17. K. Ramamritham, "Real-Time Databases", Distributed and Parallel Databases, volume 1, number 2, pp. 199-226, 1993.

18. K. Ramamritham, Raju Sivasankaran, John A. Stankovic, Don T. Towsley, M. Xiong, "Integrating Temporal, Real-Time, and Active Databases", SIGMOD RECORD, Vol. 25, No. 1, p.8 - p.12, 1996.

19. R. M. Sivasankaran, John A. Stankovic, Don Towsley, Bhaskar Purimetla, K. Ramamritham, "Priority Assignment in Real-Time Active Database", The VLDB Journal, volume 5, number 1, pp .19 - 34, 1996.

20. O. Ulusoy, "A Study of Two Transaction Processing Architectures for Distributed Real-time Database Systems", Journal of Systems and Software, volume 31, number 2, pp. 97-108, 1995.

21. J. Widom and S. Ceri, Active Database Systems : Triggers and Rules for Advanced Database Processing, Morgan Kaufmann Publishers, In.c, San Francisco, 1996.

22. J. Widom, "The Starburst Active Database Rule System", IEEE Transactions on Knowledge and Data Engineering, volume 8, number 4, pp. 583-595, 1996.

23. M. Xiong, J. Stankovic, K. Ramamritham, D. Towsley and R.M. Sivasankaran, "Maintaining Temporal Consistency : Issues and Algorithms", In Proceedings of First International Workshop on Real-time Databases: Issues and Applications, California, 1996.

24. M. Xiong, R. Sivasankaran, J.A. Stankovic, K. Ramamritham and D. Towsley, "Scheduling transactions with Temporal Constraints: Exploiting Data Semantics", In Proceedings of 1996 Real-Time Systems Symposium, Washington, December, 1996.

25. P. S. Yu, K. L. Wu, K.J. Lin and S.H. Son, "On Real-time Databases: Concurrency Control and Scheduling", Proceedings of IEEE, volume 82, number 1, pp. 140-157, 1994.

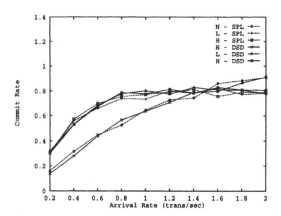

Fig. 5. SPL vs DSD under Deferred Mode with Different Workload

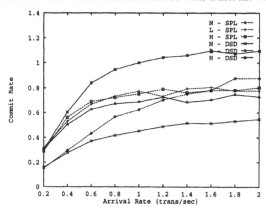

Fig. 6. SPL vs DSD under Immediate Mode with Different Workload

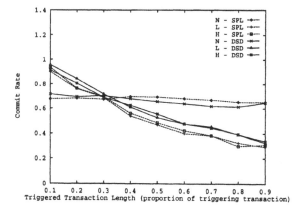

Fig. 7. SPL vs DSD under Deferred Mode with Different Triggered Lengths

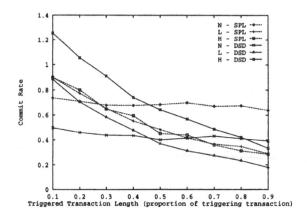

Fig. 8. SPL vs DSD under Immediate Mode with Different Triggered Lengths

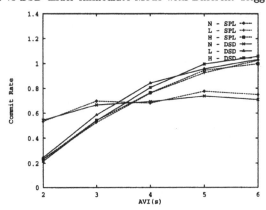

Fig. 9. SPL vs DSD under Deferred Mode with Different AVIs

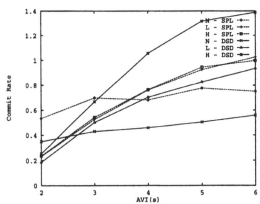

Fig. 10. SPL vs DSD under Immediate Mode with Different AVIs

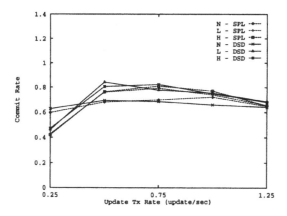

Fig. 11. SPL vs DSD under Deferred Mode with Different Update Rates

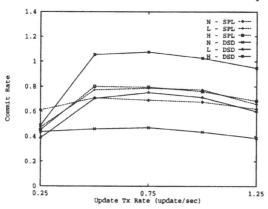

Fig. 12. SPL vs DSD under Immediate Mode with Different Update Rates

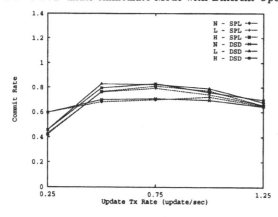

Fig. 13. SPL vs DSD under Deferred Mode with Different Update Rates

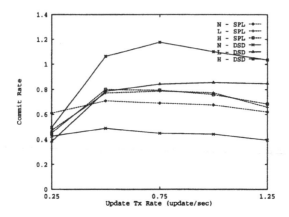

Fig. 14. SPL vs DSD under Immediate Mode with Different Update Rates

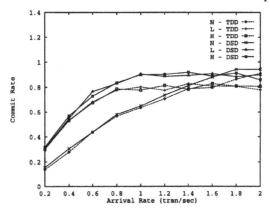

Fig. 15. TDD vs DSD under Deferred Mode with Different Workload

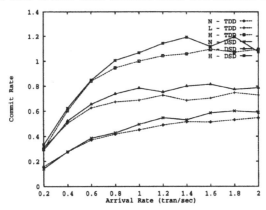

Fig. 16. TDD vs DSD under Immediate Mode with Different Workload

Buffer Management in Active, Real-Time Database Systems
Concepts and an Algorithm

Igor R. Viguier and Anindya Datta*

Department of MIS
University of Arizona
Tucson, AZ 85721
{igor,adatta}@loochi.bpa.arizona.edu

Abstract. Active, real-time database systems (ARTDBs) have attracted the attention of researchers in recent times. Such systems are envisioned as control systems for environments as diverse as process control, network management and automated financial trading. Sensors distributed throughout the system report the state of the system to the database. Unacceptable state reports typically results in corrective actions being triggered with deadlines. Thus ARTDBs incorporate both real-time as well as active characteristics. In this paper we study buffer management in ARTDBs and propose some principles that should govern such policies. Buffer management is recognized as not being a well studied area in active, real-time systems. As a result of our work, we postulate a new buffer management scheme that relies on two strategies: prefetching and priority-based buffer allocation and replacement. Subsequently, we report the result of studies of the performance of our proposed policy.

1 Introduction

Active, real-time database systems (ARTDBs) have attracted substantial amounts of interest in recent times (Datta 1994). Such systems amalgamate the properties of real-time systems and active systems. Specifically, ARTDBs are characterized by triggered transactions that arrive with deadlines. The most widespread envisioned use of ARTDB is in control systems, i.e., systems that monitor and control external environments. Examples of such systems are process control systems such as nuclear reactor control systems, automated stock trading systems, telecommunications network management systems, etc. A common theme in all these scenarios is that automatic control actions must be taken in response to semantically incorrect operation of the system. Such reactive behavior is usually operationalized by Event-Condition-Action (ECA) rules (Dayal et al. 1988) with time constraints. A nice feature of ARTDBs is the potential for the

---

* The work of this author was supported in part by a small grant awarded by the Office of Vice president for Research and the University of Arizona Foundation, University of Arizona

use of "canned transactions" (Ramamritham 1993). Usually, control systems are "closed loop" systems where two primary classes of transactions dominate: (a) *state reporting transactions*, where distributed sensors report the values of pre-determined data items (e.g., process sensors reporting the state of environment variables such as temperature, pressure, reaction kinetics in reactors); and (b) *control action transactions* which are fired in response to unacceptable system behavior detected by analyzing the reported system state. Because both these transactions classes consist of transactions whose instances arrive repetitively, it is possible to determine the read/write sets of these transactions a priori. We will exploit the "canned transaction" phenomenon in this paper.

Data buffering is an important issue in any database systems including ART-DBs. Due to the fact that databases are usually too large to reside completely in memory, data is mostly disk resident. The principle of intelligent data buffering consists of retaining a strategic part of the database in main memory such that transactions do not have to go to disk often to fetch data, thereby reducing response times. In general data buffering is based on the principle of transaction reference behaviors (Kearns et al. 1989).

Buffer management refers to a collective set of strategies that dictate what data is held in memory and for how long. The two basic components of any buffer management policy are *buffer allocation* and *buffer replacement* (Effelsberg et al. 1984). Buffer allocation strategies attempt to allocate buffer frames to transactions, while buffer replacement policies attempt to identify victim frames, i.e., candidate frames for replacement. In non-real-time systems the goal of buffer management is to reduce transaction response times. In real-time systems a good buffer management strategy should reduce number of transactions missing their deadlines.

In spite of extensive buffer management studies in traditional, non-real-time database frameworks (Dan et al. 1990; Dias et al. 1989; Effelsberg et al. 1984; Elhardt et al. 1984; Sacco et al. 1986), not much is reported in real-time database system (RTDBS) contexts. In all, we were able to identify three research articles (Carey et al. 1989; Huang et al. 1990; Jauhari et al. 1990) that report "priority" cognizant buffer management algorithms. The work reported in Huang et al. (1990) is the only one that considers a real-time context. The other two consider prioritized buffer management in the context of a "DBMS with priorities" (not RTDBSs). Three priority cognizant buffer management algorithms are postulated: *Priority-LRU* (PLRU) and *priority DBMIN* in Carey et al. (1989) and *Priority Hints* (PH) in Jauhari et al. (1990). Priority DBMIN primarily applies to *query processing* and not *transaction processing* and is thus not directly relevant to our work in this paper. Both PLRU and PH apply to prioritized transaction processing and are therefore considered relevant. As mentioned above, these algorithms were not developed in the context of a RTDBS. Moreover, the above algorithms consider "static priorities", i.e., transaction priorities (which in turn translate into frame priorities) are always the same. In RTDBSs however, as is well known, transaction priorities often change during the course of their lifetimes (e.g., in the *Earliest Deadline* (ED) (Liu et al. 1973) algorithm, priorities increase as transactions get closer to their deadlines). Due to the non-real-time nature of the aforementioned algorithms, i.e. PH and PLRU, as well as the static nature of the associated priorities, these are not directly applicable to RTDBS scenarios. We believe that the issue of buffer management in RTDBSs is quite open — moreover, there appears to be room for improvement especially by assuming some pre-knowledge about transaction. In this paper we demonstrate that it is possible to design better performing real-time buffer management schemes.

The remainder of this paper is organized as follows: in Sect. 2, we describe an execution model for real-time, active transactions followed by a general discussion of buffer management issues in active, real-time database systems in Sect. 3. We present our algorithm, called PAPER, in Sect. 4. In Sect. 5 we describe our performance results, followed by Sect. 6 where we conclude by summarizing the paper.

2 Execution Model for Active Real-Time Transactions

In this section we explain, briefly, a model of execution of real-time triggered transactions, which forms a significant part of the workload in a ARTDB. Note that we make the canned transaction assumption, i.e., the read and write sets of incoming transactions are known. The system model we consider in this paper may be regarded as comprising of finite sets $D\{d_1, d_2, \ldots, d_n\}$ of *data items*, $C\{c_1, c_2, \ldots, c_m\}$ of pre-defined *triggering conditions* and $T\{t_1, t_2, \ldots, t_k\}$ of pre-defined *triggered transactions*. Triggering conditions are formulae consisting of a term or conjunction of terms. Each term is of the form d_i <logical operator> l, where d_i is a data item and l is a constant[1]. An example of a triggering condition is: *temperature $\geq$ 1000*. If a data item $d_j \in D$, appears in triggering condition $c_i \in C$, then d_j is said to *participate* in c_i. Transactions in T are triggered by the satisfaction of triggering conditions in C. Certain transactions upon execution may update data items which may result in the satisfaction of triggering conditions, resulting in the triggering of more transactions. Thus the system may be regarded as consisting of data items, triggering conditions and transactions that interact with each other in a pre-defined manner.

To facilitate the representation of the above model, we use a structure that we have termed a *triggering graph* (TG). TGs capture the relationships between the sets D, C and T explained above. A formal definition is provided below.

Definition: *A triggering graph (TG) is a 6-tuple (D, C, T, E, W_p, W_t) representing a (weighted) tri-partite graph with vertex set $D \cup C \cup T$ and edge set $E \subseteq ((D \times C) \cup (C \times T) \cup (T \times D))$. W_p, the satisfaction function, denotes a mapping from $(D \times C)$ to the set of probability values. W_t, the time interval function, denotes a mapping from $(C \times T)$ to the set of non-negative real numbers. A marked TG is a TG in which a nonempty set of vertices $V \subseteq D$ is identified as being "marked".*

An example TG is shown in Fig. 1. Figure 1 may be interpreted according

---

[1] l maybe another data item as well, but that case is a trivial extension of the case reported.

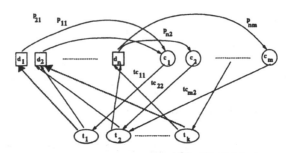

Fig. 1. A triggering graph

to the explanation of our model given above. The square nodes denote the data items, the circular nodes model the triggering conditions, while the oval nodes model the triggered transactions. The edges in the TG represent the relationship between the node sets. The edge set $E_{DC} \subseteq (D \times C)$ models the *participates* relationship explained above. The weights on these edges denote the probability that the update of a data item results in the satisfaction of the corresponding consistency constraint.

Several *coupling* modes have been suggested between triggering and triggered transactions, e.g., *immediate, deferred, detached* etc. (Dayal et al. 1990). It has been pointed out by several researchers (e.g., Branding et al. 1995; Berndtsson et al. 1995) that immediate and deferred coupling modes have several negative properties to be supported in real-time databases. Hence in this paper, we only consider the detached coupling mode, which does not impose additional unpredictable execution time to the triggering transaction. The execution model of this paper supports both parallel detached mode with casual dependencies and sequential detached mode with casual dependencies. In addition, exclusive detached mode with casual dependencies can be included for handling contingency transactions.

When utilizing the parallel casually dependent detached coupling mode, there are certain restrictions that must be satisfied: (1) triggered transactions being **serialized after** the triggering transactions, (2) **concurrency** between triggering and triggered transactions, (3) **commit dependency** between triggering and triggered transactions, and (4) **abort dependency** between triggering and triggered transactions. A straightforward implementation of parallel casually dependent detached coupling mode in a database system that uses locking could lead to potential deadlocks because the read and write sets of the triggered rule often intersect the read and write sets of the triggering transaction. For this reason we enforce restriction (1) above.

3 Buffer Management in Active, Real-Time Database Systems

Before actually presenting the algorithms, we discuss some of the issues involved in *active, real-time database systems* (RTDBSs) and the reasons why existing policies are deemed inappropriate in such systems. We begin by developing some general guidelines for buffer management in a simply real-time context, then extend this to encompass active systems.

3.1 Buffer Management for Real-Time Databases Systems

Achieving a low page fault rate is a common accepted goal of most buffer management algorithms (Silberschatz et al. 1994). Our algorithm does not depart from this common philosophy, as will be discussed below. However, certain characteristics of real time database systems need to be examined.

Transaction Deadline: Transactions in a RTDBS typically arrive with time constraints. As a result, the primary performance goal of the RTDBS is the achievement of a low miss ratio, rather than the traditional "low average response time" criterion (Abbott et al. 1992). This important difference has guided the exploration of new scheduling and concurrency protocols in RTDBSs. Our intuition suggests that for the same reason, buffer management needs to be reexamined as well.

Deferred Disk Writes: Conventional DBMSs defer disk writes, i.e., committed pages are not written to disk immediately, but either wait until when their carrying buffer is victimized through a page fault, or are written en-masse by an asynchronous write engine (Kearns et al. 1989; Teng et al. 1984). Both methods, however, present some undesirable side effects when applied to temporally constrained transaction processing. In the "write-on-demand" scenario, the actual cost of the disk-write operation is effectively transferred to the demanding transaction. This occurs regardless of the transaction's time constraint, which is clearly undesirable. If, on the other hand, an asynchronous write engine is used, it effectively allocates itself exclusive use of disk resources periodically. During this time, all active transactions are effectively suspended, which is also clearly undesirable when these transactions have time constraints.

Clean and Dirty Frames: In most algorithms that we are aware of, no distinction is made during victimization between clean and dirty frames. Suppose there are two pages p_1 and p_2 which are deemed to be equally available as victims, but p_1 is dirty while p_2 is clean. A traditional buffer management policy would choose as its victim whichever of p_1 or p_2 came first in its internal structure. In other words, in conventional buffer management algorithms, both pages have the same likelihood of being reused. We believe that this should not be the case in time constrained applications. Rather, in real-time scenarios, the clean page p_2 should clearly be victimized first, since this would potentially save a costly disk write.

From the above discussion, the following two principles should appear as clearly desirable for buffer management policies in RTDBSs:

1. A buffer management policy for a ARTDB should victimize pages that will only be used by transactions that are further away from their deadlines and,

2. Given any set of pages that are equally likely candidates for replacement, the clean frames should be victimized first.

3.2 Buffer Management for Active Systems

Having investigated the requirements that timing constraints place on buffer management, we turn our attention to how the active nature of ARTDBs can be exploited to improve buffer efficiency.

It has been recognized in the literature (Stankovic 1988), that prefetching based strategies (as opposed to demand paging) appear to be appropriate for some real-time systems. Also by analyzing the triggering graph for a particular ARTDB, it is possible to anticipate, with a certain degree of uncertainty, what transactions may be triggered. For example, if a transaction t_i, arrives in the system, using the write set of t_i we can mark the appropriate D nodes in the TG (recall the discussion in Sect. 2), and extract the subgraph induced by the nodes reachable from the marked nodes. Clearly, the C nodes in this subgraph are the triggering conditions that may be satisfied by the updates of the marked D nodes. Moreover, the T nodes in this subgraph are the transactions that would be triggered were the conditions actually satisfied. Subsequently, following the appropriate $(T \times D)$ edges one can re-mark appropriate D nodes that would be touched by the triggered transactions and start the entire process again. In this way, an n-step lookahead could be performed, and a set of data items (and consequently a set of data pages) may be identified. In addition, by simple probabilistic analysis one can easily compute the probabilities that particular transactions would be triggered and consequently particular data items needed. This could be very simply done using the weights of the $(D \times C)$ arcs, i.e., the p_{ij} values. Thus, given the arrival of a transaction into the system, it is possible to predict, with associated probabilities, which data pages may be needed subsequently. Disk requests for these data pages can hence be sent to the disk subsystem.

Clearly, thus, prefetch page requests compete for disk resources with demand page requests. However, the pages loaded by prefetch requests might not be used for a while (since the transaction that would touch them might not have been triggered). It is even likely that these pages will never be touched, if the corresponding transaction is never triggered or is aborted. Moreover, a demand request might have been issued by a transaction that is close to its deadline. In this situation, servicing a prefetch request might cause the transaction to miss its deadline. Thus, all demand page requests should have higher priority than prefetch requests. In other words a prefetch request should get served only when the appropriate disk is free, i.e., not serving a demand page request. The next logical question therefore is: are the disks free often enough in order for prefetching to have an impact. We ran extensive experiments under a wide range of operating conditions to verify the appropriateness of prefetching. It turns out that even under extreme load conditions disk utilization was rarely more than 80%. In other words, there were significant opportunities for prefetching to work.

We must also consider frame allocation and replacement in a prefetching context. Clearly, a prefetching policy should not overwrite pages that *will* be used by transactions that are currently active in the system with pages that *might* be used by transactions that are yet to be triggered. If this were not the case, a transaction might be starved by prefetching and thus made to miss its deadline. In other words, a prefetching algorithm should only replace pages that are of no use to any of the live transactions in the system. In addition, it can easily be assumed that we will be unable to satisfy every prefetch request as all demand page requests should be processed with higher priority than prefetch requests. Therefore, it makes sense to prioritize the prefetch requests in order to make it more likely that "more urgent" requests will be served before "less urgent" ones. Similarly, prefetched pages should be ordered as well so that "more urgent" pages will not be replaced by "less urgent" ones. These prefetch request and page priorities should be based on the probability that the corresponding transaction will be triggered and expected deadline of this transaction. For instance, pages that correspond to transactions that are less likely to be triggered should be replaced more readily than pages loaded for transactions that are more likely to be triggered. Similarly, pages that correspond to untriggered transactions whose expected deadline is further away should be replaced instead of pages loaded for transactions whose expected deadline is closer.

From the above discussion, prefetching appears as a viable option in ART-DBs. This prefetching, and the associated buffer management, should be based on the following principles:

- Given that transaction data access and triggering patterns are predefined (recall the triggering graph), it is possible to anticipate, with some associated uncertainty, future transaction arrival patterns, given the current state of the system. This knowledge can be used to prefetch data items that are likely to be required in the near future.
- Because of the uncertainty associated with prefetch disk requests and the fact that demand requests are triggered by transactions under time constraints, all prefetching should occur only when the corresponding disk resource is free from all demand-based activities. In other words, any demand request should have a higher priority than a prefetch request.
- Activities related to transactions that might be triggered in the future should be prioritized depending on both the probability that the corresponding transaction will be triggered and the expected deadline of that transaction, were it to be triggered.

3.3 Buffer Model

In this paper, we present a policy that follows the above principles. Under our buffer model, each transaction is allocated a piece of memory as its working space. We regard each of these memory spaces as the private buffers of active transactions. We work under the assumption that there is enough memory space for private buffers for all concurrent transactions in the system. This notion of private working space provides two benefits: (a) it helps recovery using the after image journaling approach (Huang et al. 1990); and (b) it captures intra-transaction locality of transaction reference behavior (Kearns et al. 1989).

Between the pool of private buffers and the disks on which the database is resident, lies the *global buffer* space. This global buffer is shared by all concurrent transactions. The global buffer space captures two different locality of reference behaviors: *inter-transaction locality* and *restart-transaction locality* (Kearns et al. 1989). Figure 2 illustrates the data buffering architecture assumed in this paper. Our buffer management algorithm is titled PAPER — *Prefetching*

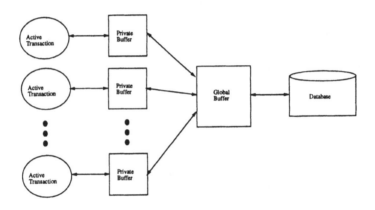

Fig. 2. Buffer model

*A*nticipatorily *and* *P*riority *basE*d *R*eplacement. As its name implies, it is based on the principles developed in sections 3.1 and 3.2. In the next section, we describe PAPER in some detail.

4 The PAPER Algorithm

There are two distinct but interrelated components of PAPER – buffer allocation/replacement and anticipatory prefetching. In both components, a central factor of the algorithm is the *virtual deadline* of transactions to be triggered, which PAPER uses both for differentiating between the frames that correspond to this transaction and for prioritizing the associated prefetch disk requests. We thus begin the discussion of PAPER by presenting the way in which these virtual deadlines are assigned. After this, we present the organization of the global buffer pool upon which PAPER relies. Finally, we describe the algorithm in some detail.

4.1 Virtual Deadlines

As was discussed in the previous section, there should exist some way of differentiating between transactions that will potentially be triggered. In PAPER, this takes the form of *virtual deadlines*. A virtual deadline encapsulates both the probability that the associated transaction will be triggered and the expected deadline that this transaction will have, if triggered.

The philosophy behind these priorities is the following: by performing a 1-step lookahead on the triggering graph, as described before, one can generate the set of data items (pages) that will be required by transactions that may arrive along with the probabilities that these transactions will be triggered. Based on this information, and the known time constraints associated with triggered transactions, it is possible to compute a virtual deadline for each page to be accessed by a potential transaction. We illustrate the process of virtual deadline computation through an example:

Example: Let transaction t_i enter the system at time A_{t_i} with deadline D_{t_i}. Assume that the 1-step lookahead mentioned above outputs the information that t_i will trigger t_j and t_k, with probabilities p_j and p_k and time constraints c_j and c_k, respectively. Additionally assume that it is known that t_j and t_k would be triggered at times Tr_j and Tr_k, respectively. In that case the deadlines of t_j and t_k would be $Tr_j + c_j$ and $Tr_k + c_k$ respectively. Also, it is easily intuitively understood that *prefetch priorities*, i.e., the urgency with which the data items belonging to a transaction's working set would be needed is (a) directly proportional to the triggering probability of that transaction; and (b) inversely proportional to the deadline of the transaction. Based on this logic, the prefetch priority of the data items (pages) corresponding to t_j's working set is $p_j/(Tr_j + c_j)$. Similarly, the prefetch priority of the data items (pages) corresponding to t_k's working set is $p_k/(Tr_k + c_k)$. The only problem with the scenario described above is that the triggering times of t_j and t_k are not possible to predict, i.e., Tr_j and Tr_k are unknown. Indeed, a trigger could occur towards the beginning of the lifetime of the triggering transaction or towards the end of its lifetime. Since this depends on both the access pattern of that transaction and on system dynamics, triggering times are effectively impossible to predict. Therefore, in PAPER, we *estimate* the trigger times by making the assumption that triggerings will happen, on average, at the midpoint of a transaction's allowed lifetime, i.e., halfway between its arrival time and its deadline. For t_j and t_k, that time is the midpoint of the allowable lifetime of t_i. In other words, we make the assumption that $Tr_j = Tr_k = (D_{t_i} + A_{t_i})/2$. Then the prefetch priority of each data item in t_j's working set is $p_j/((D_{t_i} + A_{t_i})/2 + c_j)$. Similarly, the prefetch priority of each data item in t_k's working set is $p_k/((D_{t_i} + A_{t_i})/2 + c_k)$. In PAPER, we do one more "tweak" to the method outlined above to get our priorities. Basically, we prioritize by taking the inverse of the above expressions. One can easily see that the inverses give the *virtual deadlines* associated with each page request and can be used to prioritize the request. The virtual deadline for transactions t_j and t_k of the above example will be $((D_{t_i} + A_{t_i})/2 + c_j)/p_j$ and $((D_{t_i} + A_{t_i})/2 + c_k)/p_k$, respectively. □

Having described the way in which virtual deadlines are computed, we now turn our attention to the organization of the global buffer upon which PAPER relies.

4.2 Global Buffer Organization

In PAPER, the global buffer is divided into three different "pools", each of which contains a different sort of page. We distinguish between pages that are likely to be used by a currently executing transaction (*reuse* pages), those that might be used by a transaction to be triggered (*anticipated* pages), and those that are not expected to be used by any transaction (*free* pages). Upon page fault, PAPER will victimize a free page if any is available. Otherwise, it will replace an anticipated page, again if any is available. Otherwise a reuse page will be used. The three corresponding buffer pools are the *reuse*, *anticipated*, and *free* pools, described below.

Reuse Pool Organization: From the discussion in Sect. 3, it is clear that transactions that are close to their deadline should not see their pages be replaced. We say that any buffer *reuse* page that is likely to be used by a transaction is "owned" by that transaction. Since there might be more than one transaction that claims such ownership over any given page, we assign each page the deadline of its *principal owner*, i.e., the owner with the smallest deadline. The *reuse* pool is thus sorted in order of earliest deadline, such that pages with the latest deadline principal owner are victimized first.

Also, since a given transaction may claim principal ownership of more than one page, multiple pages may have the same deadline. We distinguish between such pages according to their dirty bit. Following from our discussion in Sect. 3, PAPER victimizes clean frames before dirty ones. The complete key upon which the *reuse* pool is sorted thus becomes the pair (d_p, b_p), where d_p is the deadline assigned to page p and b_p is the clean bit of p, where b_p is null if the page is dirty and 1 otherwise.

Anticipated Pool Organization: In PAPER, frames are released from the *reuse pool* when no existing transaction intends to use the page any further. At this stage, the frame might be made available for replacement, be it for the servicing of page faults for existing transactions or the servicing of prefetch requests in anticipation of potential transactions. Yet, some of these released frames are likely to contain pages that will be needed by transactions to be triggered. Such frames are thus, instead, placed in the *anticipated pool*. This pool holds all frames that contain pages that either have been prefetched or have been requested for a prefetch and are not currently owned by an active transaction. The *anticipated pool* lies between the *reuse* and the *free pool*, i.e., the frames located there are less likely to be used than frames in the *reuse pool*, but less likely candidates for replacement than frames in the *free pool*.

Within the *anticipated pool*, frames are sorted in order of decreasing virtual deadline, such that the frame with the largest virtual deadline is selected for replacement first. Since there might, as is the case in the *reuse pool*, be more than one frame with the same virtual deadline, frame cleanness is also taken into consideration in the sorting. The complete sorting key for the *anticipated pool* thus consists of the pair (VD_R, *clean_bit*). Note that the frame data structure used here is thus the same as for the reuse pool, consisting of a (virtual) *deadline*, a *clean_bit*, and the associated *FrameID*.

To know which pages are candidates for prefetching, PAPER keeps a simple *Prefetch_count* array of prefetch request counters. Each time a transaction requests a prefetch on a page, the corresponding entry in the *Prefetch_count* array is incremented by one. Upon termination, the transaction decreases the appropriate prefetch counter for each entry in the list.

Free Pool Organization: No frame ordering is present in the free pool. It is simply divided into two subpools: a *clean* pool, and a *dirty* pool. Each pool follows the simple *first-come, first-serve* (FCFS) policy for replacement, i.e., that pages that arrived earlier are victimized earlier. Also, as was the case for the *reuse* pool, we first select victims from the *clean* pool while it is not empty.

4.3 Buffer Allocation and Replacement in PAPER

The buffer allocation and replacement policy of PAPER is based on the discussion in Sect. 3.

Having examined both the way in which virtual deadlines are computed and the organization of the global buffer upon which PAPER relies, we are now in measure to describe the allocation and replacement policy itself. This policy is implemented as a set of four procedures, which are executed at different stages of the lifetime of a transaction. These are presented below.

- **System Entry:** Upon arrival of a transaction t_i to the system, its *usage set*, $\mathcal{U}_{t_i}$, is computed. This set consists of all (p_j, n_{i_j}) where p_j is a page in the working set of t_i and n_{i_j} is the number of times t_i will need to touch p_j. Also, each page p_j in $\mathcal{U}_{t_i}$ is examined to determine if it is in memory and t_i is its principal owner. If this is the case, it is repositioned accordingly in the *reuse* pool.

  In addition, a 1-step lookahead is performed on t_i, which yields a set of data items that might be needed by transactions triggered by t_i. Each one of these data items is given a virtual deadline, which is computed as discussed in Sect. 4.1. Based on these virtual deadlines, prefetch requests are dispatched to the appropriate disk and prefetch pages that are in the *free pool* are moved to the *anticipated pool*.

- **Page Touch:** On each page reference thereafter, t_i updates its usage set, $\mathcal{U}_{t_i}$, as it accesses the pages in its working set: on each access to a page p_j, the corresponding n_{i_j} is decreased by 1, until it reaches 0, at which time (p_j, n_{i_j}) is removed from $\mathcal{U}_{t_i}$. When this occurs, if the page has another principal owner, then it is simply repositioned in the *reuse* pool according to that owner's deadline. If, on the other hand, it has no other owners, it is moved to the *anticipated pool* if it is a candidate for prefetching, and to the appropriate *free* pool, otherwise.

- **Transaction Termination:** When a transaction terminates PAPER removes from the system all prefetch requests that the transaction emitted on arrival. Upon termination, a transaction will have triggered all its children (which, upon arrival, will have moved the necessary frames into the *reuse pool*) and not-triggered some potential children (which will thus not need the pages tagged for prefetch by the parent transaction). This is performed whether or not the transaction terminated after completion.

  When a transaction t_i terminates after committing, it should be clear that, having performed all its operations, it will own no pages. If, however, there occurs an abnormal termination or restart (e.g., through deadline expiry or through the validation phase of an optimistic CC algorithm), then PAPER actively empties the usage set $\mathcal{U}_{t_i}$, along with any effects t_i might have upon buffer frames. This is done as follows. For each element of the transaction's $\mathcal{U}$ set, if the terminating transaction was the primary owner of the page and the page has not yet been swapped out, then if there exists a new principal owner for the page, the corresponding frame is relocated in the *reuse* pool, otherwise, it is simply moved to the *free* pool.

- **Page Replacement:** To complete our description of the buffer allocation and replacement of PAPER, we present the replacement policy. The procedure followed is very simple. If there is a frame in the *clean free* pool, then the corresponding page is replaced. Otherwise, if there is a frame in the *dirty free* pool, then its page is written to disk and the new one brought in. If there were no pages in either *free pool*, then the *anticipated pool* is examined. If it contains any frame, then the highest-virtual-deadline frame is selected. Finally, if no frame was available in any of the above pools, then the highest-deadline frame from the *reuse* pool is selected. Whether the page came from the *anticipated* or the *free* pool, the dirty bit is checked and, if it is set, the corresponding page is flushed to disk before the new page is brought in.

Having examined the buffer allocation and replacement policy of PAPER, we turn our attention the mechanism by which pages corresponding to anticipated transactions are loaded into the global buffer.

4.4 Prefetching in PAPER

In PAPER, we do not send the prefetch requests directly to disk. Rather, they are sent to a number of prioritized queues maintained inside the system. There is one queue for each disk. Whenever the demand queue for a disk is empty, the highest priority prefetch request is served from its associated prefetch queue. The primary motivation for holding prefetch requests in specialized queues is that we want to have more control on the prefetch requests than on the demand page requests. There are two reasons for this:

- Depending on the level of activeness of the underlying ADBMS, there might be a lot more prefetch requests generated per arriving transactions than demand page requests. If the prefetch requests were allowed to proceed directly to the disk queues, these queues would grow indefinitely. However, by holding these requests in controllable queues, we can control the rate of growth by eliminating requests that are outdated.
- Because of the large number of prefetch requests generated, it is likely there would be a large amount of redundancy, e.g., the same page may be requested several times. Thus, it is necessary to be able to exert some amount of control in order to reduce these redundancies.

Our proposed solution can be summarized as follows: All demand requests have higher priority than all prefetch requests. If a disk queue is empty, the highest priority request from its corresponding prefetch queue is serviced. Before sending a prefetch request to disk, PAPER checks if the page already exists in buffer. If this search succeeds, the prefetch request is temporarily ignored and the next one checked. A prefetch request R is represented in PAPER by a pair (p_R, VD_R), consisting of the page, p_R, to be brought into memory and the *virtual deadline*, VD_R, assigned to this requested page through the computation presented previously. Each disk δ has an associated *prefetch_queue$_\delta$* where prefetch requests particular to that disk are placed. Each such queue is sorted so that requests having the earliest VD_R will be serviced first. The procedure by which these prefetch requests are serviced is the following one.

Servicing Prefetch Requests: Whenever a disk δ becomes idle, the prefetch request with the lowest deadline in *prefetch_queue$_\delta$* is serviced as follows. An available clean victim frame in which to insert the page to be prefetched is first identified. This frame is, of course, taken only from either the *Clean_pool* of the *free pool* or the *anticipated pool* itself. If there exists no such frame, then the procedure simply exits. Otherwise, *prefetch_queue$_\delta$* is searched for a request for a page that is not currently in memory. Once such a request is found, if its virtual deadline is earlier than that of the page in the victimized frame[2], then the request is actually serviced, the frame is then inserted into the *anticipatory pool*, and the prefetch request is removed from the *prefetch_queue$_\delta$*.

Having presented the details of our proposed algorithm along with the reasons for implementing such a policy, we now turn to the experiments performed to test the validity and appropriateness of the principles underlying PAPER. This discussion begins with a presentation of the model used to study the different versions of the algorithm.

5 Performance

We have built a comprehensive simulation model of a ARTDB using SIMPACK (Fishwick 1995), a C/C++ based simulation toolkit. For a complete discussion

---

[2] For this purpose, frames located in the *free pool* are given an infinite deadline. This ensures that they will always be used as victims for prefetching.

of our simulation model see (Datta et al. 1996). On this model we have conducted extensive performance studies of PAPER. We have compared the performance of paper to LRU (Effelsberg et al. 1984), and two well known real-time databases buffer management algorithms, namely Priority-LRU (PLRU) (Carey et al. 1989), and Priority-Hints (PH) (Jauhari et al. 1990). In this section we report some of the results. These results seem to indicate that PAPER outperforms the other algorithms in most cases. The performance metrics used are the usual metrics employed to measure the performance of real-time database systems, namely *miss ratio*, along with page fault rates. These two metrics are defined as:

- Miss Ratio (%) = $\dfrac{\text{Number of transaction aborts}}{\text{Number of transaction aborts and commits}} \times 100$
- Page Fault Rate (%) = $\dfrac{\text{Number of page faults}}{\text{Number of page requests}} \times 100$

Also, to evaluate the performance of the prefetching component of PAPER, we measure the prefetch request service rate, defined as:

- Prefetch request service rate (%) = $\dfrac{\text{Num. prefetch requests serviced}}{\text{Num. prefetch requests submitted}} \times 100$

Though we conducted a wide range of experiments (see Datta et al. 1996) we only report a baseline case in this short paper. In the baseline model, our intent is to isolate the effect of memory contention by making buffer the bottleneck resource. The corresponding parameter settings are shown in Table 1.

Notation	Meaning	Value
NumCPU	Number of CPUs	8
NumDisk	Number of Disks	16
ProcCPU	CPU time per page	10 ticks
ProcDisk	Disk time per page	20 ticks
PrivPool	Size of Private Buffer Pool	800 pages
GBuf	Size of Global Buffer Pool	800 pages
DBSize	Database Size	40000 pages
DiskFrac	Global Buffer Size in relation to Disk Size	2 %
NumItemsPerPage	Number of data items per page	4
WriteProb	Probability that a page that is read will also be updated	0.1
SizeInterval	Range of Transaction Sizes in number of pages accessed	[1,30]
SRInterval	Slack Ratio Interval	[2.0,6.0]
NumTrigCond	Number of Triggering Conditions	300
NumTrigTran	Number of Triggered Transactions	300

Table 1. Parameter values for the baseline model

The result of the experiment is shown in figures 3A, and 3B. Figure 3A shows the effect of varying arrival rate on miss ratio. Note that the arrival rate is that of non-triggered transactions. however, this rate directly affects the arrival of triggered transactions in the system, and therefore, is a good indicator of the system load.

The curves of Fig. 3A have the "S" shape characteristic of real-time database management systems. At sufficiently low non-triggered transaction arrival rates,

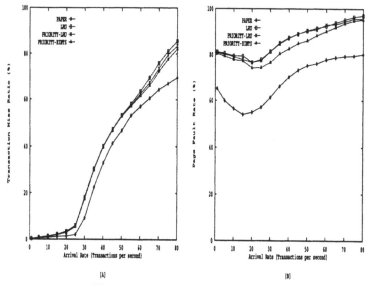

Fig. 3. Baseline experimental results

such a system is able to schedule resources so that almost all the offered work-load can complete within time constraints. Deadline misses are caused by rare data contention or resource contentions. As the arrival rate increases, resource contention causes transactions to have to wait in the system queues for an in-creasingly longer time, until the system reaches its *overload point*, characterized by a sudden sharp increase in the miss ratio curves.

Figure 3A shows that PAPER consistently outperforms the other algorithms. The overload point is pushed from approximately 24 transactions per second for PH and LRU to about 29 transactions per second for PAPER. Also, under overloaded conditions, PAPER attains a miss ratio substantially lower than the other protocols. For instance, at an arrival rate of 40 transactions per second, PAPER causes the system to only miss about 33% of the offered workload, while PH looses 40% of the transactions.

These performance gains can be understood by examining Fig. 3B, which shows the page fault rates corresponding to Fig. 3A. The "V" shape exhibited by these curves is characteristics of the combined effects of two, inversely pro-portional causes:

– At very low arrival rates, there are only a few transactions active in the system at any one point in time. As a result, the probability that a given page needed by an active transaction has been referenced by another currently or recently active transaction is relatively low. In short, there exists little inter-transaction locality of reference and, in the presence of a small buffer, executing transactions must load most pages they require from disk. This intuition explains the relatively high page fault rates observed at very low arrival rates in Fig. 3B. As workload increases, then, the concurrency in the system at any point in time increases as well. This results in an increased inter-transaction locality of reference, and thus in a declining page fault rate. This phenomenon is the cause of the declining part of the page fault rate curves.

- As the transaction arrival rate increases, however, so does the total number of unique pages that are referenced by concurrent and recent transactions. In other words, the union of the working sets of these transactions grows. In the presence of limited memory, this entails that, as workload increases, the length of time that a page will remain resident decreases as cache contention increases. This phenomenon, which is negligible at very low arrival rates, becomes more important as concurrency increases. This intuition explains the ascending side of the "V" shaped curves of Fig. 3B.

Thus, at low arrival rates, the effects of low inter-transaction locality of reference dominate those of low cache contention. As workload increases, however, this phenomenon is reversed: the increasing number of page faults due to cache contention override the growing number of cache hits brought about by locality of reference.

Having explained the overall shape of the page fault rate curves, we now turn our attention to the differences that appear between them, from inherent differences in effectiveness. LRU, which only uses information about the order of page references, seems to perform the least well, reaching page fault rates of up to 95%. At the other extreme, PAPER, which takes into account transaction priorities, predicted reference patterns and the known operations of a transaction, seems to perform extremely well, especially at low arrival rates, reaching page fault rates of only 55%. It would thus seem that the performance of a buffer management algorithm for active, real-time database systems is linked to the amount of relevant information it utilizes.

The most significant reductions in page fault rates, however, occur with PA-PER. At low arrival rates, PAPER reaches down to about 55%. The increased performance is due to the anticipatory components of PAPER. From Fig. 3B, it is clear that performance improvements from prefetching attain their highest levels at low arrival rates. To illustrate this phenomenon, we present Fig. 4. This plot represents the number of prefetch requests that were actually serviced, and corresponds to the plots of Fig. 3.

As can be seen, the number of pages that were brought into memory in anticipation of the access patterns of future triggered load first increases at low non-triggered arrival rates. This is simply due to the correspondingly growing number of non-triggered transactions that arrive to the system which trigger a respectively growing number of prefetch requests. Most of these requests are serviced until the point where contention for the disks is too large. After this point, even though the amount of submitted prefetch requests increases, the number of requests that are serviced decreases since the operations of executing transactions are given priority over those of our prefetching module.

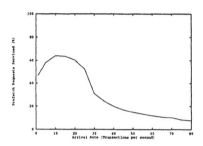

Fig. 4. Active prefetching in PAPER

6 Conclusion

In this paper, we presented PAPER, a buffer management algorithm designed to study the needs of ARTDBs. The algorithm consists of a priority-based buffer management policy coupled with a prefetching mechanism. The buffer management policy relies on the system priority of the active transactions to determine proper allocation and replacement of pages. The second component of PAPER, the prefetching mechanism, utilizes the "canned-transaction" properties associated with ARTDBs to try to reduce the number of page faults of triggered transactions. The proposed algorithm was simulated, and the results from this simulation clearly show that PAPER outperforms other DBMS buffer management policies: less transactions miss their deadlines. However, this superiority, although always present is not always significant. It appears that prefetching, in particular, cannot provide significant performance improvements except in some cases.

References

R. Abbott and H. Garcia-Molina. Scheduling Real-Time Transactions: Performance Evaluation. *ACM Transactions on Database Systems*, 1992.

M. Berndtsson and J. Hansson. Issues in Active Real-Time Databases. In *Proceedings of the International Workshop on Active and Real-Time Database Systems*, June 1995.

H. Branding and A. Buchmann. On Providing Soft and Hard Real-Time Capabilities in an Active DBMS. In *Proceedings of the International Workshop on Active and Real-Time Database Systems*, June 1995.

M.J. Carey, R. Jauhari, and M. Livny. Priority in DBMS Resource Scheduling. In *Proceedings of the 15th VLDB*, 1989.

A. Dan, D.M. Dias, and P.S. Yu. An Approximate Analysis of the LRU and FIFO Buffer Replacement Schemes. In *ACM SIGMETRICS*, May 1990.

A. Datta. Research Issues in Databases for Active Rapidly Changing data Systems (ARCS). *ACM SIGMOD RECORD*, 23(3):8–13, September 1994.

A. Datta, S. Mukherjee, and I. Viguier. Buffer management in real-time active database systems. Available as a Technical Report from http://loochi.bpa.arizona.edu, 1996.

U. Dayal and B. Blaustein et al. The HiPAC Project: Combining Active Databases and Timing Constraints. *ACM SIGMOD RECORD*, 17(1):51–70, March 1988.

U. Dayal, M. Hsu, and R. Ladin. Organizing long-running activities with triggers and transactions. In *Proceedings of the ACM SIGMOD Conference on Management of Data*, 1990.

D.M. Dias, B.R. Iyer, J.T. Robinson, and P.S. Yu. Integrated Concurrency-Coherency Controls for Multisystem Data Sharing. *IEEE Transactions on Software Engineering*, 15(4), April 1989.

W. Effelsberg and T. Harder. Principles of Database Buffer Management. *ACM Transactions on Database Systems*, 9(4), December 1984.

K. Elhardt and R. Bayer. A Database Cache for High Performance and Fast Restart in Database Systems. *ACM Transactions on Database Systems*, 9(4), December 1984.

P.A. Fishwick. *Simulation Model Design And Execution: Building Digital Worlds*. Prentice Hall, 1995.

J. Huang and J. Stankovic. Real-time Buffer Management. Technical Report COINS TR 90-65, University of Massachusetts, Dept. of Computer and Information Sciences, 1990.

R. Jauhari, M. Carey, and M. Livny. Priority-hints: An algorithm for priority-based buffer management. In *Proceedings of the 16th Conference on Very Large Databases, Brisbane, Australia*, pages 708–721, Los Altos, CA, August 1990. Morgan Kaufman pubs.

J.P. Kearns and S. DeFazio. Diversity in Database Reference Behavior. *Performance Evaluation Review*, 17(1), May 1989.

C. Liu and J. Layland. Scheduling Algorithms for Multiprogramming in a Hard Real-Time Environment. *Journal of the ACM*, January 1973.

K. Ramamritham. Real-Time Databases. *Distributed and Parallel Databases: An International Journal*, 1(2):199–226, 1993.

G.M. Sacco and M. Schkolnick. Buffer Management in Relational Database Systems. *ACM Transactions on Database Systems*, 11(4), December 1986.

A. Silberschatz and P.B. Galvin. *Operating Systems Concepts, 4th ed.* Addison Wesley, 1994.

J.A. Stankovic. Misconceptions About Real-Time Computing. *IEEE Computer*, pages 10–19, September 1988.

James Z. Teng and Robert A. Gunaer. Managing ibm database 2 buffers to maximize performance. *IBM Systems Journal*, 23(2):211–218,, 1984.

Parallel Event Detection in Active Database Systems:
The Heart of the Matter

Ulrike Jaeger

Humboldt-Universität zu Berlin
Institut für Informatik
10099 Berlin
Germany
jaeger@dbis.informatik.hu-berlin.de

Johann K. Obermaier

ABB Corporate Research AG
CHCRC.C2
Segelhof, CH-5405 Baden
Switzerland
johann.obermaier@chcrc.abb.ch

Abstract. This paper proposes a strategy for parallel composite event detection in active database management systems. Up to now, event detection is sequential and totally synchronized, and thus preserves the timely order of events during the detection process. However, in distributed and extensible applications events may occur simultaneously in parallel unsynchronized streams. In order to adapt composite event detection to those new requirements we relax the timely order of events to a partial order and process parallel event streams. As a consequence, composite event detection must deal with unsynchronized and parallel event compositions. Our approach introduces a hybrid parallelization strategy for composite event detection in Active Database Management Systems that respects the timely order of events.

1 Introduction

This paper discusses basic approaches to parallel detection of event compositions. Although it characterizes several techniques by means of a simple cost model, it emphasizes on the aspects of order preserving parallelism and does not cover performance issues. Parallel detection of event compositions is a facet of the SMILE approach [Jae95] which extends the concepts of active database management systems (ADBMS) in order to meet the requirements of event driven, long lived, distributed, and partially connected applications. Events might occur simultaneously and could be processed in parallel. We adapt techniques and optimizations from query execution in relational database management systems. However, queries and composite events differ fundamentally. The semantics of query execution is set oriented, whereas composite event detection is based on open streams of events. Cardinality and frequency of incoming events is unpredictable. Event compositions often base on a order-sensitive combinations, e.g. sequences. Parallel detection destroys the timely order of events and compositions.

Up to now, ADBMS detect events and event compositions sequentially. The existing execution models guarantee a timely ordered detection process, but become inefficient if many events and event compositions are involved.

The remainder of this paper is organized as follows: Section 2 sketches the state of the art in ADBMS with an emphasis on composite event detection by operator graphs. Section 3 discusses parallelization techniques developed for query execution in relational DBMS. We illustrate the different techniques by examples for detecting composite events. We discuss the special problems that arise in composite event detection if we naively adapt parallel query execution strategies. As a solution, Section 4 introduces our hybrid parallelization strategy for composite event detection. Section 5 discusses related research. Section 6 contains our conclusion and future work.

2 State of the Art in Composite Event Detection

ADBMS extend the regular DBMS functionality by *event-condition-action rules*, called *ECA* rules [DBM88]. An *event* represents the successful execution of some operation within the database system or application. The *condition* tests the context state when the event occurs. The *action* is executed, when the condition evaluates to true. The application defines and produces *atomic events*, and requests for atomic as well as complex *composite events*. The event detector component in ADBMS collects and distributes atomic events, and detects event compositions.

2.1 Basic Concepts

Events and History. An event is a "happening of interest" [GJS92b] within the ADBMS or its application. Events occur repeatedly, therefore those events are instances of a given event type. Events are ordered by global time stamps. The ADBMS attaches a time stamp to each event. The time stamps are isomorphic to ℕ. In contrast to most ADBMS approaches, our approach also integrates simultaneous events.

We denote event types by capital letters. Instances of an event type are represented by tuples, having a set of attributes like type, time stamp and others. In this paper we focus on type and time information only, therefore denote an atomic event as an aggregate $<typename>.<timestamp>$. For example, $A.4$ is an instance of type A, bearing the time stamp 4. Throughout this paper we use capital letters for type names as well as for the set of instances of those types.

During runtime, the ADBMS receives atomic events and collects those in a timely ordered history. For example, a history of event instances of types A, B, C, D is: $\langle A.1, B.4, C.5, D.5, D.7, C.8, A.9 \rangle$ We will refer to this history throughout this paper.

Event Compositions. Events issued by the application are atomic events. Composite events are constructed from atomic or other composite events according to the semantics of event operators. Composite events are typed as atomic events. A composite event type X refers to a certain expression of constituent event types — except X, as recursion is not allowed — and operators. A composite event instance x is a typed representation for a combination of constituent event instances. Languages for event compositions provide a variety of operators ([BZBW95], [PW93], [WC94]). Without discussing those languages, we classify event operators into three groups:

- *constructors* combine events from different sources to form new result tuples.
- *collectors* collect events from different sources and merge them without constructing a new event tuple.
- *selectors* receive events from one source and select a certain subset without constructing a new event tuple.

In this paper, we focus on a common subset of event operators as examples for each operator class. Let A, B be event types:

- *BEFORE (A,B)*: instances of A are composed with instances of B if $a \in A$ happens before $b \in B$, i.e. time stamp of $a <$ time stamp of b. The operator is a constructor for triples $(a, b, t) \in A \times B \times TIME$, where t is the time stamp of b.
- *AND (A,B)*: instances of both A and B are composed, no matter what timely order. The operator is a constructor for triples $(a, b, t) \in A \times B \times TIME$, where t is the time stamp of the most recent of the two constituent events.
- *OR (A,B)*: instances of either A or B, no matter what timely order. The operator is a collector of events from $A \cup B$. The result of *OR* is a heterogeneous set of instances of both types A and B.
- *FIRST(A)*: the oldest instance of A. The operator is a selector of events for a single $a \in A$, with timestamp of $a \leq$ time stamp of $\tilde{a}$, $\forall \tilde{a} \in A$.
- *LAST(A)*: the most recent instance of A. The operator is a selector of events for a single $a \in A$, with time stamp of $a \geq$ time stamp of $\tilde{a}$, $\forall \tilde{a} \in A$.

We denote composite event types by capital letters as well. Instances of a given composite event type have the list of constituent events and a time stamp as arguments. For example, $Z.5(A.2, B.5, 5)$ is an instance of the composite event type Z, based on the composition $Z = AND\ (A,B)$. $Z.5$ inherits the time stamp 5 from the most recent constituent event $B.5$.

Composition Semantics. The detection operates on sets of constituent events and produces sets of compositions. SENTINEL ([CKAK94], [Kri94]) was the first ADBMS to provide a set of explicit language concepts to define which subset of possible combinations is required. The semantics of event composition is described by so called consumption modes. The composition semantics determines the behavior of constructor operators, like *BEFORE* and *AND*. There are many variations of composition semantics (cf. [Beh95], [Kri94]). In this paper we refer to the most general consumption semantics, called *ALL*, and the most common consumption semantics in ADBMS, called *CHRONICLE*.

Constructors with *ALL* semantics are based on the Cartesian product of constituent events. Combinations are constructed according to the operator semantics. For example, *ALL (AND (A,B))* results in a set S with: $|S| = |A| * |B|$ and $S \subseteq A \times B \times TIME$

Constructors with *CHRONICLE* semantics produce a subset of the *ALL* result: combination of events also means consumption. If an event is combined for a composite event, it is not reused for others. *CHRONICLE* describes the stream based behavior of most of the event detection implementations in ADBMS. For example, input events for *AND* are combined and consumed in fist-in-first-out (*fifo*) order.

An ADBMS provides composite event detectors that automatically collect and combine constituent events of the event composition. In this paper, we discuss the stream based operator graph approach as used in SENTINEL ([CKAK94], [Kri94]), REACH [BBKZ92], ADL [Beh95], SMILE [Jae95], and others ([PW93], [WC94]). Variations of the graph approach are: finite automata in ODE ([GJS92b], [GJS92a]), and modified colored Petri nets in SAMOS ([Gat95], [GD92], [GD94]).

Operator Graphs. An operator graph is represented by a set of nodes and edges. An edge indicates a stream of totally ordered entries. Entries are appended at the end of the stream and received from the head. A node is either a leaf, a root, or an operator node. A detection graph forms a tree.

- A *leaf node* is labelled by an event type. It represents the perception of constituent events of that type. It has one input stream for the required constituent event type and one output stream. *LEAF(<type>)* performs selections on input streams, thus it is a selector operator.
- An *operator node* represents an operator of the event language. It receives entries from a set of input streams and composes new result entries according to the operator definition. Some operators need internal buffers. The result composition is sent to the output stream. The output stream is input stream for another node.
- A *root node* has one input stream and a set of output streams. The root prepares each entry for output to consumers. The output of *ROOT(<type>)* is a stream of composition instances of type <type>. It sends the result to the application and other consumers of the composition. The root is a selector operator.

Example. Throughout this paper we refer to the detection tree for the composition *X=(OR(A,BEFORE(B,AND(C,D))))* as shown in Figure 1.

2.2 Composite Event Detection

Throughout this paper we use a very simple cost model:

- Each operator performs its work on a stream entry within one time unit, called tick.

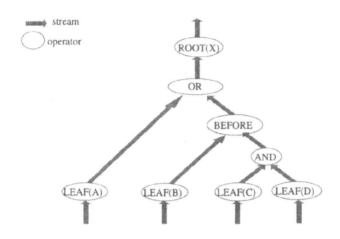

Fig. 1. Example detection tree

– Propagation along streams takes no time.

For illustration, we show the behavior of operator trees as tables. Vertically we show the counter for ticks. Horizontally we show the operators of the operator tree. A field in the table contains the result of an operator at a special tick. Leaf operators receive constituent events from a given history. Each entry is represented by the aggregate *<type>.<time stamp>*. Operator nodes receive and combine incoming event. The result is a composition represented as a tuple *(<constituent events>, <time stamp>)*. Example: Table 1 shows the sequential behavior of a operator section for *BEFORE (A, B)*. At tick 1 *LEAF(A)* accepts $A.14$, at tick 2 *LEAF(B)* accepts $B.17$. At tick 3 the *BEFORE* operator produces the composition of $A.14$ and $B.17$, bearing the time stamp 17.

ticks	LEAF(A)	LEAF(B)	BEFORE
1	A.14		
2		B.17	
3			$(A.14, B.17, 17)$

Table 1. Example table for *BEFORE(A,B)*

Composite event detection in ADBMS so far is sequential and centralized ([Beh95], [BBKZ92], [CKAK94], [Gat95], [GD92], [GJS92b], [Jae95], [Kri94], [PW93], [WC94]). For composite events the detection process advances step by step with each constituent event. The composite event detector accepts events in a totally ordered stream. For the sequential synchronized execution of the operator graph, we assume that new constituent events are sent to the leaf nodes synchronously. For each input entry the operator tree performs all possible operators, and produces results possibly up to the root. New input is accepted by the tree only if no further construction of results is possible. This strategy synchronizes event composition and guarantees that no event can overtake previous events during the detection process. For the *ALL* semantics constructor operators like *AND* and *BEFORE* have to buffer their input streams and reuse them for new combinations. For the *CHRONICLE* semantics the operands are not buffered. Input streams are received, combined, and consumed.

Sequential Example. Table 2 shows the execution of the example detection tree of Figure 1 on the history ⟨ *A.1,B.4,C.5,D.5,D.7,C.8,A.7* ⟩ using the *ALL* semantics. For brevity we omit the root.

ticks	A	B	C	D	AND	BEFORE	OR
1	A.1						
2							A.1
3		B.4					
4			C.5				
5				D.5			
6					$(C.5, D.5, 5)$		
7						$(B.4, (C.5, D.5, 5), 5)$	
8							$(B.4, (C.5, D.5, 5), 5)$
9				D.7			
10					$(C.5, D.7, 7)$		
11						$(B.4, (C.5, D.7, 7), 7)$	
12							$(B.4, (C.5, D.7, 7), 7)$
13			C.8				
14					$(C.8, D.5, 8)$		
15						$(B.4, (C.8, D.5, 8), 8)$	
16							$(B.4, (C.8, D.5, 8), 8)$
17					$(C.8, D.7, 8)$		
18						$(B.4, (C.8, D.7, 8), 8)$	
19							$(B.4, (C.8, D.7, 8), 8)$
20	A.9						
21							A.9

Table 2. Sequential example for *ALL(OR(A,BEFORE(B,AND(C,D))))*

Sequential CHRONICLE Example. Table 3 shows the execution of the same detection tree and history using the *CHRONICLE* semantics. Here, *B.4, C.5,* and *D.5* are consumed by combinations. We indicate the deletion from the operator's buffers by a star (∗) at consumption time. Entries above the ∗ are thus marked as consumed. For example, $B.4$ is consumed at composition time tick 8. With consumption, $C.8$ and $D.7$ cannot lead to new complete composite events as they would in the *ALL* semantics.

ticks	A	B	C	D	AND	BEFORE	OR
1	A.1						
2	∗						A.1
3		B.4					
4			C.5				
5				D.5			
6			∗	∗	$(C.5, D.5, 5)$		
7		∗			∗	$(B.4, (C.5, D.5, 5), 5)$	
8						∗	$(B.4, (C.5, D.5, 5), 5)$
9				D.7			
10			C.8				
11			∗		$(C.8, D.7, 8)$		
12	A.9						
13	∗						A.9

Table 3. Sequential example for *CHRONICLE(OR(A,BEFORE(B,AND(C,D))))*

2.3 Problems of Sequential Event Composition

The examples shows the effects of synchronization:

- Synchronized sequential event detection is *time order preserving*. Each row shows one result, meaning: each operator execution blocks other operators. In each column the results are timely ordered. The execution does not destroy the timely order, due to synchronization. For example, in Table 3 the event $A.9$ is accepted only after $C.8$ has caused results up to the *OR* operator. $A.9$ cannot overtake predecessors which would corrupt the timely order of the result tuples.
- Synchronized sequential event detection is *not efficient*. Since only one operator is active at a time, the others are idle. The small example shows a tendency that can be generalized for real world applications where many events occur. The *ALL* semantics causes exponential increase of intermediate results within the tree. New events will be accepted with increasing delays.

We looked for ways to speed up the composite event detection. In long running applications the number of events and intermediate result explodes exponentially. The sequential execution leads to considerable delays in composite event detection, especially for the *ALL* semantics. As our environment is distributed, we discuss the effects of possible parallel event detection.

3   Two Basic Paradigms for Parallel Event Detection

Parallelization is especially useful for operator trees as introduced in section 2. Stream based operators are well suited for parallel execution. We could relax the synchronization: while operator nodes compute results, the tree accepts new events and computes result sets in parallel to produce the complete set of final results much faster.

In general, operator trees can be executed in parallel by three different strategies: First, *inter-tree-parallelism*: each detector is executed as a single process, all detectors run in concurrent processes. Second, *inter-operator-parallelism*: each operator in a tree is executed in a single specialized process. Third, *intra-operator-parallelism*: each operator is executed by a set of concurrent processes, ideally one for each data entry. All three parallelization strategies can be combined. Inter-tree-parallelization alone leads to a heavy workload for each process, since a single process evaluates all data entries from a leaf to the root in a single sequential program. Both inter- and intra-operator-parallelism add to a much finer granularity and diminish the workload for each process such that we achieve a much better load balancing between processes. In this section, we investigate inter- and intra-operator parallelism and apply it to our language operators for examples. We call the first *pipelining parallelism strategy* (PPS), the latter *universal parallelism strategy* (UPS).

3.1   Pipelining Parallelism Strategy (PPS)

Each operator is performed by a specialized process. Operators are connected by sequential streams. We assume that events are sent to the leafs in partial timely order.

After a start-up delay all operators receive and produce entries concurrently. However, PPS has a serious load balancing problem: while the workload for each operator increases towards the root, the grade of parallelism decreases. The root is a bottleneck with heavy workload. For our operator categories execution works as follows:

- Selector operators like *LEAF* and *ROOT* receive a single input stream, select the appropriate entries and send them to the output stream. For example, the leaf operator for type *A* pipes all entries of type *A* to the output stream.
- Constructor operators like *AND* and *BEFORE* have buffers for each input stream. For each input entry *e* of one operand the buffer of the other operand is searched for appropriate partners. For example, *BEFORE* searches the buffers for entries with appropriate time stamps, and combines pairs. For each entry there may be a set of matching pairs. That set is sent to the output stream; one at a time. Then the entry *e* is added to the corresponding buffer.

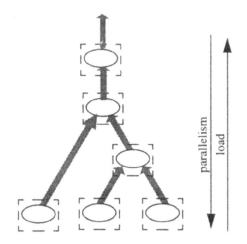

process boundaries

stream

operator

ticks	A	B	C	D	AND	BEFORE	OR
1	A.1 B.4						
2			C.5 D.5				A.1
3	A.9		C.8 D.7		$(C.5, D.5, 5)$		
4					$(C.5, D.7, 7)$	$(B.4, (C.5, D.5, 5), 5)$	A.9
5					$(C.8, D.5, 8)$	$(B.4, (C.5, D.7, 7), 7)$	$(B.4, (C.5, D.5, 5), 5)$
6					$(C.8, D.7, 8)$	$(B.4, (C.8, D.5, 8), 8)$	$(B.4, (C.5, D.7, 7), 7)$
7						$(B.4, (C.8, D.7, 8), 8)$	$(B.4, (C.8, D.5, 8), 8)$
8							$(B.4, (C.8, D.7, 8), 8)$

Table 4. PPS example for $ALL(OR(A, BEFORE(B, AND(C, D))))$

parallelization paradigm operators are interpreted as processes, and stream entries as passive data. In UPS we interpret each stream entry as a process, and the operator tree as passive data. UPS requires a shared everything architecture. The operator tree information is stored in shared memory, and is globally known to each process. For the model, each stream entry is a process. It reads the universal tree information and performs all operations along its path from a leaf to the root node.

Of course, a realistic implementation cannot evaluate each event as a single process, but requires a suitable organization of processes and resources as proposed in [MOW97]. For this paper, we do not discuss resource organization but the general idea of PPS. For the three operator categories execution works as follows:

- If a process performs a selector operator, the process checks the event information If the selection predicate is fulfilled the process resumes for this entry. If not, it terminates.
- Constructor operators are performed symmetrically from both sides — called *left* and *right* — of the input streams. If a process performs a constructor operator coming from input stream *right*, it creates a data entry and appends it to the buffer of *right*. Next, it searches the buffer for *left* for partners, creates new processes for each matching pair, and terminates. As an example, *AND* combines all entries in one buffer to each new entry of the opposite operand, and vice versa.
- If a process performs a collector operator, it passes the collector and resumes.

UPS achieves both pipelining and intra-operator parallelism, because each entry process performs all operators. Between operators the streams are used in a pipelining manner. The fine granularity overcomes the problems of the PPS, because no operator is a bottleneck.

Example: we use the same scenario as in table 4. Each event is a process. Table 5 shows the content and position of an event process. The process for $A.1$ passes the $LEAF(A)$ operator, and next performs the OR operator, which takes one tick. It is now in the output stream of the OR operator, therefore shown as

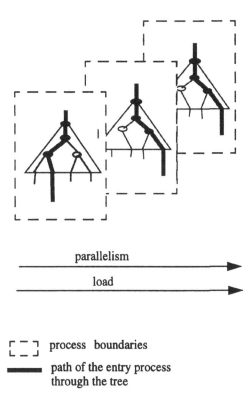

parallelism

load

```
r ¬   ¬
L _  J    process  boundaries

━━━━     path of the entry process
          through the tree
```

Fig. 3. Universial Parallelism Strategy

"result". The result of *AND* at tick 4 is a set of events, all computed in parallel. That set proceeds further in parallel. That is why UPS needs less time than PPS which proceeds one tuple at a time. Especially for the *ALL* semantics, UPS will lead to substantial performance improvements and is a tempting technique.

3.3 Parallel Event Detection and Timely Order

Parallelization overcomes the synchronization delays of sequential execution. Unfortunately, parallel computation may corrupt the timely order of events. We cannot simply adapt parallelization techniques developed for parallel query evaluation in relational DBMS. There, the semantics is set oriented and the base relations are complete. In contrast, composite event detection is based on open — often infinite or silent — streams of events. Cardinality and frequency of incoming events is unpredictable. Timely order is essential:

- Some operators are based on timely order, e.g. *BEFORE*.
- The consumption mode *CHRONICLE* (and variations as described in [Kri94]) requires timely ordered input streams.

ticks	A	B	C	D	AND	BEFORE	OR
1	A.1	B.4					
2			C.5	D.5			A.1
3	A.9		C.8	D.7	$(C.5, D.5, 5)$		
4					$(C.5, D.7, 7)$ $(C.8, D.5, 8)$ $(C.8, D.7, 8)$	$(B.4, (C.5, D.5, 5), 5)$	A.9
5						$(B.4, (C.8, D.5, 8), 8),$ $(B.4, (C.5, D.7, 7), 7),$ $(B.4, (C.8, D.7, 8), 8)$	$(B.4, (C.8, D.5, 5), 5)$
6							$(B.4, (C.8, D.5, 8), 8),$ $(B.4, (C.8, D.7, 8), 8),$ $(B.4, (C.5, D.7, 7), 7)$

Table 5. UPS example for $ALL(OR(A, BEFORE(B, AND(C, D))))$

– Timely order is an important optimization precondition, e.g. *FIRST* produces the result immediately if the input stream is timely ordered.

Therefore we have to find a strategy that respects the timely order of events, if necessary. We now discuss the behavior of PPS and UPS regarding timely order in more detail. As a proposition, we assume the input to the leaf operators to be timely ordered. Generally, we observe the following in operator trees:

1. The structure of the operator tree is unbalanced, i.e. the path lengths differ significantly. We do not assume that processing takes no time, therefore each operator along a path adds to the computation delay. Entries of short subtrees may overtake entries of deep subtrees.
2. The entry load is unbalanced. Due to the open streams, frequency of entries differ among streams. Some constructor operators have to compute more combinations than others. The delay allows other streams to overtake.

PPS and Timely Order. PPS fills and processes streams one tuple at a time. As a consequence, the detection process along one path in the tree is order preserving. However, streams among each other are not synchronized. For reasons described in (1) and (2), events may overtake. For example, A.9 arrives at the OR operator ahead of others with older time stamps (see Table 4, tick 4). As a consequence, the output streams of binary operators will not be ordered by time, unless we block all binary operators and sort the result before resuming.

UPS and Timely Order. In UPS both streams and operators are processed in parallel. Any given order will be destroyed by the execution. In addition to the problem of overtaking as in PPS (see Table 5, tick 4), operators are passed in parallel by several processes. For example, event processes for C.5, D.5, D.7, and C.8 perform the *AND* operation and subsequent operators along the path to the

	ALL(Y)	CHRONICLE(Y)
ALL(X)	Y and X : UPS	Y and X : PPS
CHRONICLE(X)	Y : UPS X : PPS	Y and X : PPS

Table 6. Parallel strategies for *ALL* and *CHRONICLE* combinations

root in parallel, that is, in unpredictable order, depending on resource load (see Table 5, ticks 4 to 6).

4 The SMILE Solution

We propose a combination of UPS if possible, and PPS if necessary. In order to cope with the problems of open streams, we introduce an extension to PPS, called *heartbeats*.

Not all the operators rely on timely order, and the *ALL* semantics for composite event detection is based on sets and produces sets of combinations without any order restrictions. Therefore UPS is a suitable parallelization strategy for *ALL*. The resulting compositions will be produced in arbitrary order, but quickly.

In composite event detection with *CHRONICLE* semantics the timely order of events is essential. The operands have to be sorted before producing results. Sorting might consume any performance improvement of the parallel execution. Since PPS is at least order preserving along paths in the operator tree, we may simply combine heads of timely ordered input streams. Unfortunately collector operators will not produce an ordered output because input streams may overtake each other. The *OR* operator has to sort the input before piping it to the output stream.

The sort itself is sensitive to the unpredictable behavior of open streams, which we call *frequency skew*: one operand is producing frequent results while the other does not. Collector operators have to wait for entries from the silent operand in order to decide which events can be sent to the output stream.

4.1 Hybrid Parallelism

We execute a detector tree according to its semantics either in UPS for *ALL*, or PPS for *CHRONICLE*. A detector might combine both semantics. In that case we differentiate the subtrees accordingly. Given a composition Y based on composition X, we combine the strategies as shown in Table 6. The switch from on strategy to another is done by a special stream operator *ACTIVATE* which create a new process for each incoming entry (switch from PPS to UPS) and, symmetrically, a *SORT* operation that sorts incoming process data and transforms it to passive data (switch from UPS to PPS).

As stated before, unary operators are processed by PPS without any further extensions to the strategy. In order to produce sorted results for binary operators, we have to collect and sort entries in buffers before producing new results after comparing the time stamps. We propose sort-merge joins instead of naive *fifo* construction for constructor operators like *BEFORE* and *AND*.

In oder to overcome the frequency skew problems discussed above, we introduce heartbeats as an extension of the PPS strategy. Heartbeats are dummy events comparable to dummy signals in network environments.

4.2 Heartbeats

A heartbeat is a special event of type H that is produced globally by the ADBMS itself. A heartbeat bears a time stamp as any regular event. The heartbeat type H is a subtype of all other types. For each *CHRONICLE* and *OR* combination in an event expression, copies of a heartbeat event are sent to the leafs of the subtree of *OR* operator. All operators accept heartbeats and send them to their output streams without further selection or construction.

Since streams in PPS in are timely ordered, the heartbeat $H.t$ with time stamp t indicates that the entries in that stream preceding $H.t$ are older or equal than t, while the entries following $H.t$ are younger or equal than t.

As soon as a collector operator receives identical heartbeats from its input streams, the buffers are merged — including one copy of the heartbeat — and sent to the output stream. The buffers are flushed.

Example: based on the history of events: $\langle$ A.1, A.2, A.5, A.8, A.11, A.13, A.14, A.15, B.16,...$\rangle$ we want to detect compositions *CHRONICLE(OR(A,B))* in a history of atomic events. Without heartbeat, all instances of A would have to wait for the first instance of B. In order to speed up the *OR* operator execution, we insert two global heartbeats to the history: $\langle$A.1, A.2, A.5, H.6, A.8, A.11, A.13, A14, A.15,B.16,H.16, ...$\rangle$.

ticks	LEAF(A)	LEAF(B)	OR
1	A.1		
2	A.2		
3	A.5		
4	H.6		
5	A.8		
6	A.11	H.6	
7			A.1
8	A.13		A.2
9	A.14		A.5
10	A.15		H.6
11	H.16	B.16	
12	...	H.16	
13		...	A.8
14			A.11
15			A.13
16			A.14
17			A.15
18			A.16
19			B.16
20			H.16
21			...

Table 7. Heartbeat example

Table 7 shows a section of the execution. Both leaves eventually receive and propagate H.6, see ticks 4 and 6. *LEAF(B)* sends the heartbeat as its first entry, since B.16 has not yet occurred. As soon as *OR* has received H.6, it merges all buffered entries into the output stream. Since the right operand buffer contains no entries of type B, it sends the buffered section of A.1,A.2, and A.5, followed by the heart beat, see ticks 7 to 10. During the following period *OR* receives and buffers instances from both A and B before the next heartbeat $H.16$. The buffers are merged without waiting for the heartbeats, and $B.16$ is sent along with instances of A.

The example illustrates that collector operators like OR now produce events at discrete heartbeat pulses. The heartbeat limits buffer space and enables the detector to produce possible event compositions as early as possible. In contrast to sequential detection, which immediately produces the first composition instance, the heartbeat pulse might delay composition instances for at most one heartbeat. But PPS then will produce results much faster than a sequential execution.

5 Related Research

At first view the issue of complex event detection with operator trees is closely related to the processing of time-series in temporal data base systems (cf. [SS87], [TCG⁺93]), or the processing of general sequence data (cf. [SLR96]). In those areas the timely order of data is essential. But temporal queries process completely stored data. This correspond only to composite event detection in a persistent history of past events, whereas the immediate detection of new composition instances from open streams is a new issue here.

Parallel processing in relational DBMS has been a research topic for a long time ([DG92], [Val93]). Relational DBMS are good candidates for performance improvements by parallelization because of the set-oriented nature of relations. The sequence-oriented second nature of time-series spoils set-oriented parallelization in temporal database systems. So, research for temporal databases is taking very first steps towards parallel processing ([KBO90], [MOW97]). The considered parallelization strategies are only feasible for stored data, and not for continuous processing as needed for composite event detection.

Most ADBMS approaches propose centralized, sequential detection of composite events. As an exception, Schwiderski et al. [SHM95] discuss time stamping and timely order of results in distributed composite event detection based on operator trees with the $CHRONICLE$ semantics. The trees themselves are distributed across sites. The approach introduces two detection algorithms: a synchronized algorithm where operator nodes request for each input entry from other sites and an asynchronous algorithm where nodes accept input entries irrespectively of timely order. The synchronized algorithm enforces timely order of results, which may lead to unpredictable delays due to failure of sites. In that case, delays may completely block the operator. Entries are buffered and merged comparably to our PPS approach. Parallelization itself is not the scope of the paper, but the distributed detection process leads to concurrent evaluation. In contrast, our approach assumes centralized event detection. We propose a parallel strategy suitable for the $CHRONICLE$ and the ALL semantics, respecting timely order of events, and use both PPS and UPS.

6 Conclusion and Future Work

Our hybrid approach for parallel event detection is a useful optimization for applications where many trees have to cope with frequent and unsynchronized events. The paper discusses the parallelization with the help of a subset of event operator languages. The basic discussion of collectors, constructors, and selectors can be extended and applied to other ADBMS languages as well.

While UPS is suitable for the general *ALL* semantics, PPS with heartbeat extension is used for *CHRONICLE* semantics, as an example for time preserving parallelism. Our prototype implementation currently is based on the parallel programming language C-Linda [CG89], having a network of 6 SPARCstations with 8 processors in total. Both PPS and UPS are implemented for the discussed example operators.

Future work will investigate the dynamics of heartbeats in more detail. The frequency of heartbeats depends on elapsed time and the number of events already arrived at the buffers. The detector may dynamically increase the frequency if its buffers overflow, or decrease if the operators receive too many heartbeats. We may produce more than one global heartbeat for all detectors and use individual heartbeats for each disjoint *OR* subtree in the forest. This allows us to adjust the heartbeat frequency to the behavior of individual subtree streams.

References

[BBKZ92] A.P. Buchman, H. Branding, T. Kudrass, and J. Zimmermann. REACH: A REal-Time, ACtive and Heterogenous Mediator System. *IEEE Bulletin of the Technical Committee on Data Engineering*, Vol. 15(No. 1-4), December 1992.

[Beh95] H. Behrends. *Specification of Event Driven Activities in Data Information Systems*. PhD thesis, University of Oldenburg, Germany (in German), October 1995.

[BZBW95] A.P. Buchmann, J. Zimmermann, J.A. Blakeley, and D.L. Wells. Building an Integrated Active OODBMS: Requirements, Architecture, and Design Decisions. In *Proc. 11th Intl. Conf. on Data Engineering*, Taipei, Taiwan, March 1995. IEEE, IEEE Computer Society Press.

[CG89] N. Carriero and D. Gelernter. How to Write Parallel Programs: A Guide to the Perplexed. *ACM Computing Surveys*, Vol. 21(No. 3), September 1989.

[CKAK94] S. Chakravarthy, V. Krishnaprasad, E. Anwar, and S.K. Kim. Composite Events for Active Databases: Semantics, Contexts and Detection. In *Proc. Int'l. Conf. on Very Large Data Bases VLDB*, Santiago, Chile, 1994.

[DBM88] U. Dayal, A. Buchmann, and D McCarthy. Rules are objects too: a knowledge model for an active, object-oriented database system. In *Proc. 2nd Int'l. Workshop on Object-Oriented Database Systems*, Lecture Notes in Computer Science 334. Springer, 1988.

[DG92] D. J. DeWitt and J. Gray. Parallel Database Systems: The Future of High Performance Database Systems. *Communications of the ACM*, 35(6), June 1992.

[Gat95]   S. Gatziu. *Events in an Active, Object-Oriented Database System*. PhD thesis, Univerisity of Zurich, Switzerland, 1995.

[GD92]   S. Gatziu and K.R. Dittrich. SAMOS: An Active Object-Oriented Database System. *IEEE Quarterly Bulletin on Data Engineering*, 15(1-4), December 1992.

[GD94]   S. Gatziu and K. Dittrich. Detecting Composite Events in Active Database Systems Using Petri Nets. In *IEEE RIDE Proc. 4th Int'l. Workshop on Research Issues in Data Engineering*, Houston, Texas, USA, February 1994.

[GJS92a]   N. Gehani, H.V. Jagadish, and O. Shumeli. Composite Event Specification in Active Databases: Model and Implementation. In *Proc. 18th Int'l Conf. on Very Large Data Bases*, Vancouver, Canada, Aug 1992.

[GJS92b]   N. Gehani, H.V. Jagadish, and O. Shumeli. Event Specification in an Active Object-Oriented Database. In *Proc 1992 ACM-SIGMOD Conf. on Management of Data*, San Diego, California, Jun 1992.

[Jae95]   U. Jaeger. SMILE — A Framework for Lossless Situation Detection. In *Proc 1995 Int'l Workshop on Indformation Technologies and Systems*, Nijenrode, The Netherlands, December 1995.

[KBO90]   S. Karimi, M. Bassiouni, and A. Orooji. Supporting Temporal Capabilities in a Multi-Computer Database System. In *Proc. Int'l Conf. on Databases, Parallel Architectures and Their Applications* , Miami Beach, Florida, USA, March 1990.

[Kri94]   V. Krishnaprasad. Event Detection for Supporting Active Capabilities in an Active OODB: Semantics, Architecture, and Implementation. Master's thesis, University of Florida, USA, 1994.

[MOW97]   S. Manegold, J. K. Obermaier, and F. Waas. Load Balanced Query Evaluation in Shared-Everything Environments. In *Proc. European Conf. in Parallel Processing*, Passau, Germany, August 1997.

[PW93]   N. Paton and M. Williams, editors. *Rules in Database Systems.*, Workshops in Computing. Springer, September 1993.

[SHM95]   S. Schwiderski, A. Herbert, and K. Moody. Composite Events for Detecting Behavior Patterns in Distributed Environments. *TAPOS Distributed Object Management*, July 1995.

[SLR96]   P. Sheshadri, M. Livny, and R. Ramakrishnan. The Design and Implementation of a Sequence Database System. In *Proc. Int'l Conf. on Very Large Data Bases*, Bombay, India, September 1996.

[SS87]   A. Segev and A. Shoshani. Logical Modeling of Temporal Data. In *Proc. ACM SIGMOD Int'l Conf.*, San Francisco, California, USA, May 1987.

[TCG+93]   A. U. Tansel, J. Clifford, S. Gadia, S. Jajodia, A. Segev, and R. Snodgrass. *Temporal Databases — Theory, Design, and Implementation*. Benjamin/Cummings, Redwood City, CA, USA, 1993.

[Val93]   P. Valduriez. Parallel Database Systems: Open Problems and New Issues. *Distr. and Parallel Databases*, 1(2), 1993.

[WC94]   J. Widom and S. Chakravarthy. *Proc. Intl. Workshop on Research Issues in Data Engineering RIDE 1994*. Morgan Kaufman, Houston, Texas, USA, February 1994.

Toward Duration-Based, Constrained and Dynamic Event Types

Claudia L. Roncancio

Lab. LSR - Institut National Polytechnique de Grenoble
BP 72, 38402 St. Martin d'Hères Cedex - FRANCE
e-mail: Claudia.Roncancio@imag.fr
Phone: (33) 4.76.82.72.81
Fax:(33)4.76.82.72.87

Abstract. We propose in this paper an event model supporting duration-based, constrained and dynamic event types. We believe that many real applications using active DBMS strongly need the possibility of defining and handling higher level events. Our model aims to provide such a kind of events, with a more natural programming interface, making easier the mapping of real events into events supported by the DBMS. The proposed model is intended to be used in a DBMS with temporal and active capabilities. Dynamic event types are particularly interesting in such a system.

1 Introduction

Active database management systems (ADBMS) (Widom et al. [WiCe96], ACT-NET [ACT96]) perform operations automatically in response to events. The "active behaviour" in this systems is usually defined through Event-Condition-Action rules. The event part, or more precisely the event type, specifies what brings the rule to be triggered. Several projects have worked on the definition of event types (Chakravarthy et al. [ChMi94], Gatziu et al. [GaDi93], Meo et al. [MPC96]).

Most existing event definition languages offer a low abstraction level, close to the system. This is essentially due to implementation reasons: the ADBMS must always be able to detect events in an unambiguous manner. As a consequence, many events are difficult (and in some cases even impossible) to describe in these languages, despite their expressiveness.

We propose in this paper an event model providing duration-based events as well as the possibility to associate conditions within them. Moreover, it allows to define dynamic event types. It is an attempt to facilitate the task of the user when defining events.

One of the main characteristics of the proposed model is that it integrates the fact that events have a duration, as in real life. This is not commonly found in active databases where events are considered as being "instantaneous" (Collet et al. [CoCo96], Gatziu et al. [GaDi93]).

Events, we consider, can have a duration which can be greater than an instant. We have defined operators for composing events with a duration-based semantics. These operators are an adaptation of the operators proposed by certain active databases (Chakravarthy [ChMi94], Collet et al. [CCR96], and [CoCo96], Gatziu et al. [GaDi93]) and the operators of Allen [Allen83].

The study of several applications (Front et al. [FRG96]) has confirmed the importance of masks within the event type definition. Masks are boolean conditions concerning the context associated to the event. Event types with masks allow a better description of logical events. We integrate in our proposal masks in the style of Berndtsson and Lings [BeLi95] or Gehani et al. [GJS92].

The last important element of our proposal is the introduction of dynamic event types. Until now, event types were always specified statically by using the database schema definitions and, for temporal events, by giving dates. What we propose now is to allow the use of data (stored in the database) *as* event types. We exploit the fact that temporal data have intrinsically an event nature. Dynamic event types depends on the database state. Our proposal also allows to correlate data to temporal events. To our knowledge, these facilities are not supported by actual event models.

We believe that this idea of dynamic event types opens many interesting possibilities and seems to be useful in several contexts, in particularly if the ADBMS offers temporal facilities.

Our work could apply to any active system regardless of the data model. In the following we place our proposal in an object oriented context as it offers more possibilities for event expressions and allows us to rely on previous work related to NAOS (Collet et al. [CoCo96] and [CCR96]).

The paper is organized as follows: section 2 presents motivation of our work. Section 3 details most aspects of our event model, including composite event definitions and filters. Section 4, introduces dynamic events. Section 5, discusses on implementation issues and section 6 presents related work. Section 7 closes the paper with conclusions and research directions.

2 Motivation

The main motivation of our work is to propose an event model integrating the best features of classic event models with some other features that allow to specify events at a higher level. Duration-based events are the first element introduced in this objective. For instance, let A and B be events. In our model, it is possible to specify the following event:

A during B

In classic models, such an event would be specified as something similar to:

begin-of(B); begin-of(A); end-of(A); end-of(B)

where ; corresponds to the sequence operator. Moreover, it would be necessary to make sure that the event end-of(A) (respect. B) corresponds to the appropriate begin-of(A) (respect. B). Let us give a concrete example of duration-based events. If a user wishes to be notified when a program is compiled, then the relevant event is the compilation, that takes a certain time to be completed. Most active databases doesnt't support such an event but only event types corresponding to the "beginning of the compilation" and "end of the compilation". These events have a duration which is negligible. Now suppose that the user wants to be notified when the program source is modified during its compilation. In most existing event languages it is difficult and sometimes impossible to specify such a situation.

The second element introduced in our model are masks. The usefulness of masks in event types seems to be clear. Nevertheless, let us illustrate it with an example from a medical application. One may be interested in the event "the temperature of a patient is more than 40°C". If the corresponding event type does not include a mask, the event will only be "modification of the temperature", being necessary to test if the temperature is greater than 40°C during the evaluation of the condition part of the rule. A mask associated to the event will allow to define with more precision the desired events.

Finally, our model proposes dynamic event types. Indeed in many applications where temporal data is stored in the database, this data often corresponds to events. Here events are not operations on data but the data itself. Consider for instance a database storing information concerning passports. Each passport has a property (`Passport.expiry_date`) storing the date at which the passport expires. Now, we want to execute an action at this date, using an active rule for this purpose. Notice that in ADBMS, temporal events are expressed explicitly as " *1/1/1997* " or " *2 days after E* ", where E denotes an event. So if we want to trigger rules at the expiry date of a passport, we have to define a rule per passport giving explicitly the date at which it expires. Furthermore, this is insufficient as temporal events generally never have a context, making difficult to identify and refer to the appropriate passport. In summary, defining such an event is rather cumbersome.

We propose in our model the possibility to directly use data stored in the database to define event types:
`on Passport.expiry_date do ...`
This specifies a dynamic event type corresponding to the temporal events defined by the expiry date of passports. The event type will be dynamically "instantiated" with the expiry date of each passport present in the database. That means that an absolute temporal event will be automatically created using the appropriate dates. See section 4 for more information.

Generally stated, our work was motivated by our will to integrate the work done in the active database and temporal database fields. We think that many application areas need DBMS including temporal and active facilities (Ramamamritham [RSSTX96]). This does not simply mean putting together the results of both fields in a single system but trying to perform a more consistent integration. Our work proposes a step forward the integration of active and temporal databases.

3 Duration-based events

3.1 Intuitive definition of duration-based events

An event type defines a class of a "happening of interest" taking place over time. Some events are not instantaneous having a duration going from the instant when the event starts until the instant when it disappears. For example, compiling a program could be seen as an event which corresponds to an interval of time. We call this interval *occurrence period*, the two bounds of the interval being the points in time where the compilation starts (beginning of the event) and ends (end of the event).

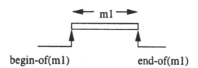

begin-of(m1)   end-of(m1)

Fig. 1. Duration-based event

In the active database domain, events are usually considered with an "instantaneous" semantics. That means that events happen at a point in time and it is not possible to refer to its duration. The (primitive) events considered in this context are mostly in the form "beginning of" and "end of" an operation (e.g. a method call, an update). They do not have a duration but the operation itself does. In real life, all operations have a duration. We propose an event model general enough as to allow the reasoning on the duration of events. The duration may be only an instant (e.g. the "beginning of something" event) or an even longer time (e.g. a method or a transaction). The chronon (Jensen et al. [JCGSS92]) is the shortest duration of time supported by the system and is the duration associated to instantaneous events.

Note that duration-based events can be considered as a level on top of instantaneous events.

Events are usually classified as primitive or composite. Our proposal uses the same classification. Section 3.2 presents primitive events. Section 3.3 introduces composite events defining operators to compose events with a duration-based semantics.

3.2 Primitive logical events

We consider hereafter primitive events as logical because we give them a duration-based semantics as it occurs in reality.

Database and application events Database events are related to read/write operations on objects, method calls and transaction executions. Application events are mainly events issued by program executions. The duration of event instances may vary. If, for example, we are interested in the execution of method m1 of class C, we express this as

    on C.m1()
    do /* some action */

The event will be notified at the end of the execution ofm1, the occurrence period being the time interval while the execution takes place (see Fig. 1). The occurrence period is part of the context of the event. So it may be used in any other part of the active rule (see 3.4).

The usual modifiers begin-of and end-ofare also integrated. For example:

    on begin-of C.m1() ...

These modifiers may be applied to primitive events, the duration of the resulting event being 1 chronon. In this way, events usually expressed with the instantaneous event specifications continue to be supported.

Temporal events Temporal events play an important role in many application areas. It is important to integrate in event models facilities for time handling which have already been well defined by the temporal database community (Fauvet et al. [FCS96a]. So, we integrate temporal concepts as *instants*, *durations* and *intervals* in the definition of event types. Time values may be specified at a different granularity: year, month, day, hour and minute. For instance:

    4/11/1997

and

    6/1997

are two valid instants. The first one uses the granularity of the day while the second one the granularity of a month. Note that 4/11/1997 is also an interval at a finer granularity (see Fauvet et al. [FCS96a] for a complete definition of instants). The occurrence period of this event is, the entire duration of the day (from 0:00 to 23:59).It will be notified at the end of the day. The begin-of (resp. end-of) modifier may be used to specify events corresponding to the beginning (resp. end) of the time value. Their granularity[1] in this case is the minute.

An interval is specified by two instants as:

    [1/1/1997, 31/5/1997]

An interval is a temporal events. Its occurrence period is the interval itself.

A duration[2] is an amount of time with known length. The supported duration unities are minute, hour, day, week, month and year. For instance:

    "6 weeks 2 days".

Durations are not events but may be used to define time spans in an event type. It is possible to specify relative events as *"8 days after the sale"*. These events are considered composite (see 3.3).

Periodic events are also supported. The period and the validity interval are specified as follows:

---

[1] Technically it would be possible to consider the second, but we submit that in our context the minute is sufficient.

[2] called positive span in Jensen et al. [JCGSS92].

`every 2 months from 1/1/1997 until 12/31/1997`

It is also possible to use the keyword during to introduce the validity interval:

`every 2 months during 1997`

The occurrence period of the events (and therefore their duration) is defined by the period.

We intend to integrate the work reported in Canavaggio and Dumas [CaDu97] in our model in order to allow different specification forms for temporal values such as "April 11,1997" and "11/4/1997".

External events Active DBMS usually include external events with an instantaneous approach. An external event type is defined by a name and a list of parameters which are then used in rules. For example,   on *alarm* do...

Event instances are signaled by the user to the DBMS, by means of a single notification in the style of:

`notify("alarm");`

In our model we maintain this kind of external event and introduce a new kind of external events which represents external events having a significant duration (e.g., a surgical operation). These kind of events are signaled with two notifications corresponding to the beginning and the end of the event. When the notification of the beginning is performed, the ADBMS return an event instance identifier. The notification of the end of the external event must include this identifier in order to allow the matching with beginnings. For example, for the external event *surgical_operation*, we specify parameters corresponding to the operation room number and the person in charge of this room. The notification of the beginning of the operation will be:

`notify_start("surgical_operation", 203, "Ortiz")`

The system returns an event instance identifier, i, used in the notification of the end:

`notify_end("surgical_operation", i ).`

The use of duration-based external events in ECA rules still the same than for instantaneous events. For example,

`on surgical_operation( room, person) do ...`

The two notifications related to the event define its occurrence period. It is also possible to use the modifiers begin-of and end-of.

3.3 Composite logical events

Composite events are defined using primitive events and composing operators. We have reviewed the operators proposed for "instantaneous" events (in the style of Chakravarthy [CKAK94], Collet et al. [CoCo96] and Gatziu et al. [GaDi93]) and we integrate new features for the duration-based semantics of events.

Allen [Allen83] considers a complete list of the different temporal relations among intervals. These relations are usually considered with a boolean semantics. We propose event operators based on these some temporal relations: in addition to the boolean semantics we propose an event semantics.

The composite event operators issued from temporal relations between intervals are: precedes, overlap, during, equal, meets, starts, and end. The logical operators are conjunction (**and**) and disjunction (**or**). Another useful operator we propose is the absence (**abs**). The definitions of these operators are given hereafter.

Fig. 2 illustrates events defined with temporal relation operators. White lines correspond to the operands and black lines to the resulting event. Time grows from left to right. Lines illustrate the occurrence period (*op*) of events ; the length of the line is the duration of the event. The black line shows the occurrence period of the resulting composite event. Recall that *op* is a time interval. *begin-op* is a function returning the left bound of the *op* of an event; *end-op* returns the right bound.

For the sake of completeness, we have defined the event semantics with all the temporal relations. Nevertheless, it may not be necessary to differentiate all the situations. Some of them could be merged. For the time being, we have not studied a full set of applications to determine which operators are essential. The operators are:

precedes: A precedes B
The end of event A precedes the beginning of event B.
$op(A \text{ precedes } B) = [\ begin\text{-}op(A), \ end\text{-}op(B)]$

during: A during B
Event A happens during event B (i.e. A starts after the beginning of B and ends before the end of B).
$op(A \text{ during } B) = [\ begin\text{-}op(A), \ end\text{-}op(A)]$

overlaps: A overlaps B
The beginning of A is before the beginning of B and the end of A is during B or vice versa.
$op(A \text{ overlaps } B) = [\ latest(\ begin\text{-}op(A), \ begin\text{-}op(B)),$
$$earliest(\ end\text{-}op(A), \ end\text{-}op(B) \ ) \ ]$$

starts: A starts B
The beginning of A and B are simultaneous. This operator is commutative.
$op(A \text{ starts } B) = [\ begin\text{-}op(A), \ latest(end\text{-}op(A), \ end\text{-}op(B)) \ ]$

equal: A equal B
The beginning of A and B are simultaneous as are their ends. The **equal** operator is commutative.
$op(A \text{ equal } B) = [\ begin\text{-}op(A), \ end\text{-}op(A)]$

ends: A ends B
The end of A and B are simultaneous. The **ends** operator is commutative.
$op(A \text{ ends } B) = [\ \mathbf{earliest}(begin\text{-}op(A), \ begin\text{-}op(B)), \ end\text{-}op(A) \ ]$

meets: **A meets B**
    The beginning of B is immediately after the end of A.
    op (**A meets B**) = [*begin-op(A), end-op(B)*]

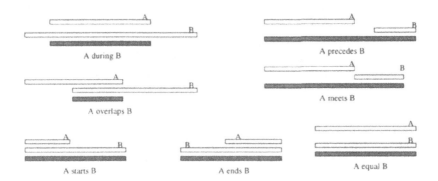

Fig. 2. Semantics of events using temporal relation operators

or: **A or B**
    Either **A** or **B** happens. The occurrence period of the disjunction corresponds to the event that happens.

and: **A and B**
    A and **B** both happen, in any order.
    *op(***A** **and** **B***)* = [*earliest-of(begin-op(***A***), begin-op(***B***)),*
                    *latest-of(end-op(***A***), end-op(***B***))]*
    Note that the temporal relation among **A** and **B** can be any of those presented in the preceding paragraphs. Nevertheless, **A and B** is not really equivalent to the disjunction of **A precedes B, A overlaps B**, etc. because of the occurrence period definition.

+: **A +**Δ
    A time span Δ (or duration, see 3.2) after the end of event **A**.
    *op(***A** **+**Δ*)* = [*end-op(***A***), end-op(***A***)+*Δ]

*absence:*abs(**A**)
    This expresses that event **A** does not happen; it is absent.
    This operator is often named negation (Collet et al. [CoCo96], Gatziu et al. [GaDi93]) but as its semantics do not correspond to logical negation, we consider that for the user, the word absence is more explicit. **abs**(**A**) is a special case, by itself, it is not an event. It can only be used within a context which delimits the time interval (monitoring interval) where the absence of **A** must be verified. For example, consider **B**, an event type with a complete defined occurrence period.

`abs(A) during B`

is a well defined event type. The event occurs if A does not occur during the occurrence period of B. The occurrence period associated to `abs(A) during B` is identical to that of B. On the other hand:

`abs(A) precedes B`

is not a well defined event type because only the right bound of the monitoring interval is defined. Only completely bounded event types are accepted. The bounding rules for all the operators are described in Poitou [Poi96].

To finish this section, one should note that events usually expressed in "instantaneous" systems are still available by using begin-of and end-of primitive events.

Event notification In presenting the different composite events we have not detailed when, exactly, the events are recognized and notified. In the following this point is called nt (notification time). We specify the nt for each operator[3].

`A precedes B`
  $nt = end\text{-}op(B)$
`A during B`
  If primitive-event(B) or time-event(B)[4]
  then $nt = end\text{-}op(A)$
  If composite-event(B)[5] then $nt = end\text{-}op(B)$.
`A overlaps B`
  Same as during.
`A starts B`
  $nt = latest(\ end\text{-}op(A),\ end\text{-}op(B))$
`A ends B`
  Same as starts
`A equal B`
  $nt = end\text{-}op(A) = end\text{-}op(B)$
`A meets B`
  $nt = end\text{-}op(B)$
`A or B`
  If A happens then $nt = end\text{-}op(A)$ else $nt = end\text{-}op(B)$
`A and B`
  $nt = latest(end\text{-}op(A),\ end\text{-}op(B))$
`A +Δ`
  $nt = end\text{-}op(A) + \Delta$
`abs(A)`
  The nt of an event containing an `abs(A)` is the nt of the event defining the monitoring interval.

---

[3] In some cases the nt of an event is later than its $end\text{-}op$.
[4] Including events of the form C + X
[5] Excluding events of the form C + X

3.4 Masks

Masks are conditions integrated into the event specification. They are not intended to replace the condition part of the rules but to allow the user to better specify the triggering situation in the event portion. Several of real life events(Front et al. [FRG96]) need such a mask to be expressed and when the active system does not support this feature, the condition part of the ECA rule is used for this purpose. That makes rule writing and understanding more difficult.

Masks are conditions on the parameters of the event, on the context or on the time at which it occurs. In general, the information associated with an event is available through a name (a pseudo-variable[6]) given by the user, for example e in the following where we suppose that appointment is a method of the class Service :

on Service.appointment(patient, date)e ...

The parameters of an event depend on its type. In the above example, the actual parameters of the method are available and can be denoted by

e.patient and e.date

If the events in which we are interested are, for example, the appointments of children, then we would formulate that as follows:

Service.appointment(patient, date)e {e.patient.age < 12}

Context information is available through functions which can be applied to the delta element. These functions are the following:

obj(): returns the identifier of the object concerned by the event (e.g. the receiver for method events).

trans(): returns the identifier of the transaction where the event occurred (e.g. trans(e)).

appli(): returns the identifier of the application where the event occurred.

These functions are not defined for all event types. For example, they are not available for temporal events. A complete definition can be found in Poitou [Poi96].

The occurrence period (functions op, begin-op and end-op) and notification time (function nt) are also available.

Masks are expressions written as a conjunction or a disjunction of terms. A term is of the form:

<event_data> <op> <constant> |
<event_data> <op > <event_data> |
same obj| same trans | same appli

where <event_data> is any of the data of the event context (described in the preceding paragraphs), <op> is a comparative operator (<, =, ...) and <constant> is a constant value. The terms starting with same are a simplification to express that the whole event applies to the same object, transaction or application.

To conclude this section we would like to comment that a good support of masks contribute to the optimization of the active system. A more precise event

---

[6] delta element in Collet et al. [CCS96]

specification avoids useless rule selections and triggering which can be quite time consuming (Berndtsson and Lings [BeLi95], Geppert et al. [GBLR96]).

4 Dynamic events

Event types defined in section 3 and in the known related works, are explicit or *static event types*. They are static in that (apart from masks) the event type is completely specified using elements of the database schema (e.g. *update of the attribute x of object of class y*) and constant values. It is not possible to dynamically integrate data into the event type. Let us consider a database containing data about students grants. They are granted for a precise time period which is stored in the database. If we want an action to be triggered when the beginning of the student grants arrive, we would like to use an ECA rule with the event *"the beginning date of a student grant"*. The usual method in active systems is to explicitly give the date corresponding to this event. For example, if a grant begins the 1 january 1997, a rule such as

    on 1/1/1997 do ...

has to be defined. Note that

- in this specification there is no relation between the event (the date) and the student grant which begins at this date. No context is as of yet associated to temporal events in the existing proposals [7].
- For each grant, the user has to define an absolute event type corresponding to the beginning date of the grant. For that, he/she has to query the database to get the dates.
- If the beginning of a grant is modified the user has to modify the corresponding event/rule.

To overcome these difficulties and to allow the expression of events in a more natural way, we introduce dynamic event types. The basic idea of dynamic event types is to automatize the last two points given above. For dynamic event types, the system automatically queries the database to dynamically create the appropriate (static) event types.

In the preceding example, suppose that `Grant.beginning` designates the attribute storing the date at which the grant begins. We introduce the dynamic event type `Grant.beginning`. The current corresponding temporal static event types are calculated by the system depending on the database state.

Consider the case of a database storing data related to projects. A project (see Example 1 hereafter) is defined by its name, participants, the starting date, the deadline, the duration of the specification phase and the period devoted to programming.

```
Class Project inherit Object
tuple ( name: string,
```

---

[7] to the best of our knowledge !

```
participants: set( Person),
starting_date: Instant,
 deadline: Instnt,
 spec_time: Duration,
prog_periode: Interval )
```

Example 1: Class Project.

In Example 1, Instant, Duration and Interval are classes implementing these temporal concepts (as in Canavaggio and Dumas [CaDu97]).

Now, to trigger an action at the deadline of each project, we use a rule as follows:

```
on Project.deadline
do { /*action1*/ }
```

Project.deadline is a dynamic event type which specifies a set of temporal static event types. This set is created dynamically by selecting the deadline of each project of the database. If for example, the database stores 2 projects named α and β whose deadlines are respectively the 28 June 1997 and the 31 December, 1997, the system will create two temporal static event types corresponding to these dates. The rule, defined above, will be triggered twice:

– the 28 th June, 1997 for project α and
– the 31 st December 1997 for project β.

Please, note the "dynamic" nature of our new kind of event types: they depend on the database state. Modifications of the data can imply modifications to the set of temporal static event types associated to each dynamic event type. For example, if the deadline of a project is modified or a new project is inserted into the database, all relevant updates are propagated to the set of temporal static event types corresponding to each dynamic type.

We use the term *dynamic event types* but one could also consider them as "generic" event types as each type (e.g. Project.deadline) is instantiated with different values leading to "bound" event types (e.g. 6/28/1997).

More concretely, we propose to express temporal events (including durations) by using temporal values stored in the database. For example:

```
on Project.starting_date + Project.spec_time {same object}
do ...[1]
```

This dynamic event type specifies the events corresponding to the date after the specification phase which begins at the starting date of the project.

Syntactically, dynamic event types are path expressions [8] which ends in a component of a temporal type: durations, intervals or instants. For example in [1], we use Project.starting_date of type Instant and Project.spec_time of type Duration. Of course, the context of use defines type restrictions.

---

[8] Objects can not be traversed.

Because of implementation issues, a dynamic event type have to depend on a single entity. For example, the following event [2] is not accepted whereas [1], above, is.

    on Project.starting_date + Project.spec_time [2]

In section 3 we have seen that a context is associated with events and it can be referred to through pseudo variables. But no context was defined for temporal events. For dynamic event types we introduce again the possibility of using contexts. That means that the temporal static event types generated for each dynamic event type have a context. For example, the following rule uses a dynamic event type with a pseudo-variable i to refer to the event context:

    on Project.deadline i [3]
    do { /* send a mail to the participants of the project */ }

Through i, the concerned Project object will be available in the condition and action parts of the rule (as for static event types of section 3). Considering the database with the α and β projects, the triggering of [3] the 6/28/1997 will have the object α in its event context whereas the triggering at 12/31/1997 will have object β. For example, the event context allows, the direct retrieval of the list of participants of the project which finishes.

Dynamic event types introduce a new way of specifying temporal events and they integrate well in the model proposed in section 3. In particular, composite event types can include static and dynamic[9] event types. For example:

    on Employee.raise_salary() during summer_holidays

Here, summer_holidays is an entity in the database of type Interval and raise_salary a method of class Employee. Another example, in a medical context:

    every 4 weeks during Patient.pregnancy_period

where Patient.pregnancy_period is a property of type interval.

The dynamic feature is orthogonal to the event model; it could be integrated to other event models supporting temporal events. Nevertheless, we think that the use of duration based events facilitates the integration of temporal data stored in the database.

Although not introduced in this article, with dynamic events it will also be possible to support relative events specifying an instant before another. For example, *3 weeks before the end of projects* (Project.deadline - 3 weeks) or, in a medical context, *two months before the delivery of the baby*. This kind of event seems to be quite useful, in particular for planning activities in any domain.

5   Implementation

The proposed model may be implemented on top of an ADBMS supporting events with instantaneous semantics. Our implementation of the event model is an extension of the event handler of NAOS 2.2.3 (Collet et al.[CCFR97]). This event handler works on "instantaneous" events and has two components: (a)

---

[9] The dynamic part can not depend on several objects

the *event detector* which is responsible for the detection of primitive database events and (b) the *event manager* which is responsible of user and time events and the detection of composite events. Both components must be modified for the support of duration-based events.

The event detector is integrated into the O2 engine. It has to be modified in order to include more information in the context associated with events. The new information is mainly a transaction identifier for all event instances occurring within a transaction, the occurring time of events, and an *execution identifier* for events related to methods and programs. The *execution identifier* allows to recognize, for instance, which "end-of method" event matches to which "begin-of method" event. Notice that the method name and the value of all the parameters are contained in the context of the event instance but they are not precise enough[10] to be used as an execution identifier.

The event detector notifies primitive events with an "instantaneous" semantics. Primitive duration-based events are identified by the event manager. They are handled as composite events. The composite event detector works on a graph representation of event types (Collet et al. [CoCo96]). Primitive "instantaneous" event instances are injected in the leaves of the graph. Then, these events flow upward, following the edges through internal nodes which construct composite events. There is one type of node per event operator and for the primitive duration-based event types. A node devoted to the recognition of a primitive duration-based event of type E receives the instantaneous events corresponding to the begin-of(E) and end-of(E). It verifies the correspondence to a single instance of E and if this is the case, then the context of the new instance of type E is calculated and the instance flows up through the graph.

For the evaluation of masks the first implementation we considered is the evaluation of the mask at the end, when an event is completely recognized. The mask is associated with the root node of the detection tree of the event type. This solution is not very efficient because it implies the buffering of a number of useless intermediate events. We intend to apply here an optimization technique often used in query evaluations: the mask is decomposed into terms and each term is evaluated as soon as possible. This means that a term is associated with the node of the tree the closer to the leaves where it can be evaluated.

For the implementation of dynamic event types we consider them as derived events and use active rules to maintain derived data. The implementation consists of the following main steps:

1. Instantiation of a dynamic event type with the corresponding values: we get the explicit temporal values to be used.
2. Creation of the corresponding static event types.
3. Creation of active rules intended to propagate updates to the static event types created in step 2. If the value used in the event type comes from an attribute A of an object O, then any modification of A will have a repercus-

---

[10] Not to mention that using this information as execution identifier would be a more time costly solution.

sion on the event type. Note that update propagation is always possible as dynamic event types depend on a single entity.

When the static event types are created, the detection mechanism is similar to the one currently implemented in NAOS for temporal events (Collet et al. [CCFR97], Fayolle [Fay97]). One of the most important differences is that for dynamic event types, the system associates a context with the corresponding temporal events.

The temporal event detector launches separate processes and uses directly operating system facilities. Dynamic event types are not already implemented but, as far as we are, we dont see particular efficiency problems.

6 Related Work

Several works have been done on event models. Among them (in object oriented contexts) Samos (Gatziu et al. [GaDi93]), Ode (Gehani et al. [GJS92]), Snoop/Sentinel (Chakravarthy et al. [ChMi94]), Acood (Berndtsson and Lings [BeLi95]), NAOS (Collet et al. [CoCo96]) and Chimera (Meo et al. [MPC96]). They propose primitive events and different constructors for composite events which in general include the sequence, conjunction, disjunction, negation (absence) operators. To the best of our knowledge all these works concern events with instantaneous semantics.

Samos primitive events are method, transaction, user and temporal (absolute and relative) events. The granularity of temporal events is the minute. Conjunction, disjunction and sequence operators are supported. It also proposes composite events related to occurrences of an event of type E within a time intervale I defined explicitly or using the occurring time of an event. *E in I, is signaled at the first occurrence of E during I, Times(n E) in I is signaled at the nth occurrence of E during I and NOT E in I is signaled at the end of I if none E have occurred. The context of events includes the transaction identity, the user identity, the occurring time and the object involved in the event (if relevant). Composite events may include a mask using the keyword SAME. Samos proposes a notion of monitoring interval associated with an event type.

Sentinel/SNOOP, is also an interesting work on the definition of composite events. The proposed operators are, disjunction, sequence, conjunction and periodic and aperiodic operators. The aperiodic operator A allows to express the occurrence of an aperiodic event E bounded by two events (for providing an interval). A* is similar to A but allows to accumulate the occurrences of E occurring in the interval. No notion of mask have been included.

Ode, supports E-A rules. Events include a mask which allows to express some restrictions on the event occurrences. This restriction can concern the parameters of the events.

ACOOD, is one which supports more expressive event types. They adopt an E_CCA (rather than ECA) model where event types include a condition on the event context. Event types are defined independently of rules. Implementation issues are not discussed.

In all of these systems it is difficult or not possible to express (with the event language) situations of the style "event1 during event2". Samos allow such expressions for time intervals in the place of event2. As all of the mentioned systems use instantaneous events it is difficult to detect situations where it is necessary to refer to the duration of operations[11]. To do so it would be necessary to correlate the event instances of the beginning and the end of an operation. In the mentioned systems it is difficult and sometimes impossible to verify that a "begin operation" and an "end operation" event occurrences correspond to the same operation instance (execution).

To our knowledge none of the previously mentioned systems propose a way (apart masks) to define event types using information extracted from the database: dynamic event types are not supported. Temporal events do not have a context.

In the temporal field, we find the interesting work reported in Prasad [PSW95]. They propose Condition-Action rules where the condition part is specified with a Past Temporal Logic formula. This logic offers two basic temporal operators Since and Lasttime. With respect to our proposal, they are really oriented toward "temporal conditions" whereas our proposal is more event oriented.

7 Conclusion and Future work

This paper has presented an event model which attempts to make a step toward facilitating the expression of real world events. It tries to be less dependent on system constraints than preceding works. The three principal characteristics are the fact that the duration of events is integrated, events can be constrained by the use of masks, and temporal event types can be dynamic. This last feature is achieved by the use of data stored in the database to instantiate a generic event type. We consider this last point particularly important because it opens interesting possibilities and is useful in many application domains. Implementation is in progress.

In the future, we will continue to work on dynamic event types considering more general event types and related issues on rule execution models. We also intend to study the use of our event model in historic databases and a better integration of temporal database concepts with the active component. Among them, the use of temporal elements in event type definitions. A temporal element is a finite sequence of intervals. For example, holidays over the year are the interval corresponding to summer holidays plus Christmas holidays and so on. If we have an entity holidays defined in the database, it would be interesting to be able to express events as follows:

on Employee.raise_salary() during holidays

The semantics of the event operators must be adapted. In this case the most intuitive interpretation would be to consider the temporal element as a disjunction of intervals and to distribute the during operator on all the intervals as follows:

---

[11] Operation is used here with a general sense.

(Employee.raise_salary()during I1) or

(Employee.raise_salary() during I2)...

where each Ix is the value of each interval contained in the temporal element holidays.

Another point we plan to work out is the relevance of duration-based events for synchronization in multimedia DBMS (Adiba and Mocellin [AdMo97]) and in distributed environments.

8 Acknowledgment

Grateful thanks to M-C. Fauvet and A. Poitou who participated to this work. Many thanks to C. Collet for her comments on a previous version of this paper and to C. Liem for correcting my English.

References

[ACT96] ACT-NET consortium, "The Active Database Management System Manifesto: A rulebase of ADBMS features", *SIGMOD Record*, vol. 25, num. 3, September 1996.

[AdMo97] M. Adiba, F. Mocellin, "STORM: une approche à objets pour les bases de données multimédia", *(Journal)Technique et Science Informatique*, vol. Ed. Hermes, , To appear 1997.

[Allen83] J.F. Allen. , "Maintaining Knowledge about temporal intervals", *Communication of the ACM*, vol. 26, num. 11, November 1983.

[BeLi95] M. Berndtsson, B. Lings, *Logical Events and ECA Rules*, num. Technical Report HS-IDA-TR-95-004, Department of Computer Science, University of Skövde, 1995.

[CaDu97] J-F.Canavaggio, M. Dumas, "Manipulation de valeurs temporelles dans un SGBD à objets", *Inforsid*, France, 1997.

[ChMi94] S. Chakravarthy, D. Mishra, *Snoop: An Expressive Event Specification Language For Active Databases*, Data and Knowledge Engineering, 1994.

[CKAK94] S. Chakravarthy, V. Krishnaprasad, E. Anwar, S.-K. Kim, "Composite Events for Active Databases: Semantics, Contexts and Detection", *(VLDB'94)*, Santiago de Chile, September 1994.

[CCS96] C. Collet, T. Coupaye, T. Svensen, "NAOS Efficient and Modular Reactive Capabilities in an Object-Oriented Database System", *(VLDB'94)*, Santiago, Chile, September 1994.

[CCR96] C. Collet, T. Coupaye, C. Roncancio, "NAOS 2.1 : Dealing with Composite Events ", *5th International Conference on Extending Database Technology (EDBT'96 Exhibit program)*, Avignon, France, March 1996.

[CHR96] C. Collet, P. Habraken, C. Roncancio, "Règles actives dans les SGBD", *(Journal) Ingénierie des Systèmes d'Information*, vol. 4, num. 3, June 1996.

[CoCo96] C. Collet, T. Coupaye, "Composite events in NAOS", *7th International Conference and Workshop on Database and Expert Systems Applications (DEXA'96)*, LNCS 1134, Zurich, Switzerland , September 1996.

[CCFR97] C. Collet, T. Coupaye, L. Fayolle, C. Roncancio, "Exhibition Paper, NAOS prototype - Version 2.2", *13th International Conference on Data Engineering(ICDE'97)*, Birmingham, United Kingdom, April 1997.

[FCS96a] M-C. Fauvet, J-F. Canavaggio, P-C. Scholl, *Un modèle multi-granulaire du temps pour un SGBD temporel*, Research Report 962-I, Lab. LSR, IMAG, http://www-lsr.imag.fr/publi.html , February 1996.

[FCS96a] M-C. Fauvet, J-F. Canavaggio, P-C. Scholl, "Expression de requêtes Temporelles dans un SGBD à Objets", *Proc. Journées Bases de Données Avancées*, pp. 225-252, August 1996.

[Fay97] L. Fayolle, *Définition et detection d'événements dans NAOS*, num. CNAM Report, Lab. LSR - IMAG, Grenoble, France, 1997.

[FRG96] A. Front, C. Roncancio, J-P. Giraudin, "Behavioral situations and active database systems", *Workshop on Databases: Active & Real-Time (DART'96)* , N. Soparkar and K. Ramamritham, ed., Rockville, USA, November 1996.

[GaDi93] S.Gatziu, K.R. Dittrich, "Events in an Active Object-Oriented Database System", *Intl. Workshop on Rule in Databases Systems, Edinburg*, August 1993.

[GJS92] N. Gehani, H.V. Jagadish, O. Shmueli, "Event Specification in an Active Object-Oriented Database", *ACM SIGMOD Intl. Conference. on Management of Data*, pp. 81-90, San Diego, USA, 1992.

[GBLR96] A. Geppert, M. Berndtsson, D. Lieuwen, C. Roncancio, *Performance Evaluation of Object-Oriented Active Database Management Systems Using the BEAST Benchmark*, num. Tech. Rep. 96.07, University of Zurich, Swiss, October 1996.

[JCGSS92] C.S. Jensen, J. Clifford, S.K. Gadia, A. Segev, R.T. Snodgrass, "A Glossary of Temporal Database Concepts", *SIGMOD Record*, vol. 21, num. 3, September 1992.

[MPC96] R. Meo, G. Psaila, S. Ceri, "Composite Events in Chimera", *Advances in Databases Technology - EDBT'96* , pp. 57-76, LNCS 1057, March 1996.

[PSW95] A. Prasad Sistla, O. Wolfson, "Temporal Conditions and Integrity Constraints in Active Database Systems", *ACM SIGMOD 95 San Jose California*, 1995.

[Poi96] A. Poitou, *Un modèle d'événements Duratifs*, num. DEA Report, University of Grenoble, France, June 1996.

[RSSTX96] K. Ramamritham, R. Sivasankaran, J.A. Stankovic, D. Towley, M. Xiong, "Integrating Temporal, Real Time and Active Databases", *Sigmod*, vol. 25, num. 1, March 1996.

[WiCe96] J. Widom, S. Ceri, *Active Database Systems - Triggers and Rules for Advanced Database Processing*, Morgan Kaufmann Publishers, San Francisco, USA, 1996.

Supporting System-Level Testing of Applications by Active Real-Time Database Systems*

Jonas Mellin

Department of computer science
University of Skövde
Box 408, 541 28 Skövde, Sweden
jonas.mellin@ida.his.se

Abstract. Event-triggered distributed real-time systems are prohibitively difficult to test due the required test effort. The test effort includes instrumenting the test object, and generating, executing, and analyzing the test results. The test effort can be significantly reduced by the use of an distributed active real-time database, thanks to the transaction concept and the built-in event monitor. The two major problems identified w.r.t. testing are the following. Firstly, whether the test effort is manageable. Secondly, whether the introduced run-time overhead is acceptable, i.e., no critical deadlines are missed due to testing.

1 Introduction

It is important to validate the quality of real-time systems, especially in terms of dependability with emphasis on timeliness. The monitoring requirement introduced by testing can affect the temporal behavior of a system, which may prohibit system level testing. Testing is a complement to formal analysis and inspections. Formal analysis can only be used to verify properties of a model based on some assumptions, whereas testing can be used to validate that the assumptions does not break. Moreover, testing should be automated as much as possible, because it is important to do as many tests as possible of an often immense amount of tests within a limited time. In addition, this results in the likelihood of introducing faults is reduced.

In real-time applications, databases are needed as many complicated problems require a database. That is, any problem with the following properties: i) the data should be durable, i.e., be permanent and resilient to crashes; and ii) the product of structural complexity and amount of data is high.

Active real-time databases, e.g., REACH (Buchmann et. al., 1995), and DeeDS (Andler et. al., 1996), is an extension to the traditional database concept, which offers a possibility to verify the timeliness of real-time systems without affecting the behavior of the system itself and without causing an unacceptable

---

* This work was supported by NUTEK(The Swedish National Board for Industrial and Technical Development), as part of the Distributed Reconfigurable Real-Time Database Systems Project in the Embedded Systems Program.

overhead. The reason is that an active database has a built-in event monitor, which can be used for logging.

Section 2 to 5 gives the background emphasizing the testing of distributed real-time systems. The problem definition is presented in Section 6. Section 7 discusses the approach taken in this paper. This is followed by related work and conclusions.

2 Real-Time Systems

Hard deadlines[1] are usually implemented using *time-triggered* systems, whereas soft deadlines[2] are usually implemented using *event-triggered* systems (Kopetz et. al., 1994). A time-triggered system works in lock-steps where the environment is observed at pre-determined points in time and all computations must be finished before the next observation time point. An event-triggered system, in contrast, reacts to events as they occur. Event-triggered systems are prone to event showers, which may cause an overload of the system. Event showers can be handled using filtering and smoothing[3] according to Kopetz et. al. An active (real-time) database system is event-triggered.

3 Testing — An Overview

Testing is mainly viewed as dynamic verification of systems, i.e., checking that an executing component does not break its specification.

In this article testing is a systematic activity where an attempt to show the presence of *faults* is done, whereas faults are located and removed during debugging. According to Laprie et. al. (1994) a fault is the hypothesized cause of an *error*, which is the incorrect state a component enters when a fault occurs. Moreover, a *failure* is a deviation from the specification of the component due to an error. The presence of faults can be shown by either errors or failures.

3.1 Overview of the Test Process

Fig. 1[4] depicts an overview of the test process elucidating generation, execution, and analysis phases.

The *test object* is the software component of interest, which requires instrumentation to be tested. The test object is executed and monitored by a *testbed*. The testbed logs significant events, which are compared to the expected output by a *test oracle* (Beizer, 1990) during analysis. During setup the tester produces the input and expected output.

---

[1] Missed hard deadlines results in catastrophic consequences.

[2] It is acceptable to miss a requirement occasionally.

[3] Smoothing constrains the events so that aperiodic events become sporadic.

[4] Inspired by Beizer (1990).

The *test effort* concerns instrumenting a test object, and generating, executing, and analyzing tests for the test object. According to Beizer it is paramount to make this as mechanical as possible to gain greater confidence in the quality of the test object.

Instrumentation of a Test Object. *Observability* (Schütz, 1995) refers to the problem that a monitored test object is affected by the monitoring, because the test object must be instrumented to make it possible to log information about its execution. This effect is named the *probe-effect* by Gait (1985), which is the difference in behavior between a monitored object and its unmonitored counterpart.

Hybrid monitoring, cf INCAS by Haban et. al. (1990), is a combination of software and hardware instrumentation, in which general purpose hardware is used to improve efficiency while supporting the flexibility of software instrumentation. This can be used when software instrumentation is required to a low computational cost.

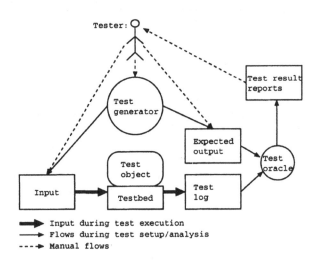

Fig. 1. Overview of testing.

3.2 System Level Testing Technique Properties

A testing technique is a systematic method to show the presence of a category of failures and errors. The black-box system level testing techniques are among the hardest problems to handle in (distributed) real-time systems, because it must be performed on the target (often an embedded system) and, according to

Schütz (1995), it is paramount to avoid the probe-effect. Thus, an operational system must contain all the necessary instrumentation for testing of temporal requirements, which are tightly connected to the behavior.

Transaction-Flow Testing. An important system level testing technique is originally called transaction-flow testing by Beizer (1990). However, this does not imply transactions in a database scope. Thus, this technique is called *activity flow* testing here to discern the meaning more precisely. An *activity* is the scope in time and space where an actor (human or non-human) performs a set of significant *tasks*, which can be internal or external to the system. Each task is atomic and made in isolation, i.e., a discrete unit of work. This technique concentrates on behavior and synchronization of activities.

3.3   Testing of Distributed Real-Time Systems

Schütz claims that the hardest problems concerning testing of distributed real-time systems are observability, reproducibility, and *representativity*. Together these can be viewed as the *testability* of a system, i.e., how easy it is to test a system. Observability is a problem in concurrent and distributed system, which is aggravated in real-time systems (see Sect. 3.1).

Reproducibility, which is tightly connected to regression testing[5], is aggravated because time is part of the input domain. That is, not only the input values but their arrival time is important. To get full reproducibility, tests must be executed using recorded time of events from test logs of previous tests, because timers deviate between executions. To get reproducibility the following categories of events are considered to be significant: i) process synchronization, e.g., blockings, suspensions, preemptions; ii) access to the system's notion of time; and iii) asynchronous interrupts. The reason is that it is paramount to know their order and/or timing to be able to determine the behavior of the system.

The representativity describes how realistic the input is. In the case of testing real-time systems the upper bound of the input domain consists of the Cartesian product of all possible input values at all possible points in time times all possible states of the system. To reduce the test-effort this Cartesian product must be reduced, while maintaining representativity. One obvious way is used in time-triggered systems is to reduce the points in time when the environment is observed by the system.

To reduce the input domain and to attain improved testability the time domain must be handled properly. First of all time points can be categorized as absolute and relative, where absolute has a common reference point in time whereas relative is only with reference to another time point. Moreover, the coupling to the input value may be either tight or loose. A tightly coupled input

---

[5] This testing strategy implies that tests should be reusable when a test object is changed.

value must occur at the specified time point, whereas a loosely coupled input value may occur within a duration from a point in time.

Schütz (1995) compares the effort to execute all necessary tests on unconstrained event-triggered with constrained time-triggered systems. This is done by comparing the number of possible environmental states ($ESTAT^6$ in (1)) that can be perceived by the system at the end of a fixed time interval g_a as a function of up to n events, which can be observed at s points. In a time-triggered system there is no synchronization within a lockstep. For a time-triggered system $s = 1$, but for event-triggered system the upper bound is described in (2), where g_{instr} is the time it takes to perform an instruction and g_{obs} is the time to handle a single observation. Note, however, that (1) gives a lower bound for event-triggered systems, because handling of simultaneous inputs is not covered. Moreover, preemptions are not covered fully either. That is, the equation is equivalent to assume no preemption scheduling, which is not realistic.

The reason, according to Schütz, for that time-triggered systems requires less effort to test is:

1. Loose coupling between value and its time, because the environment is only observed at specific observation time points.
2. The order of event occurrences between observation points is of no consequence.
3. All actions must be completed before the next observation point, i.e., no preemption is enforced.
4. There is only one possible synchronization sequence, i.e., a sequence of synchronization events that uniquely determines the result(s) of a concurrent program execution. That is, no effort must be spent on selecting important synchronization sequences.
5. Generation of synchronization sequences and test data is independent.
6. Access to global time can be made deterministic.

$$ESTAT(s,n) = \sum_{k=0}^{n} \binom{n}{k} s^k = \sum_{k=0}^{n} \binom{n}{k} s^k 1^{n-k} = (s+1)^n \qquad (1)$$

$$s_{Emax} = \frac{g_a}{max(g_{instr}, g_{obs})} \qquad (2)$$

4 Event Monitoring

Event monitoring is an integral part of an active database and is one possible way of producing the test log. According to Chakravarthy et. al (1994) an *event* is assumed to be atomic and instantaneous, i.e., either it occurs or not at all. In an active real-time database (ARTDB) events are specified using an event specification language, and can either be primitive or composite. A primitive event is a significant event generated by the system or the external environment,

---

[6] This variable is called $STATES$ by Schütz.

e.g., start of transaction or a method call. A composite event is described using operators and constituent events which may be primitive or composite, e.g., a sequence of start transaction, update variable x, commit transaction. Buchmann (1994) addresses the issue that the instrumentation of methods generating events can be made automatic in object-oriented databases (see Sect. 3.1).

4.1 Time and Order

It is paramount to be able to tell the order of events and, in real-time systems, the duration between events. If predictable remote accesses are required a real-time network is required. Moreover, a real-time network is necessary if temporal behavior of remote accesses must be monitored, e.g., for testing purposes.

In non-real-time systems logical clocks proposed by Lamport (1978) are sufficient to tell the order of related events. Moreover, vectorized logical clocks, e.g., described by Babaoğlu et. al. (1994), are sufficient to tell the order of unrelated events. However, in real-time systems real time clocks are necessary. If predictable remote accesses are required global time must be supported. To be able to tell the order of two events they must be separated by at least $2 * g$ where g is the clock precision. This is called δ_t-precedence by Kopetz et. al.

Global event detection suffers from the problem of (unpredictable) network delays in a distributed systems, site failures, and that access to global real-time is problematic, e.g., see Babaoğlu et. al. (1994 and Schwidersky et. al. (1995. To keep a global time base in a distributed system is costs in computational overhead or extra hardware. Moreover, the precision of the global time is hard get down to the precision of the local time. If all nodes in a distributed system are autonomous global event detection is less of a problem, because each node may then have their own view of the world.

5 Consistency and Replication

Immediate consistency refers to the semantics that an update to variable must be propagated to all nodes where the variable is stored before it is committed. In contrast, eventual consistency, e.g., see Ramamritham et. al. (1996) and Helal et. al. (1997), means that updates are propagated when it is feasible. In many (real-time) applications, such as naming services, and power distribution control, eventual consistency is sufficient

6 Problem Definition

The problem is to investigate how an application based on distributed active real-time databases can improve the testability of event-triggered real-time systems. That is, how to apply appropriate constraints to make the test effort manageable while maintaining the event-triggered semantics.

In spite of the fact that the results of this work is mainly for showing faults for system level testing it is conjectured that the results are useful for other testing techniques as well. Moreover, it is assumed that confidence is gained in constituents components via quality assurance methods before system level testing commences.

6.1 Assumed Requirements and Characteristics of the System

The system is assumed to handle both hard and soft deadlines. All communication between virtual nodes (VN) distributed on physical nodes (PN) are assumed to be handled by the database (see Fig. 2).

Monitoring the System. In this article a monitored real-time system is viewed as in Fig. 2. There is a local event monitor (EM) at each node in the system, which takes input from the environment, from the system itself, and signals the recipients when subscribed events occur. This event monitor may be statically allocated to a separate monitoring processor at each node. If a global event detector is needed it is assumed to exist, but it only needs access to real-time if predictable remote accesses are required. The time of occurrence of an event is assumed to be when the event is generated and not when it reaches the event monitor.

The test and debugging tools are assumed to be connected to the event monitors. Either they share the same network as the system or it needs a separate network depending on the system requirements.

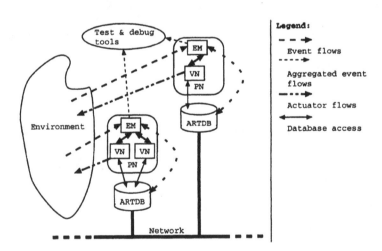

Fig. 2. A view of a monitored real-time system with two nodes.

The event monitor is assumed to be predictable. That is, it responds to all events within a bounded time and causes a known load on the system, e.g., as described by Mellin et. al. (1996). Events are assumed to be smoothed before they arrive to the event monitor and, thus, no overload on the event monitor can occur. Event criticality is assumed to be used to prioritize critical events over non-critical (Berndtsson et. al., 1995). Moreover, necessary extensions to allow other subscribers than the rule manager is also assumed to exist.

7 Approach

The approach to the problem of improving testability is to reduce the test effort and automate as much as possible by exploiting distributed ARTDB.

Firstly, all major impacts of using an distributed ARTDB are discussed. Secondly, requirements on a distributed ARTDB and its underlying components are discussed. Thirdly, a discussion on test effort and acceptable overhead is presented.

7.1 The Impacts of a Distributed ARTDB

The Impact of Transactions. The transaction support and concurrency control makes the communication between software components well-defined. The use of transactions makes it possible to constrain the possible executions. For example, if a critical transaction T_1 is executing and a non-critical transaction T_2 enters the system T_1 will not be preempted. This introduces loose coupling between time and value in certain situations (supporting reason 1 Sect. 3.3). Moreover, by increasing the locking granularity when pessimistic concurrency control is used the number of possible interleavings decreases. Hence, the test effort is reduced. This agrees well with real-time databases based on main-memory database (MMDB) system, which enhances the predictability according to Kao et. al. (1992). In a MMDB coarse locking granularity can give significant performance improvement according to Garcia-Molina et. al. (1992). This is possible if the execution time of all transactions are considered to be short.

The Impact of the Built-In Event Monitor. The built-in event monitor allows event detection and signaling for testing purposes at a low computational overhead, because the event monitor is used by the ARTDB. The event monitor can be extended with aggregation of events before signaling, because the test tools does not need to analyze the events immediately. In addition, it is possible to inject (correct or faulty) events directly into the event monitor and, thus, it is not necessary to start testing all sequences from the external stimuli to the external actuation.

Impact of Object-Oriented Active Databases. An object-oriented active database can provide automatic instrumentation specified by using an event specification language. By extending active databases with features for testing tools the test effort can be reduced thanks to this possibility.

Impact of (Event) Criticality. The different criticality of events can reduce the effort to test a system. The reason is that only transactions with hard deadlines must be tested completely as long as it is guaranteed that no soft transactions can make the system fail to meet a hard deadline.

Impact of Failures and Optimistic Concurrency Control. Both media failures and optimistic concurrency control introduces retry loops, i.e., when a transaction is aborted it is restarted. These retry loops must be bounded to make it possible to achieve full test coverage.

Impact of Database Storage. The database makes it possible to provide additional information during analysis of the test log. This additional information can be used to verify the analysis and, possibly, locate the faults. Moreover, as logging for testing must always be active this can be used as a log to try to find out why a system crashed during operation.

7.2 Requirements on Distributed ARTDBs

These additional requirements must be fulfilled by the distributed ARTDB or its underlying components.

Smoothing Events to a Observation Point Grid. By only allowing the system to view the environment at certain points in time improves testability (see reason 1 Sect. 3.3). That is, all asynchronous interrupts are delayed until the observation time point. This can be done as long as all deadlines are met. Moreover, if the order of events between observation points is of no consequence the test effort is reduced (see reason 2 Sect. 3.3).

Bounded Preemption. As mentioned in section 3.3 $ESTAT$ only expresses a lower bound for the test effort of an event-triggered real-time system. Moreover, it does not take into account internal synchronization events, e.g., blockings, preemptions. These must be included for event-triggered systems to provide an upper bound.

To calculate a conservative[7] upper bound $ESTAT$ can be multiplied by number of potential blockings and potential tasks[8] preempted from the processor. This is expressed for an MMDB by $FSTAT$ in (3). $PSTAT$ is an expression that gives the number of possible combinations of preempted processes given the following; p is the maximum number of times a task can be preempted, and q is the maximum number of concurrently executing tasks triggered by the same event type. In a time-triggered system $p = 0$ and $q = 0$.

In (6) $BSTAT$ describes the number of potential blocking combinations under pessimistic concurrency control, i.e., tasks waiting on another task to release

---

[7] It is conservative because blocked tasks are not normally preempted and vice versa
[8] Tasks and transactions are equivalent in this discussion.

locked resources. This is done by finding all possible combinations of two or more tasks out of $n * q$ possible executing tasks.

In (7) $PSTAT$ describes the number of potential preempted tasks. These are not independent, because a second preempted task may not exist in the system before the first one triggered by the same event type. The number of combinations for one event type is the sum of all combinations of preempted tasks for that event type.

In (8) the resulting equation under pessimistic concurrency control. In case of optimistic concurrency control no blocking occur and, thus, $BSTAT$ must be exchanged with a formula expressing how to handle retry loops.

$$FSTAT(s,n,p,q) = ESTAT(s,n) * BSTAT(n,q) * PSTAT(n,p,q) \qquad (3)$$

$$BSTAT(n,q) = \sum_{k=2}^{nq} \binom{nq}{k} \iff \qquad (4)$$

$$BSTAT(n,q) = \sum_{k=0}^{nq} \binom{nq}{k} - \sum_{k=0}^{1} \binom{nq}{k} \iff \qquad (5)$$

$$BSTAT(n,q) = 2^{nq} - (nq + 1) \qquad (6)$$

$$PSTAT(n,p,q) = (\sum_{k=0}^{q+1} p^k)^n = \begin{cases} \left(\frac{p^{q+2}-1}{p-1}\right)^n & \text{when } p \neq 1 \\ (q+2)^n & \text{when } p = 1 \end{cases} \qquad (7)$$

$$FSTAT(s,n,p,q) = (s+1)^n (2^{nq} - (nq+1)) \begin{cases} \left(\frac{p^{q+2}-1}{p-1}\right)^n & \text{when } p \neq 1 \\ (q+2)^n & \text{when } p = 1 \end{cases} \qquad (8)$$

The Underlying Network. The requirements on the application and testing provides information of the choice of network. In this article the three categories—non-real-time network, real-time network, and duplicated real-time network—are considered. The application requirements and preconditions of interest are: i) tightness of slack, i.e., the difference between a task's deadline and its worst-case execution time; ii) criticality of requirements, e.g., hard vs soft; and iii) immediate or eventual consistency needed. In this article the slack is tight if the monitoring overhead can cause the deadline to be missed.

The non-real-time network can be used only if eventual consistency is required in the system, or immediate consistency in conjunction with soft deadlines and a maximum number of soft deadlines are allowed to be missed. The reason is that in these cases no predictable remote accesses are needed and each node can be considered to be autonomous. A real-time network is required if immediate consistency is needed in conjunction with either hard deadlines and loose slack or soft deadlines and tight slack. The reason is that in this case predictable remote accesses must be tested. A duplicated real-time network is required when immediate consistency, hard deadlines together with tight slack is needed. The reason is that the hard deadlines may not be missed and, thus, an extra real-time network is necessary.

Access to global time. In order to make tests reproducible access to global time must be made deterministic. This problem must either be avoided, e.g., by using eventual consistency and considering nodes to be autonomous, or by implementing global time (see Sect. 4.1).

7.3 Real-Time Activity-Flow Testing

Internally an activity may be represented by a task executing a series of transaction, which supports atomicity. Thus, the semantics of the graph representation can be preserved (see Sect. 3.2). The time constraints are specified by adding how long time a token may spend from the starting task to the end task. This does not simplify generation of synchronization sequences as much as for time-triggered systems, but it does emphasize the important combinations to test (cf reason 4 and 5 Sect. 3.3).

The Basic Technique. The basic technique is to describe a system using activity-flow diagrams to identify significant activities and to test different possible activity-flow combinations of importance. That is, important synchronization sequences can be identified. This activity-flow is either used as a specification of the system or derived from the specification of the system. An activity-flow is basically a token-passing algorithm, which is usable to describe and test synchronization problems (Petersen, 1981). Each token has a type and state, which is the only information allowed to be used for choosing different routes in the activity-flow graph. This does not imply that the system is implemented using token-passing. Activity-flow testing agrees well with the requirements for reproducibility (Sect. 3.3), because it is possible to model synchronization.

Representation. An activity-flow consists of nodes describing atomic tasks interconnected with edges, which are traversed by tokens for each activity. When a token is at a node the corresponding task is being performed within the activity. Tokens may be queued at nodes, e.g., this occurs when tokens arrives faster than a task can handle them.

There may be more than one outgoing edge from a node, which implies that the node is one of the following (see Fig. 4): i) a branch node where the activity must choose an appropriate edge; ii) a birth node where one or more children activities dependent on the parent are spawned; and iii) a split node where the parent activity is split into independent activities.

Likewise, there may be more than one incoming edge to a node, which implies that the node is one of the following (see Fig. 4): i) a junction where tokens from different edges are passed to a single outgoing edge; ii) a merger node where all incoming activities are merged into one activity; iii) an absorber node where one activity is considered to be a predator which kills a prey (another activity).

Categories of Errors Shown Using This Technique. Three categories of errors can be shown by this technique according to Beizer (1995): i) activity routing errors (incorrect behavior); ii) synchronization errors, and iii) activity queue errors. In addition, real-time requirements adds missed deadline errors. Together, these cover important synchronization sequences.

Activity routing errors occurs when incorrect behavior is issued from the system. For example, an activity turns up on the incorrect flow, or a merge occurs incorrectly.

Synchronization errors occurs at nodes with more than one incoming edge. A synchronization error occurs when a combination of incoming activities does not let the correct activity pass the node. In this case tests must be applied for all possible combinations of activities flowing into a node.

Activity queue errors deal with the fact that queues are normally bounded and in some cases, e.g., some real-time systems, the queue handling is not FIFO. Faults may be due to queue boundaries, prioritized activities, and non-FIFO handling of queues etc.

Missed deadlines may be catastrophical in a real-time system. When an activity does not exit a task at the right time a deadline has been missed.

Sources of Significant Events. These should be derived from the specification and encompass synchronization events, access to time, and asynchronous interrupts (see Sect. 3.3).

The sources of synchronization events are where an activity may be blocked or preempted for any reason, e.g., the transaction may be blocked accessing a entity in the database, or the system requires support by the operator. In a database all accesses to the database are subject to issuing significant events, because the database is shared among different users (human or otherwise). Preemption is handled as blocking, because all tasks are atomic and executed in isolation. Thus, all preemptable tasks must be modeled as a sequence of tasks, where preemption can occur in between the tasks. These situations can be found by logging start, abort, request to commit, commit, blockings of transactions due to other transaction holding a wanted resource, and I/O-wait in non-MMDB, because all communication is done via the database. Moreover, preemption must be logged both for tasks and transactions. The system's access to time should be modeled as separate nodes. Asynchronous interrupts are modeled as entry nodes to the graph.

Example of Using Activity-Flow. In Fig. 3 a train track is depicted. Trains may come from either east or west. The problem is to avoid collisions and, thus, if two trains are detected (conflict detection) one of them must be redirected into the sidetrack. Sensors are depicted by boxes enumerated by A-F and can tell the direction (east or west). It is assumed that if a train enters the inner sector and no train has been detected in the opposite direction no train will come from that direction.

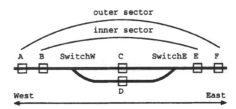

Fig. 3. Example of application for system level testing.

The conflict detection in this example can be modeled as in Fig. 4. If a train T1 enters from the west going to the east the following may scenario with variations is possible. It is assumed that nothing has happened before T1 enters from the west implying that no tokens reside in the activity-flow network. T1 passes sensor A in direction east (Aeast). An activity token $T1east$ is introduced at Aeast in the network. $T1east$ moves to birth B1, in which a child $T1east_{child}$ is born. $T1east$ moves to merger M1 (see event part of R11 in Table 1) and $T1east_{child}$ to M2. Note that a merger node does not necessarily merge two or more incoming tokens, but may merge tokens with empty tokens. In this case a merged token $T1east + empty$ moves to the branch Br1 (see action part of R11). As $T1east + empty$ should not be terminated it moves to B3. At B3 a child $\overline{T1east + empty}_{child}$ is born and moves to M1 where it serves as a memory in case a train in the opposite direction enters the outer section. $T1east + empty$ moves to M2, where it waits for a token from Beast or Fwest.

If no train comes from the opposite direction a token $T1east2$ enters at Beast, indicating that the train now has entered the inner sector. $T1east2$ moves to B4 where the $T1east2_{child}$ moves to M1 (see R12) to remove $\overline{T1east + empty}_{child}$, by merging them into $\overline{T1east + empty}_{child} + T1east2$ which goes to termination via Br1. The parent $T1east2$ moves to M2, where it is merged with with $T1east + empty$ into $T1east + empty + T1east2$. This token moves to Br2, at which the appropriate flow is followed.

If a train comes from the opposite direction a token $T2west$ enters at Fwest. $T2west$ passes B2 spawning $T2west_{child}$ and continues to M1, where it is merged with $T1east + empty_{child}$ (see R23). This merged token is terminated via Br1 (see R23). The $T2west_{child}$ moves to M2, where it is merged with $T1east + empty$ (see R23). The merged token $\overline{T1east + empty} + T2west_{child}$ moves to Br2 where the appropriate flow is taken, which must resolve the conflict.

An example of a few rules emphasizing node M1 of the implementation are described in Table 1. Detached coupling mode is assumed. Moreover, each rule has an associated temporal scope carrying necessary information for the scheduler, e.g., deadline, worst case execution time. When a token is on an edge an insert (*ins*) operation is performed, e.g., $insB1M1(t_1)$ implies that a token is placed on the edge between B1 and M1. To remove a token the delete (*del*) operation is used. The $\oplus$ operator merges tokens.

To check for activity routing errors each path must be traversed in each possible state of the graph from start to termination. To check for synchronization errors each combination of tokens to, e.g., M1 must be checked (5 input edges). This can be done by injecting events into the event monitor to trigger the appropriate rules.

The rules in Table 1 cannot handle simultaneous tokens entering from both directions (see Fig. 3). The reason is that the graph does not cover simultaneous events. Thus, by only looking at the specification it is possible to deduct that some situations are not handled properly. As the scheduler by using the temporal scope determines in which order events are handled activity queue errors must be checked too. At each node where tokens can be queued up different queues must be tested. The complexity of this last check depends on the complexity of the scheduling algorithm.

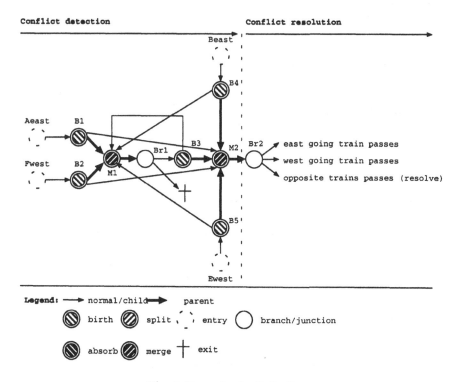

Fig. 4. Example of activity-flow.

Rule	Event	Condition	Action	Temporal scope
R11	$insB1M1(t_1)$	$\neg B3M1(t_2)$	$insM1Br1(t_1 \oplus empty)$	TS_{11}
R12	$insB4M1(t_1)$	$true$	$delB3M1(any)$	TS_{12}
R13	$insB1M1(t_1)$	$B3M1(t_2)$	$delB3M1(t_2);$ $insB1M2(child(t_1))$	TS_{13}
R21	$insB2M1(t_1)$	$\neg B3M1(t_2)$	$insM1Br1(t_1 \oplus empty)$	TS_{21}
R22	$insB5M1(t_1)$	$true$	$delB3M1(any)$	TS_{22}
R23	$insB2M1(t_1)$	$B3M1(t_2)$	$delB3M1(t_2);$ $insB2M2(child(t_1))$	TS_{23}

Table 1. Examples of rules handling node M1.

7.4 Test effort

The test effort of an event-triggered system is higher than for a time-triggered system, but, at least, (8) expresses an upper bound of the number of states to be tested. This is in contrast to Schütz who uses a lower bound on the test effort of event-triggered systems.

The test effort can be constrained by: i) only testing tasks with hard deadlines completely while making sure that tasks with soft deadlines do not make hard deadlines to be missed; and ii) selecting important synchronization sequences by using real-time activity flow testing technique. Moreover, by using an MMDB no I/O-waits must be logged and the coarse locking granularity may be employed. The latter brings down the number of possible interleavings of transactions. If the locking granularity is the whole database $BSTAT = 1$.

7.5 Acceptable Overhead

The question is whether the necessary instrumentation does not cause an unacceptable overhead. No hard deadlines may be missed due to this. However, it is important to note that there must be sufficient capacity left for the soft tasks.

The events transaction start, termination, acquire/release locks, access to time, and asynchronous interrupts (see Sect. 7.3) must be logged. In case of a non-MMDB I/O-waits must also be logged. By increasing the locking granularity and introducing eventual consistency the number of events that must be logged can be reduced significantly. Moreover, by using an MMDB logging I/O-waits can be avoided.

8   Related Work

Schütz identifies the general problems w.r.t. testing distributed real-time systems and provides solutions for testing time-triggered systems. However, he does only list the additional problems w.r.t. event-triggered systems and compares the effort of testing time-triggered vs event-triggered, which is clearly won by time-triggered systems. The reason is that time-triggered systems are compared with unconstrained event-triggered systems. In contrast, this article is concentrated on system-level testing of event-triggered systems based on distributed active real-time databases.

9 Conclusions

By using an distributed active (object-oriented) real-time database as a basis for real-time applications the testability can be improved compared to an unconstrained event-triggered real-time system. The testability of a time-triggered system is still better. However, in this article an upper bound of the test effort for event-triggered systems is presented.

The test effort is bounded by smoothing incoming events so that they are observed only at pre-specified time points, setting a bound on how many times a transaction or task may be preempted from the processor, and a bound on how many tasks triggered by the same event type may execute concurrently. Moreover, if the order of events between observations points is of no consequence the test effort is reduced. By using an MMDB as a base no I/O waits must be logged and coarse locking granularity can be used, which brings down the test effort. Transactions provide a feasible way of putting a bound on the maximum number of allowed preemptions. Optimistic concurrency control and media failures introduces retry loops. These must be bounded in order to make the test effort bounded. By using real-time activity-flow testing the test effort can be focused on the important synchronization sequences. Moreover, only tasks with hard deadlines must be tested completely as long as it is guaranteed that the system meets its deadlines under full load.

The overhead of event monitoring for test purposes can be made acceptable. This is done by reducing the amount of event types that must be logged, and choosing and sizing the network properly. In an MMDB only start, termination, acquire/release locks has to be logged. Of these events the two first is monitored already for the ARTDB. In a non-MMDB I/O-waits must be logged too.

Moreover, active object-oriented real-time databases offer automatic instrumentation by using an event specification. This reduces the work to prepare the system for testing. In addition the availability of durable data storage makes it possible to improve analysis and make it possible to analyze a system after it has crashed.

9.1 Future Work

To test active databases it would be useful to automatically derive a basis for tests from the specification, e.g., using ECA-rules to derive activity-flows. In addition, it would be useful to automatically derive important synchronization sequences from a real-time activity-flow diagram.

210

Acknowledgments

Prof. Sten Andler has provided extensive comments and invaluable advice. Moreover, Brian Lings, Prof. Sharma Chakravarthy, Bengt Eftring, Henrik Engström, and Johan Lundström has given comments on this work.

References

Andler, S. F., Hansson, J., Eriksson, J, Mellin, J, Berndtsson, M, and Eftring, B.: DeeDS Towards a Distributed Active and Real-Time Database System. *Spec. Issue on Real Time Data Base Systems, SIGMOD Record* **25(1)** March (1996)

Babaoğlu, Ö., and Marzullo, K.: Consistent Global States of Distributed Systems: Fundamental Concepts and Mechanisms, Ch. 4, see Mullender (1994)

Beizer, B.: *Software Testing Techniques.* (2nd ed.). Van Nostrand Reinhold (1990)

Beizer, B.: *Black-Box Testing: Techniques for Functional Testing of Software and Systems,* Wiley (1995)

Berndtsson, M., and Hansson, J.: Issues in Active Real-Time Databases, *Proc. Int'l Workshop on Active and Real-Time Database System (ARTDB-95),* Springer-Verlag (1995)

Buchmann, A. P.: Active Object Systems. *Advances in Object-Oriented Database Systems,* p. 201–204. Springer-Verlag (1994).

Buchmann, A. P., Zimmermann, J., Blakeley, J. A., and Wells, D. L.: Building an Integrated Active OODBMS: Requirements, Architecture, and Design Decisions. Data engineering (1995)

Chakravarthy, S., and Mishra, D.: Snoop: An Event Specification Language for Active Databases. *Knowledge and Data Engineering* **13(3)**, October (1994).

Gait, J.: A Debugger for Concurrent Programs. *Software—Practice And Experience* **15(6)**, June (1985).

Garcia-Molina, H., and Salem, K.: Main Memory Database Systems: An Overview. *IEEE Trans. on Knowledge and Data Engineering* **4(6)** (1992) 509–516

Haban, D., and Wybranietz, D.: A Hybrid Monitor for Behavior and Performance Analysis of Distributed Systems, *IEEE Trans. on Software Engineering* **16(2)** (1990) 197–211

Helal, A. A., Heddaya, A. A., and Bhargava, B. B.: *Replication Techniques in Distributed Systems* Kluwer Academic Publisher (1997)

Kao, B., and Garcia-Molina, H.: An overview of real-time database systems. *Proc. of NATO Advanced Study Inst. on Real-Time Computing.* St Marten, Netherlands Antilles. Springer-Verlag (1992)

Kopetz, H., and Veríssimo, P.: Real Time and Dependability Concepts, Ch. 16, see Mullender (1994) 411–446

Lamport, L.: Time, Clocks and the Ordering of Events in a Distributed System. *Comm. of the ACM* **21(7)** (1978) 558–565

Le Lann, G.: The 802.3D Protocol: A Variation on the IEEE 802.3 standard for real-time LANs, Tech. Rep., INRIA, BP 105, F-78153 Le Chesnay Cedex, France (1987)

Laprie et. al.: *Dependability: Basic Concepts and Terminology.* WG 10.4. IFIP, (1994).

Mellin, J., Hansson, J., and Andler, S. F.: Refining Design Constraints using a System Services Model of a Real-Time DBMS, *Proc. 1st Int'l Workshop on Real-Time Databases,* Newport Beach, California (1996) 84–91

Mullender, S. (ed): *Distributed Systems.* Addison-Wesley (1994)

Petersen, J. L.: *Petri Net Theory and The Modeling of Systems*. Prentice-Hall (1981)

Ramamritham, K., and Chrysanthis, P. K.: A Taxonomy of Correctness Criteria in Database Applications. *The VLDB Journal* **5** (1996) 85–97

Schütz, W.: *The Testability of Distributed Real-Time Systems*. Kluwer Academic Publishers (1995).

Schwidersky, S., Herbert, A., Moody, K.: Composite Events for Detecting Behaviour Patterns in Distributed Environments, *Distributed Object Management 95*, (1995)

Veríssimo, P.: Real Time Communication, Ch. 17, see Mullender (1994)

Temporal Indeterminacy in Deductive Databases: An Approach Based on Event Calculus

Luca Chittaro and Carlo Combi

Dipartimento di Matematica ed Informatica,
Università di Udine,
Via delle Scienze, 206
33100 Udine, Italy
{chittaro,combi}@dimi.uniud.it

Abstract. In this paper, we deal with the notion of temporal indeterminacy in temporal deductive databases. We adopt Kowalski and Sergot's Event Calculus (1986, 1992) as our data model. To the best of our knowledge, no previous research efforts have been devoted to introduce indeterminacy in the Event Calculus (EC). We first motivate the need for indeterminacy in real world applications. Then, after briefly presenting EC, we illustrate in detail our proposal (TIC, Temporal Indeterminacy event Calculus). From a description of events whose precise temporal occurrence is unknown, and a description of the properties initiated or terminated by those events, TIC derives intervals over which properties are necessarily valid, and intervals of indeterminacy for the initiating and terminating instants of the properties. Although we adopt EC as our ontology, the proposed ideas can be reformulated for adoption in other approaches. TIC is presented both informally and formally, and illustrated with several examples. Finally, we discuss completeness and complexity issues of TIC.

1 Introduction and Motivation.

Temporal indeterminacy refers to an incomplete knowledge of when an event happened. Temporal indeterminacy is expressed by sentences like "between 18 and 18:30", or "in the afternoon" or "at the end of January". As outlined in (Dyreson and Snodgrass, 1995), temporal indeterminacy of information may be due to different reasons: scale, dating techniques, future planning, unknown or imprecise event times, clock measurements. Furthermore, in different application fields, indeterminacy is due to more than one reason among the above ones.

Without loosing generality, let us consider as an example our application domain, that is the medical one (Chittaro and Dojat, 1997; Chittaro et al., 1997). Indeterminacy may arise due to the following reasons:

- Unknown or imprecise event times. Time occurrence of a clinical episode can be not exactly known, e.g., "between 17:30 and 18:15 the patient suffered from a myocardial infarction", "a chest pain episode happened in the afternoon of May 18, 1997".

- Clock measurements. In Intensive Care Units (ICU), there are several clocks related to the recording of different vital signs: electrocardiograms are sampled at 500 Hz; respiratory signals are sampled at lower frequencies (80 - 100 Hz); respiratory parameters related to gas analysis are sampled at 0.1 Hz; blood pressures are sampled at 60 - 80 Hz. Each event related to the recording of a vital sign is then detected within a time quantum. Events are then located with different indeterminacies on the time axis.
- Scale. Historical medical data are usually given at *different time scales* (Combi and Cucchi, 1997), e.g., "at 1:00 p.m. the patient had an episode of atrial fibrillation", "the therapy with thrombolytics started in July 1995", "On October 12, 1993 the patient had a follow-up visit". Mapping these events on the same time axis leads to temporal indeterminacy.

Research on temporal indeterminacy has been carried out both by the databases (DB) and the artificial intelligence (AI) communities. In most works, indeterminacy in locating a time point on the time axis is modeled by an interval, consisting of all the time points possibly coinciding with the considered, indeterminate time point. AI and DB research differ in focus: in the DB area the focus is on modeling, representing at high abstraction levels, storing, and querying temporal information with indeterminacy. The AI area focused more on inferring new knowledge from the given temporal information.

In DB, three different classes of approaches can be distinguished to deal with temporal indeterminacy and the uncertainty deriving from relationships between indeterminate time points:

- Approaches based on probability. For example, Dyreson and Snodgrass (1995) associate to each time point the probability that a given indeterminate instant is located there.
- Approaches based on modal operators. For example, Maiocchi, Pernici, and Barbic (1992), and Brusoni et al. (1994) define MUST and MAY operators for a query language.
- Approaches based on multiple-valued logics. For example, Combi and Cucchi (1997) use a three-valued (true, false, undefined) logic to deal with uncertainty in temporal relationships, while Gadia, Nair, and Poon (1992) use a similar logic to deal with uncertainty associated to tuples.

The subject of temporal indeterminacy is also relevant in the AI area of temporal constraints, where some authors (e.g., Dechter, Meiri, and Pearl, 1991) allow the modeling of indeterminacy in the temporal distance between two given time points. The focus of that area is on algorithms which detect inconsistencies in a generic set of temporal constraints or find a consistent solution for a set of temporal constraints.

Unlike the above mentioned authors, our main focus is on temporal databases with deductive capabilities. In this paper, we deal with the notion of temporal indeterminacy in this more complex context. We adopt the data model of Kowalski and Sergot's Event Calculus (1986, 1992), and extend it to deal with temporal indeterminacy. To the best of our knowledge, no previous research efforts have been devoted to introduce indeterminacy in the Event Calculus (EC). From a description of events whose precise temporal occurrence is unknown, and a description of the properties initiated or terminated by those events, our extension of EC derives intervals over which properties are *necessarily* valid, and intervals of indeterminacy for the initiating and terminating instants of the properties.

The paper is organized as follows: Section 2 briefly presents EC; Section 3 proposes our extension (TIC, Temporal Indeterminacy event Calculus) both informally and formally, illustrating it with several examples; Section 4 discusses completeness and complexity issues of TIC, and Section 5 sketches our current work.

2 Event Calculus with Preconditions.

The Event Calculus (EC), originally proposed in (Kowalski and Sergot, 1986), is a general approach to representing and reasoning about events and their effects. In particular, Kowalski (1992) presents EC in the context of temporal databases, comparing it with temporal relational databases. Many variants of EC have been proposed by different authors, but most further development of EC subsequent to the original proposal focused on employing time points instead of time periods, as pointed out by (Sadri and Kowalski, 1995). In this Section, we briefly present EC taking this widespread perspective.

From a description of events which occur in the real world and properties they initiate or terminate, EC derives the maximal validity intervals (MVIs) over which properties hold. The notions of event, property, time point and time interval are the primitives of the formalism: *events* happen at *time points* and initiate and/or terminate *time intervals* over which some *property* holds. Properties are assumed to persist until an event occurs that interrupts them (*default persistence*). An event occurrence can be represented by associating the event to the time point where it occurred, e.g. by means of the *happens(event,timePoint)* clause. The relation between events and properties can be defined by means of *initiates* and *terminates* clauses, such as:

$initiates(event1, property, T) \leftarrow$
  $happens(event1, T) \wedge$
  $holds(prop1, T) \wedge ... \wedge holds(propN, T).$

$terminates(event2, property, T) \leftarrow$
  $happens(event2, T) \wedge$
  $holds(prop1, T) \wedge ... \wedge holds(propN, T).$

This *initiates* (*terminates*) clause states that each event of type *event1* (*event2*) initiates (terminates) a period of time during which *property* holds, provided that N (possibly zero) given preconditions hold at instant T. The EC model of time and change is concerned with deriving the maximal validity intervals (MVIs) over which properties hold. For example, consider Figure 1a with one initiating event (marked with i) and two subsequent terminating events ($t1$ and $t2$) for a property p: p maximally holds between 1 and 3, and it cannot hold between 1 and 4, because $t1$ would be an interrupting event which would break the interval. Figure 1b presents a situation where two initiating events ($i1$ and $i2$) are followed by a terminating event (t): in this case, although [2,4] is definitely a validity interval, it is not maximal, and the MVI for the property is [1,4]. A declarative implementation of the derivation of MVIs in PROLOG can be obtained with a very concise program, e.g., see (Sadri and Kowalski, 1995). Obtaining an efficient PROLOG implementation is less trivial, see (Chittaro and Montanari, 1996) for a discussion of computational complexity aspects.

A property is assumed not valid at the left endpoint of an MVI, and valid at the right endpoint. In Figure 1a, p is thus valid for any instant greater than 1, and lower or equal than 3. As pointed out by (Chittaro and Montanari 1996), the use of preconditions in the initiation and termination of properties implicitly defines a property dependency graph, which illustrates the dependency relations among properties for the derivation of MVIs. More precisely, the *property dependency graph* is a directed acyclic graph such that:

- Each node denotes a property p;
- there exists an edge (p_j, p_i), if and only if there exists an *initiates* or *terminates* clause for p_i, having p_j as one of its preconditions.

The acyclicity requirement is introduced to ensure that the derivation process always terminates. An example of property dependency graph is illustrated in Figure 7.

Chittaro and Montanari (1996) distinguished two different ways of interpreting *initiates* clauses in the derivation of MVIs. In the first one (*weak* interpretation), an initiating event initiates a MVI, provided that the property does not already hold at the time point of occurrence. This interpretation is the one applied in Figure 1b. The alternative interpretation (*strong* interpretation) considers also initiating events as interrupting events. Applying it to the three events of Figure 1b, we would thus obtain the MVI depicted in Figure 1c. In the following, we will adopt the weak interpretation because it is more frequently found in the literature and also because it proved more useful in our application experience with patient monitoring (Chittaro and Dojat, 1997).

3 TIC: Event Calculus with Temporal Indeterminacy.

In this Section, we present our approach to deal with temporal indeterminacy. Although we adopt EC as our temporal ontology, the proposed ideas can be reformulated for adoption in other approaches. First, Section 3.1 extends the notion of event and MVI, to deal with the indeterminacy in locating events, then, Section 3.2 informally illustrates some relevant situations of MVI derivation in the case of partially ordered events. Finally, Section 3.3 generalizes the

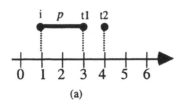

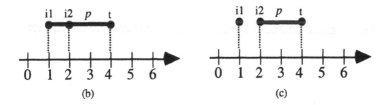

Fig. 1. Examples of (a) MVI, (b) weak interpretation, and (c) strong interpretation.

illustrated situations, and provides a formal description of TIC. Although we have used PROLOG to implement the new calculus presented in this paper, we will illustrate our proposal without committing the reader to a specific programming language.

As mentioned before, TIC is concerned with deriving *necessary* information, that is, given a set of events with indeterminate occurrence time (possibly resulting in a partially ordered sequence of events), every MVI we derive must be *consistent with any possible assignment* of all indeterminate occurrence times (total ordering of events). This is the perspective adopted in all the following sections.

3.1 Introducing Events with Indeterminate Occurrence Times.

While EC assigns a precise timestamp to any event recorded in the database, in this work we relax this constraint, by allowing also to assign an interval of indeterminacy to an event. This interval specifies the time span over which we are certain that the (unknown) timestamp is located. More formally, indeterminacy in event occurrences is represented by generalizing the second argument of *happens*. We use the *happens(event, IntervalOfIndeterminacy)* clause, where *IntervalOfIndeterminacy* (IOI) is a convex interval over which *event* necessarily happened, and is assumed to be open to the left and closed to the right (according to time interval conventions in EC). For example, *happens(e, [2, 5])* states that the occurrence time of event e is greater than 2 and lower or equal than 5. For uniformity of notation, in the special case where the timestamp is precisely determined, we denote the event occurrence as *happens(e, [t, t])*, where t is the timestamp.

The definition of MVI changes accordingly to the more general concept of event. Since a property is initiated and terminated by events, the occurrence time of these events can now be indeterminate, and an MVI has the form $\langle Start, End \rangle$ where $Start$ (End) denotes either a specific instant, when it is known, or the *minimal* interval over which the initiation (termination) of the property is necessarily located in the case of indeterminacy. The maximal interval of necessary validity for the property is delimited by $Start$ and End: if $Start$ (End) is a precise instant, it is trivially the left (right) endpoint of the delimited validity interval; if $Start$ (End) is itself an interval, then the right (left) endpoint of $Start$ (End) is the left (right) endpoint of the delimited validity interval. Therefore, a $Start$ (End) determines (i) the minimal interval over which the initiation (termination) of an instance of a property is necessarily located, and (ii) when the property initiates (terminates) to be necessary valid. For example, suppose to have only two events in the database: $happens(e1, [2, 5])$, and $happens(e2, [10, 10])$, and $e1$ initiates property p while $e2$ terminates the property. In this case, we know that the initiation of the property is necessarily located over interval [2,5] and the termination is located at time 10. We represent this knowledge, by saying that $\langle [2, 5], [10, 10] \rangle$ is a MVI for property p. Therefore, property p is necessarily valid at any instant greater than 5 and lower or equal than 10.

For conciseness, when an IOI is the interval of indeterminacy for an event which initiates (terminates) property p, we refer to the IOI as an *initiating* (*terminating*) IOI for p. We also refer to the interval of indeterminacy of the event e as IOI e.

3.2 Deriving Maximal Validity Intervals under Indeterminacy.

The most difficult problem to be tackled when introducing IOIs is that the order among events in the database can become partial. This problem arises when there are intersections among IOIs. In this Section, we illustrate how to deal with some relevant situations of intersection in order to derive MVIs for any given property. We first consider intersection among initiating IOIs, then among terminating IOIs, and finally among initiating and terminating IOIs. The general calculus presented in Section 3.3 includes, combines, and generalizes these situations.

Intersection among initiating IOIs. Let us consider a database containing some initiating IOIs for property p, such that their intersection is not empty, and each IOI has no intersection with terminating IOIs for p. It is here important to derive one single IOI for use as a $Start$ in a MVI. The solution to the problem is given by the interval whose left (right) endpoint is the minimum left (right) endpoint of the given IOIs. Indeed, property p cannot initiate before the minimum left endpoint because there are no other preceding events which initiate it, but it necessarily initiates after the minimum left endpoint, and before or at the minimum right endpoint. The latter delimits the interval of necessary validity for property p, because at least one initiating event happens before or at it, and there is no lower time that guarantees the same.

For example, take the three initiating IOIs ($i1$, $i2$, and $i3$) for p in Figure 2. In this case, we know that in each of the three intervals [1,6], [3,4], and [5,7], an initiating event happened. The derived *Start* is thus [1,4]: we know that the initiation of p is necessarily located over [1,4]. Property p cannot initiate before 1 because there are no other preceding events which initiate it, but it necessarily initiates after 1 (and before or at 4). Time point 4 is the left endpoint of the interval of necessary validity for p, because at least one initiating event happens before or at 4, and there is no lower time that guarantees the same.

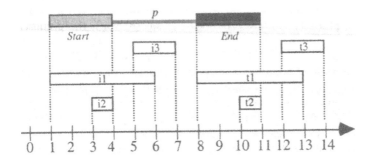

Fig. 2. Three initiating IOIs, three terminating IOIs, and the derived MVI.

Intersection among terminating IOIs. Let us consider a database containing some terminating IOIs for property p, such that their intersection is not empty, and each IOI has no intersection with initiating IOIs for p. It is here important to identify one single IOI for possible use as an *End* in a MVI. The solution to the problem is again given by the interval whose left (right) endpoint is the minimum left (right) endpoint of the given IOIs. Indeed, property p cannot terminate before the minimum left endpoint because there are no other preceding events which terminate it, but it necessarily terminates after the minimum left endpoint, and before or at the minimum right endpoint. The necessity of the validity for property p thus terminates at the minimum left endpoint, because a terminating event can happen after that point.

For example, considering the three terminating IOIs ($t1$, $t2$, and $t3$) for p in Figure 2, the derived *End* is [8,11]. Therefore, $\langle [1,4], [8,11] \rangle$ is a MVI for p.

Intersection among initiating and terminating IOIs. When an initiating and a terminating IOI for the same property have a nonempty intersection, it is impossible to establish in what order the corresponding initiating and terminating events happened. As a consequence, it is not possible to conclude anything about the necessary effects of the initiating IOI (it can be a *Start* for an MVI only if we know that the initiating event happened after the terminating one), while the terminating IOI maintains its capability of being used in an *End* with respect to previous *Starts*.

For example, Figure 3 shows four cases of intersection among IOIs for the same property, such that if we consider only the four pairs of intersecting IOIs, nothing can be concluded about the necessary validity of the property: there is no derivable MVI which is consistent with any possible ordering of indeterminate events.

Considering all the nine IOIs in the database, *i0* is a *Start* for the property, and *t1* is an *End*. These two IOIs identify the only derivable MVI in the full database, i.e. the only one which is consistent with any possible ordering of indeterminate events.

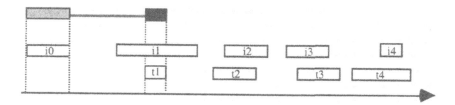

Fig. 3. Examples of intersection among initiating and terminating IOIs.

A case which requires a careful treatment occurs when initiating IOIs which intersect terminating IOIs are followed by other initiating IOIs which do not intersect terminating IOIs. Derivation of *Starts* in this case requires the consideration of the terminating IOIs besides the initiating ones. For example, consider the situation in Figure 4. We can conclude that property *p* is necessarily valid after *i2*, because *i2* has no intersection with any terminating IOI, but to determine the minimal interval for *Start*, we have to consider also *i1* and *t*. Since the ordering between events *i1* and *t* is unknown, the initiating event for the identified instance of *p* can be both *i1* (when *i1* actually precedes *i2*) and *i2* (when *i2* actually precedes *i1*). The IOI *i2* will belong completely to *Start*, while only a part of IOI *i1* will be included in *Start*, because when *i1* is the initiating event for the identified instance of *p*, it is impossible for *i1* to be located before IOI *t* (the instance of *p* initiated by *i1* would be terminated by *t*). Therefore, the *Start* for the identified instance of *p* is given by IOI [1,6]: the initiation for that instance is necessarily located in that interval.

The introduction of non-convex Starts. In the general case, a *Start* need not to be necessarily convex. This is exemplified in Figure 5, where, like in the situation of Figure 4, we can conclude that property *p* is necessarily valid after *i2*, and then we have to similarly consider *i1* and *t* to determine *Start*. Unlike the case in Figure 4, *i1* and *i2* do not overlap. Therefore, the *Start* for the identified instance of *p* is given by a non-convex interval which comprises [1,3] and [4,6]: property *p* is necessarily valid after 6, and it has been necessarily initiated over the non-convex interval [[1,3], [4,6]], obtained as the union of [1,3] and [4,6].

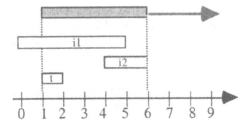

Fig. 4. Example of convex *Start*.

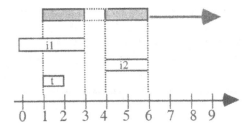

Fig. 5. Example of non-convex *Start*.

3.3 Formalizing TIC.

In this Section, we formally describe the proposed calculus in the general case. First, we focus on the identification of *Starts* and *Ends*, then we consider their coupling for the derivation of MVIs. We exemplify the definitions on the database depicted in Figure 6, which contains seven initiating IOIs and two terminating IOIs for property *p*.

We initially assume that there are no preconditions in *initiates* and *terminates* clauses. Then, after presenting all the different entities, we complete the formalization by easily introducing preconditions.

Basic Definitions. We define $initIOI(p)$ and $termIOI(p)$ as the sets of initiating and terminating IOIs for a property *p*, respectively. Formally:

$$InitIOI(p) = \{I \mid \exists e(initiates(e, p, I))\}$$
$$TermIOI(p) = \{I \mid \exists e(terminates(e, p, I))\}$$

Note that, in the case where no preconditions are used, the definitions of *initiates(e,p,I)* and *terminates(e,p,I)* clauses (described in Section 2) do not contain

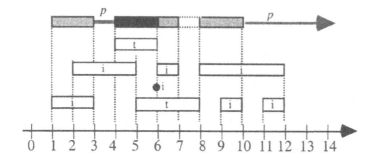

Fig. 6. A more complex example.

holds clauses. In Figure 6, we have $InitIOI(p)$={[1,3], [2,5], [6,6], [6,7], [8,12], [9,10], [11,12]}, and $TermIOI(p)$={[4,6], [5,8]}.

We now identify a subset of $InitIOI(p)$, which comprises those initiating IOIs which do not intersect with any terminating IOIs:

$$DisjointFromTerm(p) =$$
$$\{I \in InitIOI(p) \mid \neg\exists T(T \in TermIOI(p) \land I \cap T \neq \emptyset)\}$$

In the example, we have $DisjointFromTerm(p)$={[1,3], [8,12], [9,10], [11,12]}.

Given a set of IOIs S, the set $GroupedIOI(S)$ is a subset of 2^S defined as follows:

$$GroupedIOI(S) = \{G \mid G \subseteq S \land \bigcup_{I \in G} I \text{ is a convex interval}\}$$

Considering Figure 6, we have for example $GroupedIOI(DisjointFromTerm(p))$ = {{[1,3]}, {[8,12]}, {[9,10]}, {[11,12]}, {[8,12], [9,10]}, {[8,12], [11,12]}, {[8,12], [9,10], [11,12]}}, or $GroupedIOI(TermIOI(p))$={{[4,6]}, {[5,8]}, {[4,6], [5,8]}}.

The set $MaxGroupedIOI(S)$ is the set of maximal elements[1] of $GroupedIOI(S)$:

$$MaxGroupedIOI(S) = \{MG \mid MG \in GroupedIOI(S) \land$$
$$\neg\exists G(G \in GroupedIOI(S) \land MG \subset G)\}$$

In the example, $MaxGroupedIOI(DisjointFromTerm(p))$ = {{[1,3]}, {[8,12], [9,10], [11,12]}}, and $MaxGroupedIOI(TermIOI(p))$ = {{[4,6], [5,8]}}.

---

[1] From a computational point of view, it is important to underline that we are interested only in the computation of the maximal elements of $GroupedIOI(S)$. While enumerating the elements of $GroupedIOI(S)$ can require an exponential time, the enumeration of its maximal elements can be done in polynomial time by sequentially considering the IOIs in the database, associating each one to its unique corresponding maximal set.

We now define the precedes relation ($<$) and three functions on intervals (*right*, *left*, and *minprev*). The functions *right* and *left* simply return the right and the left endpoints of an interval, respectively. For example, $right([1,3])=1$, and $left([1,3])=3$. If the interval is non-convex, its right and left endpoints are assumed to be respectively the rightmost and the leftmost of the endpoints of its convex subintervals. For example, $right([[1,3],[4,6]])=1$, and $left([[1,3],[4,6]])=6$. An interval I precedes an interval I' ($I < I'$) if $right(I) \leq left(I')$. For example, $[1,3]<[5,8]$ and $[2,5]<[5,8]$ are true, while $[1,3]<[2,5]$ is false.

In order to define the function *minprev*, we first define the set *PrevIOI(I,S)*. Given an IOI I and a set of IOIs S, *PrevIOI(I,S)* is the set of those IOIs in S which come immediately before I:

$$PrevIOI(I,S) = \{I' \in S \mid I' < I \wedge \neg\exists I''(I'' \in S \wedge$$
$$I'' < I \wedge right(I'') > right(I'))\}$$

Now we can define *minprev* as the function which, given an IOI I and a set of IOIs S, returns the IOI in *PrevIOI(I,S)* with the minimum timespan:

$$minprev(I,S) = I' \in PrevIOI(I,S) \text{ such that}$$
$$right(I') - left(I') = min(right(I'') - left(I'') \mid I'' \in PrevIOI(I,S))$$

For example, if we had an IOI $[14,20]$ in Figure 6, the set *PrevIOI([14,20], InitIOI(p))* would be equal to $\{[8,12], [11,12]\}$, and *minprev([14,20],InitIOI(p))* would be $[11,12]$. Finally, we define the generic set *Intersecting(I,S)* as the set of those IOIs in S which intersect interval I:

$$Intersecting(I,S) = \{I' \in S \mid I \cap I' \neq \emptyset\}$$

In Figure 6, for example, *Intersecting([5,7],InitIOI(p))* $=\{[6,6], [6,7]\}$.

Starts. To formalize the notion of *Start*, we distinguish two different subparts of a *Start*: the first (called *Body*) is the nonempty part which can be identified by considering initiating IOIs which do not intersect with terminating IOIs, while the second (called *ext*) is the possibly empty part which considers those initiating IOIs which do intersect with terminating IOIs. The set of *Starts* for a property p, called *Start(p)*, is thus defined as follows:

$Start(p) = \{B \cup ext(B,p) \mid B \in Body(p)\}$
where
$Body(p) = \{[b1,b2] \mid MG \in MaxGroupedIOI(DisjointFromTerm(p)) \wedge$
$\quad b1 = min(left(I) \mid I \in MG) \wedge b2 = min(right(I) \mid I \in MG) \wedge$
$\quad minprev([b1,b2], InitIOI(p) \cup TermIOI(p)) \notin DisjointFromTerm(p)\}$

Each element of *Body(p)* is obtained by considering an element (i.e., a set of intervals) of *MaxGroupedIOI(DisjointFromTerm(p))*. From this element, we derive an interval $[b1, b2]$, following the criterion (minimum left and right endpoints) presented in Section 3.2 (Intersection among initiating IOIs). The constraint of weak initiation is enforced by the last line of the definition, which excludes that p is already valid due to a preceding initiating IOI: it allows only that the immediately preceding IOI (if any) is a terminating one or is an initiating one intersecting a terminating one. In Figure 6, we have $Body(p)=\{[1,3],[8,10]\}$.

Given an element B of $Body(p)$, if $MPT = minprev(B, TermIOI(p))$ does not exist, then the ext part for B is $\emptyset$, otherwise:

$$ext(B, p) = \bigcup_{I \in IT} I$$
where
$$IT = \{ \ [i1, i2] \mid I' \in Intersecting(MPT, InitIOI(p)) \wedge$$
$$i1 = max(left(I'), left(MPT)) \wedge i2 = right(I')\}$$

Given a body B for a property p, the function $ext(B, p)$ returns the corresponding second part of $Start$. To do this, it considers the terminating IOI (if any) immediately preceding B, and the initiating IOIs (if any) which intersect the considered terminating one. For each of these initiating IOIs, it excludes those points which precede the terminating IOI. The function returns the (possibly non-convex) union of the obtained intervals. In the example, $ext([1, 3], p) = \emptyset$, and $ext([8,10],p)=[6,7]$.

The set $Start(p)$ for Figure 6 is thus equal to $\{[1,3], [[6,7],[8,10]]\}$.

Ends. First, the set $End(p)$ contains the special symbol *infplus* (positive infinity), denoting a timestamp which occurs after any IOI in the database: this is introduced to ensure default persistence also in those cases where there are no terminating events for an instance of a property (the property is thus assumed to hold up to *infplus*). Second, each other element of $End(p)$ is obtained by considering an element (i.e., a set of intervals) of $GroupedIOI(TermIOI(p))$. From this set of intervals, we derive an interval $[t1, t2]$, following the criterion (minimum left and right endpoints) presented in Section 3.2 (Intersection among terminating IOIs):

$$End(p) = \{infplus\} \cup \{[t1, t2] \mid MG \in MaxGroupedIOI(TermIOI(p)) \wedge$$
$$t1 = min(left(T) \mid T \in MG) \wedge t2 = min(right(T) \mid T \in MG)$$

In Figure 6, we have $End(p)=\{[4,6], infplus\}$.

MVIs. An MVI is defined as a pair $\langle S, E \rangle$ of a $Start$ and an End, such that S precedes E, and the interval comprised between S and E is not interrupted by a terminating event:

$$MVI(p) = \{\langle S, E \rangle \mid S \in Start(p) \wedge E \in End(p) \wedge S < E \wedge \neg broken(p, \langle S, E \rangle)\}$$
$$where \ broken(p, \langle S, E \rangle) = \exists T(T \in TermIOI(p) \wedge S < T < E)$$

In Figure 6, we have $MVI(p) = \{\langle[1,3],[4,6]\rangle, \langle[[6,7],[8,10]], infplus\rangle\}$.

Note that the definition of *broken* requires that the IOI for the interrupting event is strictly between the *Start* and the *End* for the MVI. Cases where IOIs for the interrupting event intersect with *Start* or *End* are already ruled out by the definitions of *Start* and *End*.

Introducing Preconditions. In the general case, preconditions are used in the definition of *initiates* and *terminates*: the corresponding clauses thus contain *holds* predicates. To take this into account, we conclude the formalization of TIC with the definition of the *holds* predicate:

$$holds(p, I) = \exists\langle S, E\rangle(\langle S, E\rangle \in MVI(p) \wedge$$
$$right(S) \leq left(I) \wedge right(I) \leq left(E))$$

Note that the *holds(p,I)* predicate is defined using the *MVI(p)* set. Therefore, the definition of MVI for a property with preconditions is based on the definition of MVIs for its preconditions, which in turn can depend on other preconditions, and so on. Since the property dependency graph is acyclic, we have a guarantee that this recursive process terminates. For example, in Figure 7, the definition of *MVI(x)* relies on the definition of *MVI(p)* and *MVI(q)*, which both rely on the definition of *MVI(a)*. The definition of *MVI(a)* is independent from any other property.

4 Discussion.

Dean and Boddy (1988) studied the task of deriving which facts must be true over certain intervals of time in presence of partially ordered events (in our context, when properties must necessarily hold), focusing on the computational complexity of the task and showing that it is intractable in the general case. To tackle this problem, they propose to develop polynomial algorithms to compute subsets of the set of necessary facts. This criterion has been adopted in our approach. Indeed, computing *all* the necessary MVIs would have inevitably forced us in some cases to explicitly evaluate the effects of all the possible event orderings, thus falling in the intractable case. Instead of explicitly generating the possible orderings, we identified the general temporal patterns (intuitively and formally defined in the previous Sections) among initiating and terminating IOIs from which necessary facts can be derived. In some cases, e.g. if no preconditions are used in defining *initiates* and *terminates* clauses, all the necessary MVIs are recognized by the identified temporal patterns. Incompleteness arises in some situations where preconditions are used, and it may happen that a pattern can be only partially recognized unless different orderings are studied. For example, suppose that property *a* (initiated by event *ea*) indicates the availability of a resource, properties *p* and *q* (initiated by events *ep* and *eq*, respectively) need the resource to be initiated, and the initiation of *p* or *q* consumes the resource. This is formally expressed by clauses 1-5 in Figure 7a. Consider now the situ-

```
initiates(ea,a,T) ←            (1)
    happens(ea,T).
initiates(ep,p,T) ←            (2)
    happens(ep,T) ∧
    holds(a,T).
initiates(eq,q,T) ←            (3)
    happens(eq,T) ∧
    holds(a,T).
terminates(ep,a,T) ←           (4)
    happens(ep,T).
terminates(eq,a,T) ←           (5)
    happens(eq,T).
initiates(ex,x,T) ←            (6)
    happens(ex,T) ∧
    (holds(p,T) ∨ holds(q,T)).
```

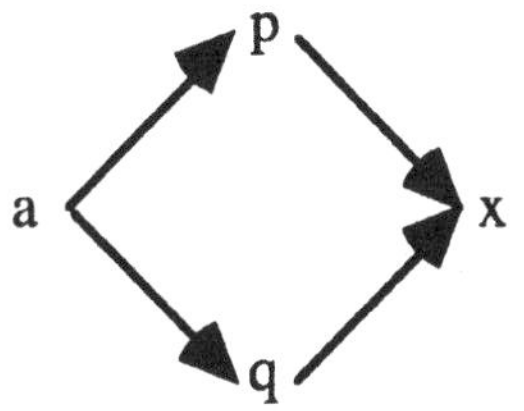

Fig. 7. (a) A set of property definitions, and (b) its property dependency graph.

ation depicted in Figure 8, where specific IOIs are given for events ea ([1,3]), ep ([6,8]), and eq ([5,9]). This situation is fully handled by TIC, which returns the MVI $\langle [1,3],[5,8]\rangle$ for property a, concluding that property a is necessarily initiated in the interval [1,3], necessarily valid in the interval [3,5], and necessarily terminated in the interval [5,8]. Correctly, TIC does not conclude anything about the necessary validity of properties p and q. Indeed, there are no MVIs for them which exist for every possible ordering of events ep and eq.

Suppose now to consider the full set of clauses in Figure 7a, thus adding a new property definition to the database: clause 6 states that property x is initiated by an event ex if p or q are valid. Furthermore, suppose to have an instance of the new event ex at 10. After introducing this new data, the output of TIC does not change, but it is now incomplete. TIC misses a necessary MVI: property x is necessarily valid from 10, because, although we cannot conclude for certain that precondition p is valid or that precondition q is valid at 10, at least one of the two must hold. In order to reach this conclusion, it would be necessary to develop the possible relative orderings of events eq and ep.

From a computational complexity point of view, derivation of MVIs in basic EC with preconditions has been shown to be polynomial (Chittaro and Montanari, 1996). With respect to that case, we add a computational load consisting in the determination of the role of each IOI in the defined temporal patterns. Even assuming a trivial implementation, this requires at worst to temporally relate each IOI to each other one: if there are n IOIs in the database, at worst n^2 pairings may be considered. Although this extra computation increases the order of complexity of the calculus, it maintains complexity polynomial.

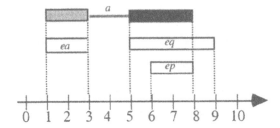

Fig. 8. An example with preconditions.

5 Current Work.

In this paper, we have presented TIC (TIC, Temporal Indeterminacy event Calculus). From a description of events whose precise temporal occurrence is unknown, and a description of the properties initiated or terminated by those events, TIC derives intervals over which properties are necessarily valid, and intervals of indeterminacy for the initiating and terminating instants of the properties.

In the previous section, we have pointed out how TIC renounces to the completeness of its output in order to achieve tractability. Our current work in this direction is aimed at precisely characterizing the relations between the set of all necessary MVIs and its proper subset computed by TIC. Moreover, we aim at identifying those restrictions on the database, for which TIC computes the full set of necessary MVIs (besides the simple case where preconditions are not used).

Finally, we are extending TIC in a seamless way to consider also information organized at different temporal granularities (e.g. seconds, minutes, hours,...).

References

Brusoni V., Console L., Pernici B., Terenziani P.: LATER: a General Purpose Manager of Temporal Information. In Methodologies for Intelligent Systems 8, LNCS, Springer, Heidelberg, 255 – 264 (1994).

Chittaro L., Dojat M.: Using a general theory of time and change in patient monitoring: experiment and evaluation. Computers in biology and medicine, Special issue on Time-oriented systems, **27**, in press (1997).

Chittaro L., Combi C., Cervesato E., Cervesato R., Antonini-Canterin F., Nicolosi G.L., Zanuttini D. "Specifying and representing temporal abstractions of clinical data by a query language based on the Event Calculus", to appear in Proceedings of the 24th Annual Conference on Computers in Cardiology, IEEE Press, Los Alamitos, CA (1997).

Chittaro L., Montanari A.: Efficient temporal reasoning in the Cached Event Calculus. Computational Intelligence, **12**, 359–382 (1996).

Combi C., Cucchi G.: GCH-OSQL A Temporally-Oriented Object-Oriented Query Language Based on a Three-Valued Logic. In Fourth International Workshop on Temporal Representation and Reasoning (TIME '97), IEEE Computer Society Press, Los Alamitos, CA, 119–126 (1997).

Dean T., Boddy M.: Reasoning about Partially Ordered Events, Artificial Intelligence, 36, 375–399 (1988).

Dechter R., Meiri I., Pearl J.: Temporal Constraint Networks, Artificial Intelligence, 49, 61–95 (1991).

Dyreson C.E., Snodgrass R.T.: Temporal indeterminacy. In Snodgrass R.T. (ed.) The TSQL2 temporal query language. Kluwer Academic Publishers, Boston, 327 – 346 (1995).

Gadia S.K., Nair S.S., Poon Y.C.: Incomplete Information in relational temporal databases. Proc. of the 18th VLDB Conference, Vancouver, Canada, 395 – 406 (1992).

Kowalski R., Sergot M.: A logic-based calculus of events. New Generation Computing, 4, 67-95 (1986).

Kowalski R.: Database Updates in the Event Calculus. Journal of Logic Programming, 12, 121–146 (1992).

Maiocchi R., Pernici B., Barbic F.: Automatic Deduction of Temporal Information, ACM Transactions on Database Systems, 17, 647 – 688 (1992).

Sadri F., Kowalski R.A.: Variants of the Event Calculus. Proc. 12th Internat. Conf. on Logic Programming (ICLP '95), MIT Press, Cambridge, Massachussets, 67-81 (1995).

Panel Sessions

Panel Session: Predictability in Active Real-Time/Temporal Databases *

Chair: Aloysius K. Mok[1]
Panel: John A. Stankovic[2], Ozgur Ulusoy[3], Jörgen Hansson[4],
Kam-yiu Lam[5], and Kwei-Jay Lin[6]

[1] Department of Computer Sciences, University of Texas at Austin
Austin, TX 78712, USA
e-mail: mok@cs.utexas.edu
[2] Department of Computer Science, University of Virginia
Charlottesville, VA 22903, USA
e-mail: stankovic@cs.virginia.edu
[3] Department of Computer Engineering and Information Science, Bilkent University
Bilkent, Ankara 06533, Turkey
e-mail: oulusoy@bilkent.edu.tr
[4] Department of Computer Science, University of Skövde
Box 408, S-541 28 Skövde, Sweden
e-mail: jorgen@ida.his.se
[5] Department of Computer Science, City University of Hong Kong
83 Tat Chee Avenue, Kowloon, Hong Kong
e-mail: cskylam@cityu.edu.hk
[6] University of California, Irvine
Irvine, CA 92967, USA
e-mail: klin@ece.uci.edu

Jack Stankovic - I thought I would try a little bit of an analogy talking about what is predictability. We look at, say, a real-time system and what has happened in the past; there are these approaches where the system had to be predictable, for safety critical systems. So people actually built their own special purpose real-time operating system to have complete control over it so they can make it predictable. Then there were lots of demands for using off-the-shelf things, so people tried to use commercial off-the-shelf operating systems like UNIX, and would it be predictable? No, it was terrible, it didn't really meet any real-time constraint - it was hard to say what the system would do.

And then there's this conversion that we take a UNIX and make it a real-time UNIX - try to undo the features that are bad for real-time performance and then do we get a degree of predictability? Well, it's somewhere in between, in fact, you get a lot better than just using off-the-shelf technology, but it still leaves something to be desired, compared to using a special purpose operating system. It is essentially a trade-off that we are giving up some degree of predictability for the benefit of using a commercial kernel that people are used to.

---

* These are transcripts of statements of the panel members, edited only for completeness, brevity, and clarity.

When we look at the database, we might see almost a similar pattern, I think. In real-time databases, if we want predictability and the people have built their own small databases for embedded systems, telecommunications, or air-traffic control, a lot of time these databases are main-memory resident, their transactions are pre-compiled, so they are really trying to be very precise about everything, building it up from scratch. You can get a fairly high degree of predictability there. However, there is a push again for using commercial off-the-shelf systems, like taking a database system and trying to use it, and running on top of a real-time operating system, getting predictability here is pretty much possible. Will this occur? I have not seen this yet, but how about a real-time DB2 database or a real-time Oracle 8 database, or will we start to see the commercial databases trying to adjust what they do to get more real-time properties, so we can get a degree of predictability? This, I do not think has happened yet.

Now, the analogy only goes so far, because of the different situations. In the top part of the real-time system, normally in these systems we know the worst-case execution times, we're trying to give guarantees. Possibly a 100% guarantee. We don't want the systems typically that large, they could be pretty large systems but generally not compared to say, large database systems. There is a fault-tolerance requirement that is typically something like "you need to handle these faults in real-time." Many times you are talking about critical applications or at least parts of the application are critical versus in the database world, the problem is not the same, a lot of times here the execution times we really do not know. We do not always have all pre-compiled transactions and even then we do not know the data sets that they are operating with. How important is it? If we do not know this, what are we talking about in predictability? So, here in these kinds of systems, predictability has these underlying issues associated with it. We go to databases, we talk about predictability, but we do not know the execution times, so we are already in trouble. If we want a probabilistic guarantee, or a best-effort behavior, we see that a lot of the metrics are percentages of deadlines, percentage of transactions that make the deadlines or metrics like that. Typically, the databases are large and heterogeneous. There is a degree of fault-tolerance - we want the ACID properties. So if something crashes, the data is still there, it is persistent. If we abort the transaction, however, the effect is as if it did not run. So there is a degree of fault-tolerance.

Generally, if things fail, the system says "Okay, time to reboot, time to recover, and after we recover then we start the system again." That model is not very effective in a lot of real-time systems that this kind of work is performed in. Besides, a lot of times the systems are not critical. We can see this in some of the metrics, such as transaction miss ratio 30% - 40%. What does that mean, what does that have to do with predictability? I think the other issue has to with what if we look at this notion of hard real-time guarantees. They and predictability are related to each other, they are not the same thing, but they are related. If you look at a spectrum of what we had in the past, then if you have a static system designed and off-line, you know all the worst case issues and problem and you analyze it off line. Then you can say that the system is predictable and that you are giving hard guarantees. But, then there were some real-time systems used in mission control with worst case execution time and worst case resource needs but they are not doing things off-line and when jobs or tasks arrive they have to decide whether they are coming in the system or not. If they come in, then the system operates predictably, all the things entered into the system are going to meet the deadlines, if they are not, then they are not allowed in the system. Is this predictable? Well, there is a degree of predictability for everything that has been accepted; we know what it's going to do, provided it has not been rejected.

Maybe we also want a statistical measure here of what percentage is not allowed in the system. We are starting to water down predictability as meaning determinism. Admission control begs on statistical guarantees, we are seeing this in the multimedia area, so that you say that your system has a certain amount of performance, it allows a certain percentage of the work to be satisfied and that work gets its full requirement, or what about you if you have re-negotiation in there and you are relaxing the requirements, but you get a statistical guarantee from the system with or without full guarantees. If you can say that, you can say my system has this kind of performance predictably, it allows this much work statistically and if you relax the requirement so well you get this kind of performance. Is that predictable? I think it is, it is just a much more relaxed definition.

You can have best-effort with analysis, meaning: Suppose we take the system and all the protocols in it are best-effort, but we look at all the workloads, anticipated workloads and we analyze the system and we say that 98% of the tasks or transactions meet their deadlines and this is what we are handing to someone. Is that predictable? It's probabilistic predictability, but it is in some sense a predictable system, and all they way down the best-effort where all the protocols are there but there was no analysis done off-line to say what the system might achieve. So, in some ways, I think that this looks a lot like a quality of service flavor, in the stuff that been done in real-time systems we do this off-line and in the admission control the quality of service was to guarantee deadline or not, and that was your binary choice. But there is more choices coming into play and as they come into play, I don't see any reason why, in systems that no longer have all the reliability and fault-tolerance requirements, that predictability can't mean a more probabilistic predictability.

Ozgur Ulusoy - Okay, I would like to express my opinions on the predictability concept. Everyone here agrees, that the two most important factors that make predictability impossible in current database systems are the I/O delay and data conflicts. For the first factor I can say that depending on the advances in the hardware technology in the near future, it can be possible to have main memory databases. Even for very large size databases. Therefore, the unpredictability due to I/O delay can be prevented. I believe that our discussion here should more focused on reducing the unpredictability due to data conflicts.

The key point, I think, in doing that is the pre-allocation of data resources. Many of you can argue that data requirements of transaction may not be known before their execution. However, I claim that it can be possible in a main-memory database system in the following way. When a transaction is submitted to the system, while parsing it with some syntactic means, it can be possible to determine which data items will be accessed by the transaction, but at a relation granularity. That means, we cannot know which tuples in each relation can be accessed by the transaction. But pre-declaration of data can be possible at a relation granularity.

It was pointed out by many researchers that large data granularities, like relation, are most appropriate in main memory database systems. So it will not be inefficient to schedule transactions at a relation level, and after the pre-declaration step we can check whether the transaction has any conflicts with other scheduled transactions and if there is no such conflict it can be started. When the transaction starts its execution it can be executed in a conflict-free manner and this is very important for the predictability, because it will not experience the overhead of conflicts such as blocking and transaction abort.

Another important concept here is that the CPU can be fully utilized for processing the operations of the transaction, which means without the overhead of conflict checks at each data access, and without the context switches between the scheduler and the transactions. So, in conclusion, I believe that in order to reduce unpredictability due to data conflict, dynamic allocation of data resources should not be the choice. Therefore pre-declaration of data is the key concept.

Jörgen Hansson - Well, I will just try to revisit some of the literature that has been published in the last couple of years when it comes to sources of unpredictability in active real-time databases. We have heard several presentations here where a deadline is associated with the transaction, and we are also familiar with some work that focuses on deadlines for data. It looks to me that when we have these active database systems, where we are making use of the ECA paradigm that has a lot of expressive power when it comes to specifying reactive behavior, and when we combine this with coupling modes, then we will really have something useful. Still the ECA rule language does not necessarily include timing constraints.

When we look at what really happens in an active real-time database system, at some point in time we have an event occurrence. Then we have an event detection, followed by firing some rules guided by which rules to evaluate, and then we focus on how to perform scheduling of the triggered transaction, which hopefully will meet its deadline. It seems to me that the work carried out so far, to some extent guarantees certain situations of transaction deadlines and data deadlines. Still, there is no such thing, as far as I know, when it comes to time cognizant event detection schemes and methods, and time cognizant or predictable processing of rule requirements, which is necessary if a transaction deadline should be relative to the event occurrence, and not the time when the event was detected by the system.

If we look into the situation when we have event showers, we will see that most events in database systems are internally generated as opposed to real-time systems that also have a degree of externally generated events. Of course, some of the event showers we can handle by specifying the maximum event arrival rate for the system, but that does not necessarily solve the problem of bounded and predictable event detection. Because, even though we specify the maximum number of externally generated events or even the number of internally generated events, there is still some degree of unpredictability in determining how much time it takes to notify a set of rules because that is also a function of the size of the rule base.

To me it looks like what we also have to look at these new sources of unpredictability in active real-time database systems. These are not really new sources, because some of them have been mentioned before in the literature. It seems to me that these have not yet been solved, and they are worthy of some discussion. It seems to me that we have to come up with predictable event detection schemes, handling the case with primitive events and then composite events. We have a situation where we have both externally generated versus internally generated events, which, I think this is a little different from the traditional database paradigm. The next question is how do we predictably and efficiently evaluate rule sets, perform rule selection, make decisions of which rules to trigger, etc., in order to make sure that the time it takes is, at least to some extent, bounded or predictable.

Kam-yiu Lam - Predictability in real-time database systems, since the transaction has deadlines, is that we would like to have all transactions completing before the deadline. For the actual issues, because the surrounding environment is always changing, we would like the system to be able to respond to all critical events occurring in the environment. How about the temporal relationships, okay the data is temporal data, so with it to maintain the temporal consistency of all time for all the data, my opinion is that it is not necessary. Only thing we have to do is to ensure that all the transactions will access temporally consistent data. We do not mind for some data to be temporally inconsistent. Because in order to maintain all the data temporally consistent, we may have to pay a lot of update transactions to distribute trivial updates all over the system.

To achieve this objective, is in my personal opinion very difficult. There exist of a lot of places that can introduce unpredictability, just as Ulusoy said before, data conflict, I/O's, the dynamic workload, or the triggering of transactions. In order to have a highly predictable system, we must gather information about the transactions and the data, the probability of triggering data requirements. And also for the data we have to define the absolute validity interval and the relative validity interval. The problem is that for some applications it may not be easy to do so. For example, about a stock trading system, how can we define performance parameters for the stock? Yes, it depends on the current situation on the stock market, it can change very quickly, so it is very difficult to predict.

Anyway, for hard real-time transactions deadlines are very important, so we must have a highly predictable system. In this way we must satisfy this requirement. Even if we have this information the hard real-time transaction also may have to be aborted due to the access of some invalid data, the data may be temporally inconsistent. In this case, even if we use some scheduling, for example rate monotonic, we still cannot guarantee that all hard real-time transactions can complete within their deadline. At least until now, we still have no solution to solve this problem for hard real-time transactions.

For soft real-time transactions it would be okay to have a statistically predictable system, just as Prof. Stankovic has said before, where for example 30% - 35% of the transactions can complete before the deadline, which we can guarantee. How about a situation when we have a mixed transaction system, i.e., the system has hard real-time transactions and at the same time the system has soft real-time transactions? In this case it becomes much more complicated, and the scheduling of the hard real-time transactions can affect the scheduling of the soft real-time transactions and in this case we may not be able to achieve a satisfactory guaranteed probability. So, what shall we do? Well, a possibility, I think is, to relax the timing constraint on the soft real-time transaction. Okay, for example, you redefine the deadline of the soft real-time transaction to be 40 seconds after its arrival, then we find that we may have 10% of soft deadlines missed in a mixed system. However, if we relax the timing constraint to be say 41 seconds, then we maybe have a better performance for the soft real-time. In this way we can prove the performance and the predictability of the system. Another way is to relax the interval for data consistency, for example we can use similarity or other solutions, for example epsilon serializability.

Kwei-Jay Lin - I have been requested in real-time to search my database, to try to actively find some answers. I think that the ways we have been doing real-time research for about 20 years, maybe 15, and one of the big lessons that we have learned and we try to teach people is that real-time does not mean "fast." Jack Stankovic has used this sentence in many different places, and we have always tried to tell people that real-time actually means bounded, that is what we mean by predictability. Predictability means that, for example, if we use scheduling, we want to bound the completion time. It does not need to always finish very fast, but it needs to be finished before the deadline. That is something that we have learned in the past 15-20 years.

On the other hand, I am not very familiar with the active part. My impression is that when people are talking about active databases, what they want is a fast way to trigger certain actions, because of events occurring. The idea of events is good, because with event-condition-action rules you do not need to search the whole database. When you have a certain event occur, immediately you can have some rule being triggered so therefore you can have fast reaction. On the other hand, if you look at just the active database systems, they are not really so concerned about bounding the time. This means that if you want to have real-time active, or active real-time, you want it to be fast and you want to have it bounded.

The other way to look at this, is to compare the two kinds of systems. In an active system, whenever you have an event, you want to bound the time it will take for something to start off. Therefore, we try to bound the triggering time so that is immediate. Then, depending on your system, you can generate actions. In real-time systems, on the other hand, we do not really care about when something is triggered, but we want to be able to bound the completion time. So again, if we want to marry these two, the real-time and the active part, we are trying to bound the trigger time as well as the completion time, which again is very difficult.

Now, the third way to look at the question that Al Mok has posed is to look at what we are talking about here. Are we talking about active real-time database systems or are we talking about real-time active database systems? I think it is very smart in this workshop to have just "active *comma* real-time *comma*," so therefore both of them are kind of and/or. There is no way to say that one is more important than the other. If you want to build active real-time database systems, then what we are trying to do is that we have a real-time database system, then we want to put the active property or active mechanism into the real-time database so that it can improve the real-time capability, which is the predictability.

Therefore the question now, if you want to do this kind of research, should be: "How do we use triggers or ECA rules to help improve the real-time property of a real-time database system?" The other way to look at this question is that, if we have an active database, how do we put the real-time property in, or how do we use real-time mechanisms to help active database systems. I think Al Mok has been working on the rule-based system, and how to bound the completion time. I think both are valid approaches to try to solve this problem.

Personally, I feel that if you want a real-time database you probably should start with a real-time system, because if you design an active system and then try to make it real-time it is very difficult. Some scenarios may illustrate how difficult this problem is. I am thinking of, in terms of my working environment, what kind of people we have that are like real-time systems, and what kind of people we have that are like active systems. I have these two different kinds of people that I work closely with. One is my secretary and the other group of people are the graduate students. Which one do you think is real-time and which one do you think is active? If a student is active it is okay, because if you give him some idea then he immediately jumps on it and he is so excited about your new idea. We also know that graduate students are not always real-time, in the sense that they not always produce the results before the deadline of a conference submission. On the other hand, the other kind of person is the secretary. We want him/her to be able to meet our deadline, so we don't really care exactly when they start, but we are more concerned about when they deliver the result. So again, the question now is how do you build a real-time active database, or an active real-time database. How do you make a graduate student behave like a secretary or how do you make a secretary behave like a graduate student?

Panel Session: Practical and Industrial Experience in Active Real-Time Databases *

Chair: John A. Stankovic[1]
Panel: John A. Stankovic[1], Anindya Datta[2],
Martin Kersten[3], and Sten F. Andler[4]

[1] Department of Computer Science, University of Virginia
Charlottesville, VA 22903, USA
e-mail: stankovic@cs.virginia.edu
[2] Department of MIS, University of Arizona
Tucson, AZ 85721, USA
e-mail: adatta@loochi.bpa.arizona.edu
[3] Centrum voor Wiskunde en Informatica (CWI)
Kruislaan 413 1098 SJ Amsterdam, The Netherlands
e-mail: mk@cwi.nl
[4] Department of Computer Science, University of Skövde
Box 408, S-541 28 Skövde, Sweden
e-mail: sten@ida.his.se

Jack Stankovic - The title of this panel is "Practical and Industrial Experiences in Active Real-Time Databases". Based on this title, the first thing I thought was "well, are there any practical and industrial experiences that we can really talk about?" Certainly, for the active aspect, triggers are used in a lot of systems. For example, a lot of commercial systems have triggers; you have systems like DB2, POSTGRES, HiPAC, Sybase, and SQL3, each with triggers as part of them. So there is a lot of activity in the active DB aspects, and, consequently, a lot of experience.

The notion of "real-time" and "active" together is being pursued by some companies. I know personally of groups and people at Honeywell, Mitsubishi, IBM, Hughes Aircraft, and Lockheed Martin, all of whom are looking at this, i.e., having research groups and investigating the active and real-time aspects. But there is not much experience yet for this combination of ideas. On the other hand, we do have the notion that there are a lot of applications out there for active real-time databases. At the various workshops that have been held over the last few years, there is a vast array of applications where there are claims that the real-time active model is needed. Air traffic control, aircraft mission control, and spacecraft control are examples. And I think that I listed in our last meeting in California at RTDB'96 about twenty different application areas that people at this meeting were claiming that their work on active real-time databases was applicable for.

---

* These are transcripts of statements of the panel members, edited only for completeness, brevity, and clarity.

So the idea is that there are some experiences with active and real-time databases in a research setting, many companies are interested, there are potentially lots and lots of applications, but is there truly any experience with the real-time part, or the combination of the two? I think there is some, but it is not encouraging to date. I know of two systems. One was the system called DBx which was really a small embedded systems database focused on military applications. The database was main-memory resident, the transactions were pre-declared, and the actions were periodic. So in this application everything was well defined and it was more of a "how do we deal with the data problem in this application", rather than a full database management system. But, nevertheless this company seems to have failed commercially, although there could be many reasons for this unrelated to the technology.

EagleSpeed is the second system, very similar to DBx, and implemented by Lockheed Martin. EagleSpeed basically was for navy submarine warfare systems. The idea is that in these kinds of critical real-time systems, the data problem is getting more and more complicated. So how are we going to deal with it? Well, database management people have nice schemas, they have organized ways of dealing with complicated data. So, can we use that? But once we look at commercial tools we find that they are not appropriate because they do not have predictability, among other problems. So what the designers of these systems do, is they build their own embedded real-time database. When they do this it tends to be focused on the particular application, in this case the navy submarine warfare system. I talked to one of the designers and he said that they looked around, but that they couldn't find any commercial system that was applicable. They wanted deterministic transactions, real-time performance, and main-memory data. This is very similar to what DBx did. The designers were also trying to search for commercial applications. As far as I know, they have not been successful in moving it out into the commercial world.

So for my last transparency I have listed some questions. What is holding back the commercial use of active real-time database results? Is it that we just don't have good solutions yet? We do have answers, we do have solutions, but maybe they are not really effective enough. Or, is it that the commercial world doesn't need these solutions yet (or ever)? Or, maybe there is another possibility, that they are just not convinced yet and they simply need to be convinced. Is it just a marketing problem? I think many people in our field don't look at the commercial viability enough. When you talk about critical systems and embedded systems, where there are feedback control loops and there are real equipment and actuators being controlled, there is a degree of hard real-time in these systems that is not included in many commercial database models. So for the real-time database world you need to make use of main-memory and more pre-compiled transactions. The more you know, the more predictable you can make your system. The solutions for this might not be the same solutions as for the general purpose complex database systems. So we have this mix and match problem in the kind of solutions we're developing. And in many cases, papers I've seen in our area don't distinguish between these very different kinds of systems.

Anindya Datta - My talk will be much more story-book oriented than Jack Stankovic's. For the last two years I've had quite a bit of experience in building real systems in the financial domain, so I thought that is what I'll talk on.

First of all, I have not encountered, in spite of looking, any sort of active real-time databases in the real world. Moreover, another thing I found is that when people do talk of real-time systems, like real-time database systems, they mostly refer to soft real-time, rather than hard or firm real-time. Yet, if you go and talk to these folks in companies and say that "you have this need and I can build this for you," they say that they do this already. And they swear by the system they have. They show you this little system using some Excel spreadsheet with some few macros in it and pushing some number from here to somewhere else, and they say "this solves all our problems".

Anyway, let me tell you on what basis I say what I say. A major Wall Street organization came upon my web page and they gave me a call. They said that they managed institutional portfolios and they wanted to build what they called a portfolio management system. The main difference is that with institutional portfolios, the volume is orders of magnitude larger. The institutional investment managers are a special breed, essentially because when they take a position, the market moves. So I went to New York and talked to them, and they said "why don't you work for us and build a system for us". I came back and thought about it a little bit, and I called them up and said that "I'm willing to work with you, but I don't want to be your employee. Why don't we set up something together and we can build something?" What they did was that they came to Tucson and set me up with some space and some machines. And essentially what we built, three of my students and I, was a prototype that we called an Analytics Engine. We bought about four or five commercial ticker service feeds from Reuters, Blumberg, Telerate, etc. What we wanted to do was, based on these feeds, to compute what industry folks call analytics, which essentially are mathematical formulas, mostly statistical such as standard deviations, very large means, and so on. And they said, "build this and convince us that you guys can do this." What we told them was that we would compute these analytics in real time and we would show them that the real-time values that we output would be fairly close to the true values. And it turned out that we actually built a reasonable system. They gave us eight analytics and we built an analytics engine for them, based on algorithms I wrote a paper on, which I think appeared in the most recent issue of Information Systems. And it turned out that the results we got were pretty much within 1% standard error of the true solution. And this was built on Windows NT using MS SQL Server DBMS.

So what are the major problems that we experienced? First of all we ran into major problems in the choice of the platform. Of course, I come from a UNIX background, and in my mind it was clear that if we would build this system we would go with UNIX. It turned out that NT has a huge market segment in Wall

Street now. And these people didn't want to talk to us if we said that we wanted to build this on UNIX. The problem was that we had to screw around at the OS level quite a lot. This was a bit of a problem.

Other problems that we experienced was the complexity of these analytics. If you want to compute a simple mean, it's very easy. But one or two of these analytics that they wanted us to compute were very complex, and we actually did not do as well with these as we did with the simple ones. It turns out that the more complex the analytics the less real-time behavior you need. A very complex analytic can tolerate more delay than simple analytics.

Of course, the most major problem was that while we had very nice interaction with the company's research division, basically a bunch of physicists, we had a huge problem with the actual institutional brokers. Jack Stankovic was mentioning the marketing problems, and my experience was that if you want to send this product into the financial market, which is one of the largest applications of this technology, these research types don't mean anything. The actual brokers will impact the final decision to a large degree. These people often manage billions of dollars and the CEO of an investment company would listen to his star broker before he listens to his head of research.

Essentially, our deal with this company has almost fallen through, primarily because of the problem of user acceptance. That is my practical experience.

Martin Kersten - Trying to recall some of our experiences over the last couple of years in this field, and conclusions we have drawn with respect to future activities. First, let me recall essentially the environment we are dealing with. We have essentially a small kernel, which relies on a minor relational algebra and all of ADT functionality. So this is a very small kernel. On the top we have some interfaces, but that's it. The goal of our research is to intercept on modular extensions to deal with separate application environments, etc. But that is a separate topic.

During the last couple of years we also spent quite some energy to build essentially support for temporal analysis, and also include active behavior. This is a relatively traditional schema of trying to implement a transaction-triggered event-monitoring subsystem. So what we actually did was build a model that just fit into the core of the database kernel. This essentially provided an event pool, and the event pool is nothing special. It's just one of those association tables we have in the kernel. it was filled with information on before-and-after images of operators that were fired against the kernel. Likewise, we had a simple scheduler that was looking to the event pool and at the same time trying to evaluate composite events. So in essence it was nothing more than finding a query against the event pool table. When the event finally succeeded, it would go on and fire essentially a procedure. So our question was, can we somehow make this problem minimal. so that we can realize active behavior without immediately being confronted with having to tackle all the problems from the beginning.

How expensive was it? Well, only building this little module into the kernel, it took less than ten pages of code. That was all that was needed to get it into the system, because we have a simple interpreter that interprets essentially the relational algebra of the rules. A second issue was to do quite some experimentation with "where are we using the cycles." We essentially found that the system is fast enough for the basic cycle. The basic cycle: raising the event, getting it into the pool, getting it out of the pool, and checking the event condition, is less than 0.1 ms per event. Of course we have to be a little bit careful with operating system scheduling, especially since the event pool is part of the operating system. But after this little experience we said, OK, it's fine. The basic infrastructure is for the moment fast enough.

Alongside this implementation track, we had started a number of research areas to assess essentially how we were going to build active applications. We didn't have a direct example from the industry so we were using traditional research experiments. Assuming that we have an active database so that we can express ECA rules, what are we going to do with it? The first analysis that was finished three years ago was trying to come up with analytical tools to assess the impact of specification of a number of ECA rules in order to predict the outcome. Because whenever we started to build applications that go beyond one ECA rule you need that analytical power to specify a good and coherent system. And our conclusion was that we couldn't find in the research environment efficient handles and tools to provide a user with an active database or an active application to help him analyze what he was specifying, to predict that the system in the end would behave. This was a rather negative result.

So we switched a little bit the research towards a state where we had to say "OK, let's step away from ECA rules and try to make a rich object model," where you also provide essentially a scenario mechanism where you can easily predict the outcome of the future. All this will be finished by the end of the year. And although it has improved the situation, it's far more descriptive than traditional ECA's. But if we look at the applications, and we are using the system already, we'll need a GIS environment to have the active capabilities. In images, not really, there is no eminent drive to use it. In data mining where it's most used, not either, so there is no trigger to use essentially the whole machinery to its potential, you can imagine. Even in telecom, I'm not sure, with examples I have been confronted with, that you really need to go to a rather elaborate active component. It may be relatively simple.

So despite the fact that we completely engineered out the kernel enhancements required to have fully active components, we in the end came to the conclusion that we should not invest many resources in this area, unless there is a very clear killer application available. And I'm wondering, who has the killer application that justifies essentially a further investment in this area?

Sten Andler - We started a group working on distributed real-time systems in 1993 and we were looking for problems in this area that we were really going to focus on. And with the intent of applying for research money, of course, we studied literature in the area and we talked a lot with the industry. Pretty quickly we were pointed in the direction of databases, which was pretty OK with the background that we had in databases. It wasn't difficult to motivate, because everyone we talked to said that they had a need for database functionality but no real use for conventional databases, which didn't really support the need that they had. And they all had, as we heard previously here, ad hoc solutions. They had built their own little database, often very primitive, often forgetting about all the things that we associate with a database and a database management system. These results, these little systems that they had built, were not published. Their solutions were not general. So we saw a large need for work in developing general techniques in this area. At that time, we didn't sense a very big effort of research in the real-time database that area. Since then it has become a very hot topic, I would say.

In 1994, we were funded by NUTEK to work on a project to develop techniques for distributed real-time databases. The very first year that we worked on this, we got in touch with active functionality, partly because there were activities in Skövde in that area, and partly because it's natural for real-time systems to be reactive. They react to signals and event that happen in the outside world, and the only difference from active databases is that there is also a timeliness requirement. On the other hand, real-time systems, as I said, needed the database functionality. So we thought it was a natural marriage, and inspired by HiPAC and the local synergy with the active database group, we went in that direction. In January of 1995 we defined the first version of the DeeDS architecture, which appeared as a complete technical report in May 1995 and later appeared in SIGMOD Record as an article on DeeDS, the name of our Distributed Active Real-time Database System.

We worked with the industry right from the beginning, because we asked them what the problems were. When we looked for what operating system we should implement this on, we evaluated a large number of real-time kernels and real-time operating systems. And we pretty quickly found that we didn't want to start with something that was a stripped down UNIX, something that had a lot of the baggage still of the large operating system that UNIX is today. Rather we wanted to look at systems that were developed as small kernels. Most of those had the properties that they were implemented in assembly language or not very portable. We found one that had been re-implemented in a portable way, and where we also at the same time of contact with them actually got a dialog. So this company, Enea, has been our partners since 1994, and we built our prototype on the operating system kernel that they are providing.

As far as the rest of the software is concerned, we decided to go with existing software. There was a lot of practical experience in trying to get software from other places and trying to adapt that to the needs that we had. For the object-oriented database, or object store, we used OBST, which comes from an EU project called STONE, so we cooperated with the FZI of Karlsruhe. As for the storage manager, which we needed for nested transactions and flexibility, we cooperated with Canada.

We put together a project plan to build a prototype and we're now in the technology transfer stage. We started that in the fall of 1996 when Jonas Mellin put together a series of tutorials and programming assignments, where system programmers at Enea participated, to try to get them into thinking of active real-time databases, how to solve problems, how to program things, so that they could also carry that over to their customers.

So what did we learn from this? Well, to really look not only at the academic problems, but try to find problems that are real, that industry could be interested in. At the same we learned not to get down too deep, so that you are not stuck with one single solution that works only for one single platform. So, abstract away from that particular sub-problem, and maybe abstract away from a software and hardware platform. To be successful in transferring the results, I think you have to work with an industrial partner right from the beginning of the project. It's hard to do a project in isolation and then sell it to the industry.

Author Index

Lecture Notes in Computer Science

For information about Vols. 1–1478
please contact your bookseller or Springer-Verlag

Vol. 1479: J. Grundy, M. Newey (Eds.), Theorem Provng in Higher Order Logics. Proceedings, 1998. VIII, 497 pages. 1998.

Vol. 1480: F. Giunchiglia (Ed.), Artificial Intelligence: Methodology, Systems, and Applications. Proceedings, 1998. IX, 502 pages. 1998. (Subseries LNAI).

Vol. 1481: E.V. Munson, C. Nicholas, D. Wood (Eds.), Principles of Digital Document Processing. Proceedings, 1998. VII, 152 pages. 1998.

Vol. 1482: R.W. Hartenstein, A. Keevallik (Eds.), Field-Programmable Logic and Applications. Proceedings, 1998. XI, 533 pages. 1998.

Vol. 1483: T. Plagemann, V. Goebel (Eds.), Interactive Distributed Multimedia Systems and Telecommunication Services. Proceedings, 1998. XV, 326 pages. 1998.

Vol. 1484: H. Coelho (Ed.), Progress in Artificial Intelligence – IBERAMIA 98. Proceedings, 1998. XIII, 421 pages. 1998. (Subseries LNAI).

Vol. 1485: J.-J. Quisquater, Y. Deswarte, C. Meadows, D. Gollmann (Eds.), Computer Security – ESORICS 98. Proceedings, 1998. X, 377 pages. 1998.

Vol. 1486: A.P. Ravn, H. Rischel (Eds.), Formal Techniques in Real-Time and Fault-Tolerant Systems. Proceedings, 1998. VIII, 339 pages. 1998.

Vol. 1487: V. Gruhn (Ed.), Software Process Technology. Proceedings, 1998. VIII, 157 pages. 1998.

Vol. 1488: B. Smyth, P. Cunningham (Eds.), Advances in Case-Based Reasoning. Proceedings, 1998. XI, 482 pages. 1998. (Subseries LNAI).

Vol. 1489: J. Dix, L. Fariñas del Cerro, U. Furbach (Eds.), Logics in Artificial Intelligence. Proceedings, 1998. X, 391 pages. 1998. (Subseries LNAI).

Vol. 1490: C. Palamidessi, H. Glaser, K. Meinke (Eds.), Principles of Declarative Programming. Proceedings, 1998. XI, 497 pages. 1998.

Vol. 1491: W. Reisig, G. Rozenberg (Eds.), Lectures on Petri Nets I: Basic Models. XII, 683 pages. 1998.

Vol. 1492: W. Reisig, G. Rozenberg (Eds.), Lectures on Petri Nets II: Applications. XII, 479 pages. 1998.

Vol. 1493: J.P. Bowen, A. Fett, M.G. Hinchey (Eds.), ZUM '98: The Z Formal Specification Notation. Proceedings, 1998. XV, 417 pages. 1998.

Vol. 1494: G. Rozenberg, F. Vaandrager (Eds.), Lectures on Embedded Systems. Proceedings, 1996. VIII, 423 pages. 1998.

Vol. 1495: T. Andreasen, H. Christiansen, H.L. Larsen (Eds.), Flexible Query Answering Systems. IX, 393 pages. 1998. (Subseries LNAI).

Vol. 1496: W.M. Wells, A. Colchester, S. Delp (Eds.), Medical Image Computing and Computer-Assisted Intervention – MICCAI'98. Proceedings, 1998. XXII, 1256 pages. 1998.

Vol. 1497: V. Alexandrov, J. Dongarra (Eds.), Recent Advances in Parallel Virtual Machine and Message Passing Interface. Proceedings, 1998. XII, 412 pages. 1998.

Vol. 1498: A.E. Eiben, T. Bäck, M. Schoenauer, H.-P. Schwefel (Eds.), Parallel Problem Solving from Nature – PPSN V. Proceedings, 1998. XXIII, 1041 pages. 1998.

Vol. 1499: S. Kutten (Ed.), Distributed Computing. Proceedings, 1998. XII, 419 pages. 1998.

Vol. 1500: J.-C. Derniame, B.A. Kaba, D. Wastell (Eds.), Software Process: Principles, Methodology, and Technology. XIII, 307 pages. 1999.

Vol. 1501: M.M. Richter, C.H. Smith, R. Wiehagen, T. Zeugmann (Eds.), Algorithmic Learning Theory. Proceedings, 1998. XI, 439 pages. 1998. (Subseries LNAI).

Vol. 1502: G. Antoniou, J. Slaney (Eds.), Advanced Topics in Artificial Intelligence. Proceedings, 1998. XI, 333 pages. 1998. (Subseries LNAI).

Vol. 1503: G. Levi (Ed.), Static Analysis. Proceedings, 1998. IX, 383 pages. 1998.

Vol. 1504: O. Herzog, A. Günter (Eds.), KI-98: Advances in Artificial Intelligence. Proceedings, 1998. XI, 355 pages. 1998. (Subseries LNAI).

Vol. 1505: D. Caromel, R.R. Oldehoeft, M. Tholburn (Eds.), Computing in Object-Oriented Parallel Environments. Proceedings, 1998. XI, 243 pages. 1998.

Vol. 1506: R. Koch, L. Van Gool (Eds.), 3D Structure from Multiple Images of Large-Scale Environments. Proceedings, 1998. VIII, 347 pages. 1998.

Vol. 1507: T.W. Ling, S. Ram, M.L. Lee (Eds.), Conceptual Modeling – ER '98. Proceedings, 1998. XVI, 482 pages. 1998.

Vol. 1508: S. Jajodia, M.T. Özsu, A. Dogac (Eds.), Advances in Multimedia Information Systems. Proceedings, 1998. VIII, 207 pages. 1998.

Vol. 1510: J.M. Zytkow, M. Quafafou (Eds.), Principles of Data Mining and Knowledge Discovery. Proceedings, 1998. XI, 482 pages. 1998. (Subseries LNAI).

Vol. 1511: D. O'Hallaron (Ed.), Languages, Compilers, and Run-Time Systems for Scalable Computers. Proceedings, 1998. IX, 412 pages. 1998.

Vol. 1512: E. Giménez, C. Paulin-Mohring (Eds.), Types for Proofs and Programs. Proceedings, 1996. VIII, 373 pages. 1998.

Vol. 1513: C. Nikolaou, C. Stephanidis (Eds.), Research and Advanced Technology for Digital Libraries. Proceedings, 1998. XV, 912 pages. 1998.

Vol. 1514: K. Ohta, D. Pei (Eds.), Advances in Cryptology – ASIACRYPT'98. Proceedings, 1998. XII, 436 pages. 1998.

Vol. 1515: F. Moreira de Oliveira (Ed.), Advances in Artificial Intelligence. Proceedings, 1998. X, 259 pages. 1998. (Subseries LNAI).

Vol. 1516: W. Ehrenberger (Ed.), Computer Safety, Reliability and Security. Proceedings, 1998. XVI, 392 pages. 1998.

Vol. 1517: J. Hromkovič, O. Sýkora (Eds.), Graph-Theoretic Concepts in Computer Science. Proceedings, 1998. X, 385 pages. 1998.

Vol. 1518: M. Luby, J. Rolim, M. Serna (Eds.), Randomization and Approximation Techniques in Computer Science. Proceedings, 1998. IX, 385 pages. 1998.

1519: T. Ishida (Ed.), Community Computing and Support Systems. VIII, 393 pages. 1998.

Vol. 1520: M. Maher, J.-F. Puget (Eds.), Principles and Practice of Constraint Programming - CP98. Proceedings, 1998. XI, 482 pages. 1998.

Vol. 1521: B. Rovan (Ed.), SOFSEM'98: Theory and Practice of Informatics. Proceedings, 1998. XI, 453 pages. 1998.

Vol. 1522: G. Gopalakrishnan, P. Windley (Eds.), Formal Methods in Computer-Aided Design. Proceedings, 1998. IX, 529 pages. 1998.

Vol. 1524: G.B. Orr, K.-R. Müller (Eds.), Neural Networks: Tricks of the Trade. VI, 432 pages. 1998.

Vol. 1525: D. Aucsmith (Ed.), Information Hiding. Proceedings, 1998. IX, 369 pages. 1998.

Vol. 1526: M. Broy, B. Rumpe (Eds.), Requirements Targeting Software and Systems Engineering. Proceedings, 1997. VIII, 357 pages. 1998.

Vol. 1527: P. Baumgartner, Theory Reasoning in Connection Calculi. IX, 283. 1999. (Subseries LNAI).

Vol. 1528: B. Preneel, V. Rijmen (Eds.), State of the Art in Applied Cryptography. Revised Lectures, 1997. VIII, 395 pages. 1998.

Vol. 1529: D. Farwell, L. Gerber, E. Hovy (Eds.), Machine Translation and the Information Soup. Proceedings, 1998. XIX, 532 pages. 1998. (Subseries LNAI).

Vol. 1530: V. Arvind, R. Ramanujam (Eds.), Foundations of Software Technology and Theoretical Computer Science. XII, 369 pages. 1998.

Vol. 1531: H.-Y. Lee, H. Motoda (Eds.), PRICAI'98: Topics in Artificial Intelligence. XIX, 646 pages. 1998. (Subseries LNAI).

Vol. 1096: T. Schael, Workflow Management Systems for Process Organisations. Second Edition. XII, 229 pages. 1998.

Vol. 1532: S. Arikawa, H. Motoda (Eds.), Discovery Science. Proceedings, 1998. XI, 456 pages. 1998. (Subseries LNAI).

Vol. 1533: K.-Y. Chwa, O.H. Ibarra (Eds.), Algorithms and Computation. Proceedings, 1998. XIII, 478 pages. 1998.

Vol. 1534: J.S. Sichman, R. Conte, N. Gilbert (Eds.), Multi-Agent Systems and Agent-Based Simulation. Proceedings, 1998. VIII, 237 pages. 1998. (Subseries LNAI).

Vol. 1535: S. Ossowski, Co-ordination in Artificial Agent Societies. XV; 221 pages. 1999. (Subseries LNAI).

Vol. 1536: W.-P. de Roever, H. Langmaack, A. Pnueli (Eds.), Compositionality: The Significant Difference. Proceedings, 1997. VIII, 647 pages. 1998.

Vol. 1538: J. Hsiang, A. Ohori (Eds.), Advances in Computing Science – ASIAN'98. Proceedings, 1998. X, 305 pages. 1998.

Vol. 1539: O. Rüthing, Interacting Code Motion Transformations: Their Impact and Their Complexity. XXI,225 pages. 1998.

Vol. 1540: C. Beeri, P. Buneman (Eds.), Database Theory – ICDT'99. Proceedings, 1999. XI, 489 pages. 1999.

Vol. 1541: B. Kågström, J. Dongarra, E. Elmroth, J. Waśniewski (Eds.), Applied Parallel Computing. Proceedings, 1998. XIV, 586 pages. 1998.

Vol. 1542: H.I. Christensen (Ed.), Computer Vision Systems. Proceedings, 1999. XI, 554 pages. 1999.

Vol. 1543: S. Demeyer, J. Bosch (Eds.), Object-Oriented Technology ECOOP'98 Workshop Reader. 1998. XXII, 573 pages. 1998.

Vol. 1544: C. Zhang, D. Lukose (Eds.), Multi-Agent Systems. Proceedings, 1998. VII, 195 pages. 1998. (Subseries LNAI).

Vol. 1545: A. Birk, J. Demiris (Eds.), Learning Robots. Proceedings, 1996. IX, 188 pages. 1998. (Subseries LNAI).

Vol. 1546: B. Möller, J.V. Tucker (Eds.), Prospects for Hardware Foundations. Survey Chapters, 1998. X, 468 pages. 1998.

Vol. 1547: S.H. Whitesides (Ed.), Graph Drawing. Proceedings 1998. XII, 468 pages. 1998.

Vol. 1548: A.M. Haeberer (Ed.), Algebraic Methodology and Software Technology. Proceedings, 1999. XI, 531 pages. 1999.

Vol. 1550: B. Christianson, B. Crispo, W.S. Harbison, M. Roe (Eds.), Security Protocols. Proceedings, 1998. VIII, 241 pages. 1999.

Vol. 1551: G. Gupta (Ed.), Practical Aspects of Declarative Languages. Proceedings, 1999. VIII, 367 pgages. 1999.

Vol. 1552: Y. Kambayashi, D.L. Lee, E.-P. Lim, M.K. Mohania, Y. Masunaga (Eds.), Advances in Database Technologies. Proceedings, 1998. XIX, 592 pages. 1999.

Vol. 1553: S.F. Andler, J. Hansson (Eds.), Active, Real-Time, and Temporal Database Systems. Proceedings, 1997. VIII, 245 pages. 1998.

Vol. 1557: P. Zinterhof, M. Vajteršic, A. Uhl (Eds.), Parallel Computation. Proceedings, 1999. XV, 604 pages. 1999.

Vol. 1560: K. Imai, Y. Zheng (Eds.), Public Key Cryptography. Proceedings, 1999. IX, 327 pages. 1999.

Vol. 1563: Ch. Meinel, S. Tison (Eds.), STACS 99. Proceedings, 1999. XIV, 582 pages. 1999.

Vol. 1567: P. Antsaklis, W. Kohn, M. Lemmon, A. Nerode, S. Sastry (Eds.), Hybrid Systems V. X, 445 pages. 1999.

Vol. 1570: F. Puppe (Ed.), XPS-99: Knowledge-Based Systems. VIII, 227 pages. 1999. (Subseries LNAI).